THE
Puritan Heritage

GEORGE M. STEPHENSON

Professor of History
University of Minnesota

THE MACMILLAN COMPANY

NEW YORK : *1952*

TO

LILLY STEPHENSON

PROVERBS XXXI. 28

CONTENTS

ONE

THE COMMON MAN'S UTOPIA

Tᴴᴇ key to the study of the planting of the kingdom of God in the United States of America—the vineyard planted and cultivated by the Puritans and by people of kindred spirit from every land—is the understanding that the worship of God in spirit and in truth is inseparable from the cause of civil liberty. It was to emancipate men from religion trammeled by ceremonies, formulas, and idols, administered by priests entangled in the meshes of legalism, that Jesus Christ walked among men and made the sacrifice on the cross. It has been said that if anyone wants to know what the kingdom of God and the coming of it meant in the message of Jesus, he must read and study His parables. He spoke in parables because it was not given to all to know the mysteries of the kingdom of heaven; for many prophets and righteous men did not see and hear, neither did they discern the signs of the times. In all generations theology has been used as an instrument for dispensing with religion. In America pietism and democracy went hand in hand.

The faith of the Puritans was drawn from the Bible; and their church government was molded and tempered in the crucible of persecution inherent in an old-world society, where church and state were so intertwined that it was sometimes impossible to distinguish between the temporal and the spiritual functions of the priesthood. The type of ministry in an ecclesiastical body is a barometer of its spiritual life; and in the New World the leaven of the kingdom of God leavened the whole lump. The common man was destined to come into his own in the universal priesthood of all believers. Men of meager education and of burning zeal exercised the right of "witnessing for the truth" without interference from prelates clothed with power to prescribe what one must believe in order to obtain salvation. The logic of events after the planting of the Plymouth Colony dictated the eventual repeal of statutes restricting the freedom of worship according to the light that was in each individual. There were no conventicle acts in federal and state statutes. In the fullness of time the Gospel was preached in America not only in edifices consecrated by ecclesiastical authority or built expressly for worship, but in homes, barns, schoolhouses, public buildings, and even in the great outdoors—in edifices not built by human hands—where the obscure layman preached ungowned without altar or communion table. Men unspoiled by worldly success, some of whom had been branded as heretics in their native lands, were granted hearings as citizens of a nation dedicated to the proposition that all men are created equal.

Religious liberty in the United States implied that it was the individual's own affair to worship or not to worship and that skeptic and believer alike might hold public office and were entitled to be included among respectable members of society.

The ecclesiastical hierarchies of the Old World frowned on public manifestations of excessive religious zeal as dangers to "pure doctrine" and as threats to the maintenance of discipline. A hierarchy composed of ranks and degrees of dignity and preferment, working in close alliance with the secular government, felt the lash of liberalism and nonconformity. Sacerdotalism in the various countries of Europe built about itself legal, theological, and ecclesiastical walls behind which it could defend itself against the forces of reform. If one wall were undermined, the other two would be weakened. Democracy in government foreshadowed the priesthood of the common man. The extension of the right of suffrage also clothed the laity with greater influence in the church, and the line of demarcation between the "spiritual estate" and the "temporal estate" became less pronounced. Luther cited the Epistles of St. Paul and St. Peter to support his contention that there is really no difference between laymen and priests except that of office and work. In America there was room for Christians who questioned the validity of ecclesiastical regulations and legislative enactments which denied the right of a man to teach publicly in the church or to administer the sacraments unless he was regularly called—that is, ordained according to prescribed forms and ceremonies and set apart in the clerical estate. In America laymen occupied the pulpit and shared the concern of the clergy for the care of souls; and they were not tender in expressing condemnation of ministers who were negligent in performing the duties of their office or who were not worthy of fellowship with "true believers" because they did not radiate a living faith by renouncing worldly things.

One of America's greatest revival preachers, George Whitefield, upon departing from New England in 1740, after having had a part in the Great Awakening, recorded that on many accounts that province exceeded all others in America; and for the establishment of religion, perhaps all other parts of the world; but he detected that almost all the ministers preached from notes, which he thought was proof that they had in great measure lost the old spirit of preaching. He deemed it a sad symptom of the decay of religion when the reading of sermons became fashionable. When the spirit of prayer began to be lost, he said, then the forms of prayer were invented; and this observation, he thought, was equally valid with reference to preaching. He was unsparing in condemning "unconverted ministers."

Harriet Beecher Stowe, the child of a famous and typical New England parsonage, in her delightful portrayal of life in New England in *Poganuc People,* offered similar testimony. While paying tribute to the impressive and beautiful Episcopal funeral service, she declared that there are occasions when an affectionate and devout man, penetrated with human sympathy, can utter prayers such as no liturgy can equal. There are prayers springing heavenward, from devout hearts, she wrote, that are as much superior to all written ones as living, growing flowers outbloom the dried treasures of the herbarium.

The central figure in the Great Awakening, Jonathan Edwards, believed that the extraordinary and wonderful work of the Spirit of God in that revival was a prelude to that glorious work of God, so often foretold in Scripture. In the light of Scripture and expressions of eminent men of God, "we cannot reasonably think otherwise, than that the beginning of the great work of God must be near," he said. The great preacher, theologian, and philosopher discerned many signs that made it probable that this work would begin in America, in some very remote part of the world, with which other parts had no communication but by navigation. He thought it worthy of note that America was discovered about the time of the Reformation.

In a home missionary sermon preached about one hundred years later, in 1849, Albert Barnes gave a vivid account of his visit to St. Anthony Falls, at the head of navigation of the Mississippi River, where he got a view of the greatness of his country such as he had never had in the cities and villages of the East. As he ascended the great river and viewed the boundless expanse and fertility of a land which had never been touched by the plow, he was convinced that the country had been reserved and prepared for some mighty development in the purposes of divine Providence. "God prepared the Pilgrims to make New England what it now is; he has put it in the power of this generation to make the West what it ever onward should be."

The "western mind," as he sensed it, was a strange and mighty intermingling of the minds of great power, under different propensities and views—constituting a population such as the world had never before seen in the settlement of a new land. It was a mind strongly imbued with the love of civil and religious liberty; with hatred of oppression and wrong; with the value of the simplest and purest forms of the Protestant religion; and with a desire to promote the cause of sound learning.

The Presbyterian clergyman was giving expression to the thoughts, hopes, and aspirations of countless thousands in America and Europe who thought it providential that America was discovered so late; that God had held this continent in reserve until the fullness of time when the faithful could find a refuge from persecution in a land that had freed itself from militarism and priestcraft; where the law was the protector of the meek and the poor in spirit. The humble emigrants were swept along by forces which they but faintly understood. They knew that emigrant ships had corpses in the cargo; and some of them, with fatalistic philosophy, asked: "What signifies a generation or two in the span of world history?" In common with the Puritans they were willing to suffer for conscience sake; and they harbored a rising spirit of independence and a feeling of the worth and dignity of the human soul.

The Puritan commonwealth was a radical social experiment. Their great thinkers were occupied with the final solution of the fundamental problem of society. Their theologians pondered the grandiose conception of the Millennium.

With the advance of settlement and the beginnings of communities the pioneers took the initiative in organizing congregations, building places of worship, raising money to support ministers and to defray the expenses of churches in a manner that suggests the inception of the Christian church and the simplicity and spontaneity of the apostolic age, when the Christian community illustrated the meaning of Christ's teaching that there is no essential difference between the members of His flock.

In an effort to explain the doctrine of the priesthood of the common man and to erase the arbitrary line of distinction between the "spiritual estate" and the "temporal estate"—to prove that all Christians are truly of the "spiritual estate"—Martin Luther cited a practical example and a prototype of procedures on the American frontier. The reformer stated that if a little group of pious laymen were taken captive and set down in a wilderness, and had among them no priest consecrated by a bishop, and if they were to agree in choosing one of their number and were to charge him with the duties of administering the sacraments and of preaching, the person upon whom the choice fell would be as truly a priest as though all bishops and popes had consecrated him.

The contrast between the meeting-houses on the American frontier and the cathedrals and churches in Europe, and the wide gulf between palaces, mitred carriages, and sumptuous tables of prelates and the humble cabins which gave shelter to the horseback-riding frontier preacher, is as striking as the distinction between the ancient bishops who lived by taking fish and making tents and their successors who lived a thousand years later. The clergy of the Old World formed themselves into a caste and displayed their profession in the collars of their coats. Just as the exterior of the meeting-houses in America was a symbol of the doctrine that was preached from their pulpits, so was the garb of the Puritan, the Quaker, and men of kindred spirit a protest against sacerdotalism.

Many congregations that dotted the landscape from Maine to California were in their inception and early years essentially laymen's missionary movements. A handful of spiritually-minded persons met in homes for devotional exercises—to read the Bible, to "witness for the Gospel," and to unite in prayer—in other words, in conventicles, which in the Old World were prohibited by law and were often broken up by the parish priest or by an officer of the law. In the course of time boys and girls assembled for instruction in Sunday school, a congregation was organized, and a structure to serve as a schoolhouse and chapel was built by the coöperative efforts of the pioneers. As the number of settlers augmented and the community prospered, the humble building was displaced by a more suitable meeting-house. Statistics showing the number of vacant pastorates were misleading, because ministers served many congregations and consecrated laymen took charge in the absence of clergymen. More congregations than ministers did not necessarily mean that the doors of churches were closed. A heritage from the founders of New England was the principle that piety belongs to the care of the individual without the intervention of a priesthood.

The absence of titles of nobility and of traditions rooted in an archaic society worked to the advantage of American churches. They were not cumbered with extensive landholdings, gradations of officials, scribes, copying clerks, chaplains assigned to great estates, and livings dependent on men of wealth or distinction. After the separation from Great Britain, when the colonies became states, constitutions were adopted which, with few exceptions, abolished ecclesiastical establishments which were a part of the secular government. In other words, separation of church and state was effected; and a principle was established which was rarely challenged except by prelates who were trained in a polity foreign to the atmosphere of America.

This was well stated in a discourse delivered in Albany, New York, on Independence Day, 1801, by Eliphalet Nott, president of Union College: "In these United States no civil code binds the conscience; no assuming pontiff dictates to us our faith. Happy, thrice happy land where religion stands upon its own basis, where truth is vindicated by its own weapons, and conquers by its own evidence. Here light without a veil emanates from the sun of righteousness, and salvation, without mixture, flows pure and unrestrained from its sacred source—the Gospel." This address was appropriately delivered in the first year of the administration of Thomas Jefferson, whose tombstone bears the inscription, placed there at his own request: "Here was buried Thomas Jefferson, Author of the Declaration of Independence, of the Statute of Virginia for Religious Freedom, and Father of the University of Virginia."

New England Puritanism sprang from seed sown by martyrs who revolted against the government of church and state as it was administered by the first two Stuart sovereigns and their Lauds and Wentworths. The Puritan conception of social equality and its repudiation of the doctrine that the Church of England was the true apostolic church was woven into the very existence of the people of New England. To them religion was something more than usage and obedience. They made few concessions to human nature; the soul and the spiritual life were realities. The Bible was everything, and they claimed the right to interpret it without regard to tradition or authority. The Pilgrims read the Bible in the light of Calvin's logic and legalism; but they also pondered John Robinson's statement: "The Lord hath more truth to break forth out of His Holy Word." Out of this attitude of mind and spirit came their faith in new revelations and the logical flowering of diversity of doctrines and numerous sects, which became characteristic of America. New England theology encouraged inquiry and soul-searching.

The Puritans were willing to listen to sermons which shattered smug self-satisfaction; they heard many "hard sayings"; their preachers did not always tell them what they approved. Many of their ministers were men of great attainments who proved that they set a high value on learning by encouraging the establishment of schools and academies. New England set up a system of local schools and became an oasis in which the common man and woman were able to read and write, with the result that self-government and democracy found a congenial atmosphere whether in the towns of New England or in those parts of the United States where their descendants began anew the weaving of the fabric of society. With the exception of England, the religious literature of the America of the eighteenth and early nineteenth century was the most widely diffused. Moreover, Americans were heirs to the masterpieces of English literature that were produced in the great years of Puritanism—Shakespeare, Milton, Bunyan, and a host of writers who are still read for devotion and enlightenment in secular and spiritual matters.

Horace Bushnell, one of New England's sons who chose to remain throughout most of his life a resident of Connecticut, stated in a sermon that a band of Congregational Protestants emigrating to the New World neither did establish, nor could have established, any other than a popular government. "It was Protestantism in religion producing republicanism in government," he said.

Another son of Connecticut, Lyman Beecher, who for a time cast his lot with the pioneers of the Old Northwest, in a series of public addresses, appealed to the people in the states of the Atlantic Seaboard to contribute of their means to establish educational institutions for the promotion of the religion of those who fought the battles of the Reformation and of the Revolution. He would not spread the mantle of charity over any religion which was the enemy of liberty of conscience and of free inquiry. "A despotic government and despotic religion may not be able to endure free inquiry," he said, "but a republic and religious liberty cannot exist without it." He called it an anti-republican charity which would shield any religious denomination from the animadversions of impartial criticism. "Denominations, as books, are public property, and demand and are benefited by criticism." In order to be assimilated to American institutions, he continued, a religion must be subjected to the tug of controversy and searching inspection of the public eye.

It was the irony of fate that the adherents of the three great established churches of the Old World—Episcopalians, Lutherans, and Roman Catholics—in America found themselves in the position of dissenters; and but for the complexity and diversity that grew out of the spiritual upheaval of the Reformation and the democracy inherent in Calvinism and the frontier, they would have been victims of conventicle acts that were invoked to maintain uniformity and the status quo in countries where churches were allied with despotic governments. In general, the American churches were less tolerant of human frailty than were the Catholic, Episcopalian, and Lutheran bodies; but their intolerance was more in the nature of self-discipline than in laws and ordinances; and by the beginning of the nineteenth century the medley of sects and cults had made it difficult, if not impossible, for any ecclesiastical body to impose upon any other. In the United States the conception of a universal church was shattered beyond repair. Out of the multiplicity of creeds blossomed the flower of religious freedom which recognized the dignity of the human soul and the right of private judgment. This system, or lack of system, was as much in the interest of majorities as it was to the advantage of minorities. Majorities hold no monopoly of religious bigotry. Majorities need protection against intolerant and aggressive minorities, just as minorities stand in need of protection against majorities.

The American religious settlement worked to the infinite advantage of the millions of immigrants who sought release from the trammels of an old-world society. For a time, at least, every one of these newcomers was a nonconformist; they faced the problem of orienting themselves in the new environment. They had been baptized into membership of churches whose polity and doctrine were alien to the genius of American institutions. It would be unhistorical to minimize the problems raised by the heavy immigration of the nineteenth and twentieth centuries; and it would also be unhistorical and unjust to deny that underlying the nativistic movements that periodically agitated the country were conditions that gave wholesome concern to level-headed citizens as to the safety of American institutions and ideals.

It is the glory of the founding fathers that the open spaces of America became dotted with religious experiment stations. A multitude of sects and religious diversity dictated one of the finest provisions in the Constitution of the United States: the guarantee of religious freedom—not religious toleration, which assumes a privileged church.

THE EUROPEAN BACKGROUND

PRACTICALLY everything that is known about the beginnings of the Christian Church is found in the Acts of the Apostles and in the Epistles of St. Paul. It is related of Paul and Barnabas "that a whole year they assembled themselves with the church, and taught much people. And the disciples were called Christians first in Antioch." These remnants were scattered about in the cities and towns of the Roman Empire; and because they were nonconformists—that is, did not conform to the religious mores of the time—ran afoul of the law and were persecuted. The teachings of the Founder of Christianity prompted them to live in peace with their neighbors and to settle wrongs in a spirit of forgiveness; to love their enemies and to pray for those who persecuted them. They talked about their king and prayed "thy kingdom come." Everything was spontaneous; the gift of prophecy sat upon each and every one. There was no essential difference between the followers of Christ, whose speedy coming was awaited.

After the pressure of persecution was removed from Christians, their church emerged as a great and powerful organization whose membership included the regenerate and the worldly. The church became a corporation; and theologians and schoolmen became corporation lawyers who legislated and handed down decisions which collectively made up Canon Law. The church became a state within a state, with its own bureaucracy—intolerant and jealous of its own rights; it offered a career with which it attracted men because of emoluments of money, power, and social distinction. Church and state became so intertwined that a swarm of legalists spun a web of theology, and religion was reduced to the lowest common denominator.

In every age of the church the living remnant protested against the mathematical reckoning of things spiritual, the doing of things by rule. It was not until the fourteenth century that the protest against this powerful salvation machine struck at the root of the church. Previous reforms had not been revolutionary. Reformers of the sixteenth century, like Erasmus, for example, cried out that it would be well "for us if we thought less of our dogmas and more of the Gospel." They asserted that the reading of the Bible and the early church fathers would put an end to scholastic subtleties, and Christ would be taught simply and plainly. In spite of the conservative character of the Protestant Reformation and the protests of the reformers that they were not advocating anything new—that they were only returning to the teaching of the primitive church based on the New Testament— the movement was in fact open rebellion. The keynote of the New Testament is that all external observance of the law is worthless unless it is based on the obedience of the heart. To assert a principle that implied the right of private judgment was to appeal from the authority of the church to the individual and to make it possible for laymen, learned and unlearned, to reject the authority of the priesthood.

The forerunners of Martin Luther—Wycliffe in England, Huss in Bohemia, Colet in England, and Erasmus of Dutch descent—lamented that church services had become almost entirely sacramental, to the exclusion of preaching and teaching. They would return to the reasonable and simple teachings of Christ. They recognized the necessity of making the Scriptures intelligible to the masses in translation; and they lamented that men became priests and monks without having read the New Testament.

Erasmus, who was one of the greatest scholars of all time, was about twenty years younger than Luther. An eminent scholar has said that "Luther made the Reformation that was; Erasmus, the Reformation that is to be." In 1511 was published "Praise of Folly" which made Erasmus famous among the scholars of Europe. This bold satire which spared neither priests, nor monks, nor bishops, nor popes set forth the simplicity and spontaneity of the Christian faith and stated that the Master gave His apostles examples of little children, lilies, mustard seed, and sparrows, things senseless and inconsiderable, living only by the dictates of nature and without either craft or care.

The greatest work of Erasmus was, as he said in a letter, "to restore a buried literature and recall divines from their hair-splittings to a knowledge of the New Testament." This was accomplished by the publication in 1516 of a book which scholars agree did more to prepare the way for the religious reformation than any other book published during this era. It was an edition of the New Testament, containing in two columns side by side, the original Greek and a new Latin translation of his own, which was more accurate than the Latin Vulgate which was the Bible then in use. Without this work, the translations of Tyndale in England and of Luther in Germany would have been almost impossible. Erasmus also wrote a paraphrase in Latin of all the New Testament books, except Revelation. They were translated into various modern languages, and of the English version every parish in England was supplied with a copy. The eventual translation of the New Testament into the language of the common people brought the Gospel within the reach of both learned and unlearned, and eventually destroyed or shattered the priestly despotism that brought the church so low at the time of the Reformation. The open Bible brought schism in the church. The theory that the church lies in one institution was broken, and Christendom has been divided ever since.

Martin Luther, whose life spans the years from 1483 to 1546, had but one objective: to return to the original constitution of the church and the creed of the fathers. His great contribution was in his absolute doctrine of justification by faith, and *by faith alone,* which was taught by the Apostle Paul. During the years of his stay in the Augustinian monastery, Luther read the Bible and Augustine, with his mind fixed on sin and redemption. The effect of Augustine's theology was to emphasize the evil side of man's nature and the impossibility of human effort to overcome it. Augustine accepted substantially the Pauline solution of the problem, namely, that through faith man receives the grace of God, entirely apart from works. Luther's study of the Bible and his observations and experiences as a monk and priest convinced him that the Bible had not played enough part in the lives of the people. He cited the infallible Bible as the only basis of authority in religion.

Luther's desire to remain within the fold of the Roman church was nullified by the logic of events. When pressed by his adversaries as to who was the head of the church and who was in possession of authority to decide questions of controversy, Luther stated that Christ was head of the church. His adversaries argued that the interpretation of Scripture belongs to no one except the pope. Luther appealed to the validity of Christian scholarship and denied the right of a corrupt and ignorant pope to interpret the Bible to the detriment of pious and intelligent men. He recited history which testified that popes and church councils had made contradictory statements and had wrongfully condemned articles taught by Augustine, Paul, and even Christ Himself.

Standing as a condemned heretic before the Diet of Worms in April, 1521, in a ringing reply to the demand that he recant what he had written, Luther formulated the keynote of Protestantism: "I must be convinced either by the testimony of the Scriptures or clear arguments. . . . I am bound by the Scriptures which I have quoted; my conscience is submissive to the Word of God; therefore I may not, and will not, recant, because to act against conscience is unholy and unsafe. So help me God." Luther appealed from an infallible church to an infallible book.

Luther was the type of reformer who understood his own age; he knew how far he could go. He understood that it was vital to his cause to convince the responsible elements in the German population of the conservative and constructive side of the Lutheran Reformation. The man who had exposed the hollowness of forms and ceremonies in later life was called to appear as an apologist for them because of what he conceived to be the excesses of the Anabaptists and the teachings of radicals who rejected Luther's infallible Bible and conceived of salvation as entirely an affair of the spirit. They regarded sacraments and ceremonies as of no spiritual significance. Some of them cast away entirely from sacerdotalism and espoused the primitive simplicity of the apostolic church. Luther was forced to lean heavily on the secular arm. The young Luther—the idealistic Luther—was chastened, seasoned, and sobered by the mature Luther.

The Lutheran Reformation listed heavily in the direction of institutional and sacramental religion. Throughout the Augsburg Confession, which contains the jewels of the Lutheran faith, there is a constant appeal to the authority of Scripture; but the Wittenberg theologians who drew up the document omitted no word to emphasize how much Lutheranism had in common with Catholicism. Even the Romanists were surprised at its moderate and conciliatory tone.

In the long years that followed the publication of the Augsburg Confession, the Lutheran churches became established churches, and "apologies" and "formulas," more detailed and scholastic than the Augsburg Confession appeared. The dry rot of dogma and orthodoxy set in; and spiritually-minded men and women, finding no inspiration in the established churches, turned to mysticism, quietism, and various forms of pietism.

Protestantism is heavily indebted to Luther; but the reformer more directly associated with American Christianity is John Calvin, who was born in 1509, twenty-five years later than Luther, and in a sense inherited his way of salvation and built on the foundations laid by him. Calvinism was brought to what is now the United States by the Pilgrims and the Puritans, whose spirit was expressed by John Winthrop in 1630: "Yet we may not look for great things here. It is enough that we shall have heaven, though we should pass through hell to it. We are here to enjoy God and Jesus Christ. Is this not enough? What would we have more?"

In 1536 Calvin worked out the Institutes of the Christian Religion, one of the classics of the Reformation, which was never materially changed or modified. Calvinism is a religion of the book; it is a system which does not rest on reason—only on Scripture, which Calvin took literally. More than Luther, Calvin found in the Bible a law which regulates the Christian life. Calvin believed in justification by faith, but he carried the doctrine out even farther than did Luther. He went to predestination, which became the central doctrine of churches that accepted the Institutes of the Christian Religion as the rule of faith. The essential point is that man cannot understand the ways of God, who has a plan of salvation for him as an individual from all eternity. A man is "elected" to salvation, and nothing that human nature can do is able to frustrate the purpose of the Almighty. A man is not saved by good works, but he must do good works whether it helps him or not. A man does not even know if he has faith.

Calvin held that Scripture "recognizes no other minister of the church than a preacher of the Word of God, called to govern the church, whom it now calls a bishop, now a presbyter, and occasionally a pastor." The true church consists only of the elect; but the visible church consists of both elect and non-elect. There is no salvation outside the visible church, and members must conform to its discipline. Calvin had great respect for the state, but it had no power over conscience. There must be intimate relations between church and state. But what if a conflict arises between them? This is an unanswerable question. Calvin said: "If the state abuses the power, God will raise up vengeance."

Calvinists in various countries were hard and narrow in their creed and puritanical in their manners and conduct. Their religion superseded the formal observances and duties imposed upon the individual by the Catholic system by a strict moral code enforced by self-discipline. By its emphasis on Christian intelligence, on the individualistic nature of salvation, and by its exaltation of the role of the laity in church and state, Calvinism has attracted and nurtured men of sterling character. The doctrine of election—the consciousness of adoption—raised men to supreme religious fervor and moral energy. It was of immeasurable consolation to persecuted Calvinists in all countries to know that their earthly pilgrimages had been planned from eternity and that kings and prelates were impotent before a God whose judgments were unsearchable and whose ways were past finding out.

Europe lost heavily and America gained immeasurably by the flight from persecution of Huguenots from France, of Presbyterians from Scotland, and of Independents and Puritans from England.

The vitality of Puritanism was derived from a study of the Bible. It became the sole reading of the household. The intellect was freed by this private study, because it involved private interpretation of the Scriptures. Each reader became something of a churchman himself. This cultivated individual thought and intellectual liberty. The reading of the Bible brought men into direct relation with God, without the heavy emphasis on the authority of confessions and creeds. Each congregation was a spiritual covenant. The doctrine of predestination, adoption, foreknowledge, and fatalism leveled all classes before God and enhanced the self-respect of the common man. The Puritan must be born again; he must pray without ceasing; he must refrain from the lusts of the flesh. God alone determined who should be saved. The spirit of Puritanism is in Bunyan's *Pilgrim's Progress*. It tells of the immediate experience of the soul. The Puritan held family devotions, wore plain clothing, and was clean in speech, which was liberally seasoned with scriptural terms. He abhorred the confessional, but kept a diary and daily journal, in which he made dead reckonings of his conduct—an indication of his introspective nature.

The steel in the Puritan character was tempered not only by the faith and the rigid moral code of Calvinism but by outer causes as well. Protestantism—Biblical Christianity—was threatened by enemies both within and without England. In times of trial the Puritans took courage from the books of the Old Testament, where they read about the Israelites who were not numerous, but they were right and the Lord of Hosts was with them.

The Church of England emerged from the turbulent and vexing years of the sixteenth century as a compromise in the form of an ecclesiastical establishment which included elements of Catholicism, Lutheranism, and Calvinism. The radical doctrinal divergence that followed in the train of the Lutheran Reformation did not accompany the Anglican Reformation. The most radical features of the English Reformation were the separation from Rome—the repudiation of the headship of the papacy—and the supremacy of the state over the church. The Latin mass was abolished in favor of the service in the Book of Common Prayer. For the Puritans, however, the beauty of the diction and the music of the liturgy did not compensate for the symbolism, the vestments, and the decorative altars that were a part of the service. The more extreme the Protestant the more repulsive becomes the mingling of the sensuous with the things of the spirit. The Puritans wanted to eliminate those remnants of Catholicism which were retained in the Anglican service and which suggested overemphasis on the sacramental side of religion. These remnants were the sign of the cross in baptism, the surplice, kneeling at the communion, bowing at the name of Jesus, use of the ring in the marriage service, and the observance of saints' days.

Calvin did not rule out the episcopacy in church government, but he did favor a system in which the spiritual power was vested in a council of presbyters, partly clergymen and partly laymen. In every country where Protestantism established itself there were protests against the office of bishop as such; and the indignation became bitter and personal when men clothed with the prerogatives of the office offended by their arrogance and by their subservience to the crown. Kings and prelates understood that episcopacy was more compatible with kingly absolutism and sacerdotalism than was Presbyterianism. In the very first years of the seventeenth century this question of church polity flared up when certain Puritan clergymen proposed that the bishop should consult with the synod of his diocese. The proposal so incensed James I, the first of the Stuart sovereigns, that he asserted that a Scottish Presbytery agreed "as well with a monarchy, as God with the devil." His parting shot was that he would make the Puritans conform to the Church of England or else harry them out of the land.

This threat was followed shortly by a proclamation by the king ejecting from their positions clergymen who refused to conform to the Prayerbook. This measure not only created a body of conscientious objectors who stood outside the church, but it impelled the Puritans to go farther and to attack the system itself. The controversy became so hot that it finally flamed out into civil war, and one faction of the Puritans demanded the abolition of the episcopacy with "all its roots and branches."

The term Puritan broadly included persons who wanted to "purify" the church of remnants of Romanism, but there were shades of differences among the Puritans. The greatest number were nonconformists who desired to stay within the fold of the Church of England and to set up a Presbyterian form of government. The Independents or Congregationalists sought to limit church membership to the "godly" and to set up congregations to manage themselves, leaving others to join such churches as appealed to them. The smallest and most extreme group were the Brownists, who pronounced the Established Church contrary to the Bible and separated from it. They were the Pilgrims who founded the Plymouth Colony. These extremists made few converts in England. Religious toleration was necessary to the existence of this type of Christians, because their conception of church polity clashed with the prevailing view that religious conformity was essential to national unity. They would bow their conscience to neither pope, bishop, nor presbyter.

It was this democratic principle that flowered in the United States.

The religious question in England in the seventeenth century was settled in the only possible way—religious toleration. The religious question in the United States was settled in the only possible way— religious freedom. America is heavily indebted to England for preparing the way. The passion for freedom of conscience, says George Macaulay Trevelyan in his brilliant volume *England under the Stuarts,* is the only one that ever drove the English into the paths of revolution.

Calvinism, whether professed by English, Scotch, French, or Dutch, was a militant religion. There could be no reconciliation or compromise between Calvinism and Catholicism. The rapid spread of Calvinism in England and the indelibile stamp it placed on the English-speaking peoples of the world is explained in no small part by the circumstance that in the seventeenth century Rome was in the vanguard of England's enemies and that the restoration of Catholicism was bound up with foreign intervention and with the infiltration of agents of Rome in government and society. The Puritans were irreconcilable enemies of Rome.

During the years when religion was a major political issue in England, on the continent of Europe Catholicism and Protestantism were locked in a struggle known as the Thirty Years' War, from 1618 to 1648, years big with fate for English-speaking people on both sides of the Atlantic.

It was in the reign of Charles I (1625–1649) that Archbishop Laud set out to purge out the Calvinistic strain in the Church of England which had come in the years following the separation from Rome. He was as zealous as any Romanist in maintaining that the apostolic succession of bishops was historical and essential. His defection from Protestantism and his preference for Rome is attested by his emphasis on ritual and liturgy, his reverence for saints' days, shrines, and vigils, his jealous regard for the prerogatives of the clerical estate and its claim to the reverence of the laity, his preference for an unmarried priesthood, his censorship of the clergy, his denying to them the privilege of speaking in print without permission of superiors, his preference for ceremonies over the preaching of the Gospel, and his suppression of conventicles. Laud knew that freedom to print, speak, and preach is fundamental to religious and political liberty. His partiality to ceremonialism was expressed by a bit of sardonic humor: "It is called superstition nowadays for any man to come with more reverence into a church, than a tinker and his dog into an alehouse."

We need not review in detail the long chain of momentous events which precipitated a civil war of creeds, classes, and sections combined, which was terminated by the execution of the king in 1649 and was followed by the attempt by certain Puritan leaders to build up the kingdom of God by the sword. For a period of about ten years England was virtually under a dictatorship in the person of Oliver Cromwell, the greatest Englishman of his time, both as a soldier and statesman. As a destroyer of certain laws, institutions, and abuses his work was great and permanent; as a creator of institutions, he is difficult to judge. His career proves that it is extremely difficult to force a people above its education and intelligence. He was more lenient than the laws and more liberal than most of his enemies. It is largely due to his broadminded sympathy that nonconformity took such deep root that England became the pioneer in religious toleration; that thirty years after his death the religious liberty for which he fought was established by law—in the Toleration Act of 1689.

The restoration of the monarchy in the person of Charles II (1660–1685) after the death of Cromwell was necessary as the only way to restore parliamentary government. As for the government of the Restoration Period, it has been said that it had just ability enough to deceive and just religion enough to persecute. The Church of England continued to be the handmaid of monarchy. Sermons and theological works exalted the divine right of kings and passive obedience.

Among the laws that were enacted by Parliament within five years after the restoration of Charles II, perhaps the most important for Americans is the Act of Uniformity (1662) by which about a fifth of the English clergy were expelled from their livings in the Established Church for refusing to give their assent to everything in the Prayerbook. Despite the harmful effect of this legislation on the spiritual life of the Church of England, Puritanism left an enduring mark on the laity. Family prayer and Bible study were kept up in cottages; and the Puritan Sabbath continued to be the Englishman's Sunday.

The effect of the Act of Uniformity on the Protestant world was salutary. By increasing the number of nonconformists and dissenters, and putting them outside the pale of the Established Church, a long

step was taken in the direction of religious toleration. Sects of various
shades of doctrine and belief made common cause, and England had
a permanent body of dissenters. As in the English colonies and in the
United States, a multitude of sects not only led straight to religious
liberty, but healthy—and sometimes unhealthy—rivalry between
churches and sects had a sobering effect on haughty churchmen and a
restraining influence on the numerically strongest church at a given
time or place.

Charles II was a skeptic in religion; if he preferred any religion, it
was the Catholic. What aid he had received while he was in exile was
from a Catholic monarchy. He sold himself to Louis XIV of France.
In return for French money Charles promised that at a favorable opportunity he would openly declare himself a Catholic, thinking he
could establish absolutism with French aid. He was too wise to think
he could restore the Catholic Church; but he pursued a policy of granting favors to Catholics and dissenters. He quickly learned that Protestants outside the Church of England would rather suffer disabilities
than have toleration for Catholics, whom they feared. A succession
of events, in combination with revelation of Catholic intrigues and
alleged plots, fanned the fury of anti-Catholicism. It was a glorious
opportunity for the party in opposition to the king and his brother the
Duke of York. Efforts were made to exclude from the succession the
Duke of York who was known to have embraced the Catholic religion.
Despite these efforts, in 1685 the duke succeeded his childless brother
as James II.

Brothers could hardly be more unlike than Charles II and James II.
Charles was not by nature a tyrant, nor was he cruel and vindictive.
James was by nature a tyrant, and his heart was as hard as flint. He
intended to build up a standing army to crush constitutional liberty,
to introduce French despotism, and to force Catholicism on the nation. James was under the domination of the Jesuits, whose policy and
strategy he followed. He proceeded to appoint Catholics to offices—
in universities, in the church, and on the bench. The government was
passing into the hands of Catholics. In order to throw dust in the eyes
of the people, James issued two Declarations of Indulgence, in 1687
and 1688. These declarations gave freedom of worship to dissenters
and Catholics and suspended all laws by which they were debarred

from civil and military offices. By including Protestant dissenters in the declarations, James hoped to conceal his hand and also to get support from Protestants, seeing that the Established Church, which benefitted by these restrictions, would not submit to his policy. The second declaration was ordered to be read in churches; but this was too much: the whole nation, Anglicans and dissenters, united against the king.

Encouraged by nonconformist sympathy, seven bishops in the Church of England petitioned the king against the declaration. James had them brought to trial for seditious libel. Public rejoicing over their acquittal was ominous for the king. Another event that made a profound impression in England was the revocation of the Edict of Nantes in 1685 by Louis XIV, at whose ambition and bigotry Europe had trembled for many years. The revocation of the edict of toleration which had been issued in 1598, at the termination of the religious wars in France, was followed by the most cruel persecution of the Huguenots. It was known that the edict was revoked at the instigation of the French clergy and the Jesuits. Why couldn't this happen in England? it was asked.

The events which have been briefly related, and others, both major and minor, culminated in the "Glorious Revolution of 1688." It was bloodless, but none the less a revolution. James deserted the country and fled to France, before the advancing armies of William of Orange. The revolution did not change the government of England, but it prevented James from converting a constitutional monarchy into a despotism. What it meant for England and her colonies is suggested by the contrast between the Act of Toleration passed by the English Parliament in 1689 and the revocation of the Edict of Nantes in 1685 in France.

Perhaps the greatest heritage bequeathed by the Puritan Revolution was the Authorized Version, or the King James Version, of the English Bible, which a student of literature has pronounced the greatest prose work in any language. Another able student has written that "its phraseology has become part and parcel of our common tongue— bone of its bone and flesh of its flesh. Its rhythms and cadences, its turns of speech, its familiar imagery, its very words, are woven into the texture of our literature, prose and poetry alike." The historian Green pays the following tribute to the work of the translators: "But far greater than its effect on literature was the effect of the Bible on the character of the people at large. . . . The whole nation became a church." In the light of these eulogies of the Authorized Version which was published in 1611, Thomas Cranmer's prologue to the version which was printed in 1540 was prophetic:

Doest thou not mark and consider how the smith, mason, or carpenter, or any other handy craftsman, what need so ever he be in, what other shift soever he make, he will not sell or lay to pledge the tools of his occupation, for then how should he work his feet or get his living thereby? Of like mind and affection ought we to be towards the holy scripture, for as mallets, harness, saws, chisels, axes, and hatchets be the tools of their occupation, so be the books of the prophets, and apostles, and all holy writ inspired by the holy ghost, the instruments of our salvation.

The primary version of the English New Testament, one third of which is included in the Authorized Version exactly as it was originally printed, was translated by William Tyndale and published in 1535. Tyndale reached the determination that the New Testament should be translated from Greek to English "because," as he said, "I had perceaved by experyence, how it was impossible to stablysh the laye people in any truth, except ye scripture were playnly layde before their eyes in their mother tongue."

The Geneva Bible, which was first published in 1560, was the translation chiefly used by the first immigrants to New England, because the King James Version had not then passed into general use.

Next to the Bible the book dearest to the Puritans—and perhaps to millions of Christians in all lands—was John Bunyan's *Pilgrim's Progress*. Bunyan himself is the pilgrim, whose dearly bought spiritual experience was told in simple and homely English. It could not have been written without an intense spiritual experience, a soul-testing persecution, and a profound study of the Bible. His two chief literary companions were the Bible and Foxe's *Book of Martyrs*. The years of Bunyan's boyhood were those when the Puritan spirit was at its height. During the twelve years immediately following the Restoration he was in jail, under indictment for violating a law enacted in 1662. The indictment read as follows: "That he hath devilishly and perniciously abstained from coming to Church to hear Divine service, and is a common upholder of several unlawful meetings and conventicles, to the great disturbance and distraction of the good subjects of this Kingdom." The first part of *Pilgrim's Progress* was probably written during a subsequent imprisonment in 1675–1676. His knowledge of the Bible was so intimate that its words and expression became his own; and on the margin of the *Book of Martyrs* he recorded his sympathy and respect for the victims of persecution and his hatred for the Church of Rome. Only the inspiration of genius and spirituality explains why Bunyan's book won the admiration of the "vulgar majority" and the educated minority alike.

Although Bunyan expressed abhorrence for the Quakers, in spirit he was not so far removed from them. Sacramental religion plays a minor part in *Pilgrim's Progress;* and his sermons and writings are critical of liturgies and forms and ceremonies. He detected little affinity between the form of prayer and the spirit of prayer. He said that those who have most of the spirit of prayer are to be found in jail; and those who have most zeal for the form of prayer are to be found in the alehouse.

Bunyan lived long enough to learn that in New England his masterpiece was the daily subject of conversation of thousands of Pilgrims who recognized themselves and their brethren in Bunyan's dream: Pliable, Obstinate, Faithful, Hopeful, Talkative, Mercy, Greatheart, and other characters.

Another writer whose fame is enduring represents the highest type of Puritan. John Milton's *Paradise Lost* was published in 1667, seven years after the Restoration. It is the epic of Puritanism: its theme is the problem of sin and redemption—the eternal struggle of evil against good—the text of Bunyan's dream. To the English-speaking colonists and their descendants in America, Puritan England bequeathed a literary legacy that included *Paradise Lost, Pilgrim's Progress,* and a long list of sterling writers on religious subjects.

In the seventeenth century the spiritual climate of England and the widely promulgated ideas of democracy and self-government in the realm of religion set the stage for one of the world's greatest leaders in the person of George Fox. It has been said that Quakerism has been the most devout of all endeavors to turn Christianity into the religion of Christ. The language, both oral and written, of the early Quaker apostles, including their great leader and founder, was marred by the deplorable violence of the seventeenth century; and their conduct and attitude toward those who disagreed with them was provocative; but their souls were aglow, and they traveled to the end of the road in making protest against forms and ceremonies as degrading to the life of the spirit.

The attitude of the Quakers toward the Bible was fundamentally different from that of Lutherans and Calvinists, and indeed of most other shades of Protestants. The Quakers prayerfully read the Bible and pondered its contents; but they insisted that only those who walked in the spirit of the writers could understand its message. The Quaker position was stated by Robert Barclay, who was a contemporary of George Fox and William Penn: "This is the great work of the Scriptures and their service to us, that we may witness them fulfilled in us and so discern the stamp of God's spirit and ways upon them by the inward acquaintance we have with the same spirit and work in our hearts."

The Quakers had their own vocabulary and way of life. They were not afraid of being pointed out as being "peculiar" or "different." They felt "drawings"; they avoided "steeplehouses"; they abhorred "flattering titles"; they discontinued the observance of "vain and empty customs." They wore no sign of mourning for the dead and placed no memorial stones on their graves. Their homes contained no musical instruments, and the walls were bare of pictures, although it was permissible to display pictures of Penn's treaty with the Indians and the interior of a slave ship. In keeping with the scorn for idolatrous practices and meaningless and harmful forms and ceremonies and superstitious observances of customs, times, and seasons, Quaker shops were open on Christmas Day and Good Friday. The outward rites of baptism and the Lord's Supper were not observed; but the inward experiences which they symbolized were appropriated. George Fox expressed the matter as follows: "This is a nearer and further advanced state, to be with Christ in the fellowship of His death than only to take bread and wine in the remembrance of His death." In general, the Quakers took the position that time does not change the nature and substance of things in themselves, though it may cause things to alter as to their usefulness. That is, things commanded and practiced at certain times fall of themselves when the causes for which they were commanded are removed, as for example circumcision, water baptism, and bread and wine.

Marriage is one of the seven sacraments in the Roman Catholic Church, and members of Protestant churches prefer to have the marriage rite performed by clergymen; but in most countries today they have the option of civil marriage. The Quakers, however, used neither priest nor magistrate. They taught that marriage was an ordinance of God, and that only God could rightly join man and woman in marriage; but they could not go to "hireling priests" to uphold their "false and usurped authority." The Quakers took each other as man and wife in the presence of creditable witnesses.

Quaker communities were characterized by honesty in business, by truthfulness which refused to admit the double standard by the taking of oaths, by simplicity and purity of life, and by concern for the weak and downtrodden. Hats were worn in church, in the home, and in the presence of the magistrate. The customary prefixes to proper names were omitted, and individuals were addressed as "thee" and "thou." In a time when flowery language was in vogue and extravagant compliments were used recklessly and without discrimination and sincerity, and when there was much bowing and scraping, the plain language and simplicity of behavior of the Quakers—their abhorrence of sham and pretense—were offensive and discourteous to those who stood outside. The sturdy insistence on these "peculiarities" entailed suffering and humiliation on many occasions; but it built strong and independent characters.

There were no Quaker ministers in the orthodox sense, nor was there a Quaker church in the ordinary meaning of that term. The Friends understood the word "church" as used in the Scriptures as meaning an assembly of certain people called or gathered together. In practice, the Friends gathered round men and women who exercised spiritual leadership, not by virtue of office or appointment, but a leadership awarded to them because of the inspiration and example of their lives. William Penn in his *Brief Account of the Rise and Progress of the People Called Quakers* wrote that the Friends were changed men themselves before they went about to change others. They went not forth, or preached in their own time, he said, but in the will of God. They spoke as they were moved of the spirit.

The Quakers refused to pay tithes or maintenance to a national ministry, because they believed all compelled maintenance, even to ministers, to be unlawful and expressly contrary to Christ's command: Freely you have received, freely give. They cited denunciations directed by the apostles against covetous hirelings and diviners for money. George Fox recorded in his Journal that the "black earthly spirit of the priests" wounded his life. When he heard the bell toll to call people together to the "steeplehouse," it struck at his life; "for it was just like a market-bell to gather people together that the priest might set forth his ware for sale." On another occasion, in 1648, Fox attended a meeting "wherein Presbyterians, Independents, Baptists, and Common-prayer men were said to be concerned," when a woman asked a question of the priest in the pulpit. He replied: "I permit not a woman to speak in the church." Fox then asked the priest: "Dost thou call this place a church? Or dost thou call this mixed multitude a church?"

Fox, Barclay, and Penn held a conception of the church similar to the Old Testament "remnant." Barclay taught that those who are sanctified in Christ Jesus make the church. Without them, the church ceases to be. Penn wrote that Christianity allows of no pretense whatever for persecuting any man for his religion, because no persecutor can have faith, hope, and charity. When the false church sprang up and grew vain, worldly, ambitious, covetous, and cruel, the true church fled into the wilderness, that is, from superstition and violence, to a retired, solitary, and lonely state; hidden, as it were, out of sight of men, though not out of the world, which shows that her wonted visibility was not essential to the being of a true church in the judgment of the Holy Ghost. Fox taught that there is an immortal seed of God hidden in man's soul; and he knew God as revealed in Christ—as an intimate friend and companion.

It is not to be wondered that the seventeenth century heard Fox and his disciples with amazement, ridicule, and contempt; and that Fox was taken into custody by officers of the law and for months and months languished in unspeakably filthy jails. It was a strange spectacle to see a religious meeting not held in a regular place of worship. It was equally strange—and certainly unorthodox—to see a multitude assembled out-of-doors or in a house with a chimney and without a steeple. The Quaker meeting itself was a strange phenomenon. Charles Lamb, who wrote in the early nineteenth century when the Quakers had lost some of their primitive spirit, learned that "the Abbey Church of Westminster hath nothing so solemn, so spirit-soothing, as the naked walls and benches of a Quakers' Meeting. . . . Hypocrites they certainly are not, in their preaching. It is seldom indeed that you shall see one get up amongst them to hold forth. . . . More frequently the Meeting is broken up without a word having been spoken. But the mind has been fed. You go away with a sermon, not made with hands."

Quakerism, like all religious movements and establishments, presents startling contrasts and paradoxes. It was not free from neurotic and morbid symptoms. As the name suggests, there were among the Friends individuals who were subject to uncontrollable quaking. Fox himself was afflicted with nervous instability and was subject to temporary blindness and trances, and given to seeing visions. Margaret Fell, whom he married in 1669, almost immediately after her conversion became a "quaker," which for a brief period threatened to overcome her usual poise and wisdom. Throughout the years, however, the Quakers have been known and admired for the even tenor of their ways. Had they been given to the singing of hymns, they could have sung even in the time of George Fox the hymn of the Quaker poet Whittier, who lived two hundred years later:

> Drop thy still dews of quietness,
> Till all our strivings cease;
> Take from our souls the strain and stress,
> And let our ordered lives confess
> The beauty of Thy peace.

In common with the multitude of sects and various hues of nonconformists, the Quakers were victims of hostile legislation and persecution that are associated with seventeenth-century England. With the relaxation of persecution, legal and otherwise, which was inaugurated by the enactment of the Act of Toleration in 1689, Quakerism suffered a "quenching of the spirit." Habits of thrift, industry, and honesty brought respectful treatment from the community at large; and material prosperity brought with it worldliness and love of pleasure. Eighteenth- and nineteenth-century Quakerism in both England and the United States was influenced by an extreme form of religious mysticism known as quietism. This deeply spiritual manifestation of Christianity is associated with three remarkable personalities who wrote in the second half of the seventeenth century and the early years of the eighteenth century: Madame Guyon, Fenelon, and Molinos. The Autobiography of Madame Guyon especially had a marked influence upon Quakers on both sides of the Atlantic, and upon members of other churches as well. According to the brilliant Quaker historian, Rufus M. Jones, the influence of quietism explains in part one of the unique features of later Quakerism, namely, the spontaneous and unorganized itinerant ministry.

In the first half of the eighteenth century the Quakers adopted birthright membership, which meant the transition from a membership of "believers"—a "pure" church—to a "mixed" body, composed of many whose religion was nominal. This opened the door for corruption and degeneration: wealthy members, habits of luxury, compromise with unchristian customs, and spiritual indifference.

THREE

THE PURITANS IN NEW ENGLAND

NEW ENGLAND was founded by Puritans who left England during the twelve years from 1628 to 1640, when the train of events was laid for the Puritan Revolution in England. The leaders of the twenty thousand emigrants, whose chief impulse was religious, were members of the Church of England who preferred to remain within its fold if it were purged of remnants of Romanism. They were in sharp disagreement with the Pilgrim founders of the Plymouth Colony who began their great experiment slightly less than a decade earlier on their fundamental doctrine that there should be no national church. They believed that each local religious organization—each congregation—should be separate and independent of the state, and even independent in government of other churches. The Plymouth Colony grew slowly; ten years after its establishment, in 1630, the population numbered less than three hundred. But history has borne out the prophecy of James Russell Lowell: "Next to the fugitives whom Moses led out of Egypt, the little shipload of outcasts who landed at Plymouth . . . are destined to influence the future of mankind." Their free spirit which flowered into heroism pointed the way toward church independency and the freedom of Christian men. "God hath sifted a nation, that he might send choice grain into the wilderness," said William Stoughton in his "election sermon" of 1690.

The letters and contemporary documentary material, including histories, written by the hands of Pilgrims and Puritans, reveal the low-hanging clouds of persecution and war in England and in Europe. The Thirty Years' War was rolling back the Protestant tide and Cardinal Richelieu was making war on the Huguenots.

The great John Winthrop set down the reasons to be considered for "justifying the undertakers of the intended Plantation in New England":

It will be a service to the Church of great consequence to carry the Gospell into those parts of the world, to helpe on the comminge of the fullnesse of the Gentiles, and to raise a Bulworke against the Kingdome of the Ante Christ which the Jesuites labour to reare up in those parts.

All other churches of Europe are brought to desolation, and our sinnes, for which the Lord beginnes allreaddy to frowne upon us and to cutte us short, doe threatne evill times to be comminge upon us, and who knowes but that God hath provided this place to be a refuge for many whome he meanes to save out of the generall callamity; and seeing the Church hath noe place lefte to flie into but the wildernesse, what better worke can there be, then to goe and provide tabernacles and foode for her against she comes thither. . . .

The ffountaines of Learning and Religion are soe corrupted as . . . most children . . . are perverted, corrupted, and utterlie overthroune by the multitude of evill examples and the licentious government of those seminaries, where men straine at knatts and swallowe camells, use all severity for mainetaynance of cappes and other accomplyments, but suffer all ruffianlike fashions and disorder in manners to pass uncontrolled.

Except for remnants sparsely distributed in certain countries of Europe in the seventeenth century, it was taken for granted by statesmen, ecclesiastical and secular, that church and state should be intimately united. It is all the more remarkable that the founders of the New England colonies who, with the exception of the Pilgrims, were members of the Established Church, in the New World immediately set about to found their churches upon the independent plan. It was better, according to one of the prominent founders, that the commonwealth be fashioned "to the setting forth of God's house, which is his church, than to accommodate the church frame to the civil state."

The respective groups of immigrants who were carried along by the "Great Migration" to New England were more fortunate than were most of the emigrants from Europe. It was unusual for the ecclesiastical authorities and parish pastors to interest themselves in behalf of immigrants, whom they regarded as wanton deserters from their native land, deserving of whatever fate awaited them. The clergyman who gave up a comfortable living in an established church in favor of the uncertainty and hardships of frontier life was exceptional.

The Puritan clergy were exceptional. Fortunate were the first settlers in New England that some of the ablest men in England, distinguished alumni of Cambridge and Oxford, sacrificed security and ecclesiastical preferment in answer to the call of duty to serve congregations in remote villages to which they carried the torch of culture and religion. They were prototypes of New England clergymen in succeeding generations, whose early days had been spent on the parental farm, in homes suggested by Whittier's "Snow Bound." Their pastoral duties were not incompatible with the cultivation of a small farm. Their sermons were enriched by experience with the practical things of life and gave meaning to the man who held the plow handle and to the housewife who was schooled in thrift and frugality. Religion in the Puritan meeting-house and at the family altar was dignified by respect for learning.

Most of the ministers who arrived in the earliest years of the Puritan migration held to the view that the primitive and apostolic churches were distinct political bodies—Congregational rather than Presbyterian in polity. They were complete societies, each of which had the power to censure, admit, and expel members, and elect officers. Christ was the head of the church. Churches and state were so laced together that neither church nor state was superior.

Women and children were exempted from a part in church government, according to the accepted interpretation of Scripture; therefore, only elders and brethren were constituent members competent to act in the sacred corporation. The officers of the church included two ministers, the pastor and the teacher, and two ruling elders.

The Puritan churches were preaching and teaching churches. The services were educational. The emphasis was on the sermon. In New England labor and intelligence went hand in hand, and so did religion and intelligence. The faithful assembled in the meeting-house to pray and to meditate, to sing psalms, and to hear the Scriptures read and expounded by a learned man. Once a month the Lord's Supper was celebrated—not as a sacrament but as memorial observance. In reality, the faithful met for edification, rather than for worship. Puritan New England did not reproduce the dimly lighted cathedrals, with clouds of incense, and elaborately robed priests. Vestments, liturgies, holy altars, communion tables and similar sensuous aids to the religious life were absent from the meeting-houses; the Puritan delighted in the law of the Lord, and in His law did he meditate day and night. He faced the solemn questions of human destiny without the trappings of sacerdotalism. In addition to two Sunday services, there was a weekly afternoon lecture or sermon in which the minister expounded a text taken from either the Old Testament or the New Testament.

At first the minister was ordained by the officers of each congregation by the laying on of hands; but later it became the custom to call in ministers from neighboring congregations to officiate. This ceremony —ordination by laymen—was clearly a break with the episcopal Mother Church and a recognition of congregational principles, which previously only such radicals as Separatists and Anabaptists had practiced. For example, when the vanguard of Puritans arrived at Salem in 1628, a simple covenant was adopted, without a creedal statement, and a pastor and a teacher were elected. In spite of the fact that these men had been regularly ordained by bishops in the Church of England, at Salem they were ordained by the laying on of hands. Nor did a minister without a church continue to hold his ministerial character— a radical and significant departure from the *character indelebilis* of the priesthood, according to the doctrine of the Roman Catholic Church and certain Protestant churches.

According to "worldly" standards, the social climate of New England was dreary. It is true that the Puritans regarded the popular amusements of the day as of the devil; but it must be remembered that their social life was built around the home and the meeting-house. The American home celebrated in song and story was the creation of the Puritans. There was a wholesome respect for father and mother, who in turn showed tender affection for their children. The Puritan's ideal of a Christian commonwealth was mirrored in the home. His intolerance and harsh judgments were by-products of his determination to be master of himself. His gravity and sternness were manifestations of his self-discipline and his orderly and methodical life. What gave peace, joy, and amusement to the Puritan was leagues removed from the gaiety and frivolity—and often shoddiness—of holidays and of taverns. He was happy in proportion to the things he could get along without. He was sparing of diet. Father and mother, son and daughter, dressed simply and becomingly, avoiding costly apparel. The prayerful reading of the Bible and of devotional literature made them long to lose hold on earthly things.

The peace and stillness of the Sabbath was as undisturbed as the solemnity which was heralded by the nine-o'clock evening bell. The night was made to sleep in; and shortly after sunset the community prepared for bed. Whatever may have been the origin of the maxim, "Early to bed and early to rise makes a man happy, healthy, and wise," it reflected the mode of life in early New England.

The Puritans lived by statutes as strict as those of Leviticus and Deuteronomy. The moral codes enacted into statute law in the New England colonies were expressions of enlightened public opinion. Like the strict regulations in Calvin's Geneva, they were not imposed on an unwilling community. Moreover, Puritan law and justice were tender of children and dumb animals and were full of human kindness.

The common school system of America is a gift of Puritan New England. Within a few years after the first settlements, steps leading to the establishment of a system of education were taken; and by the beginning of the third quarter of the seventeenth century all the New England colonies excepting Rhode Island had provided compulsory education, which included instruction from the primary school to the university. In 1636 Harvard College was founded with the primary purpose of instructing students in the knowledge of God and Jesus Christ "as the only foundation of all sound knowledge and learning."

In Harriet Beecher Stowe's novel, *The Minister's Wooing*, portraying New England life at the close of the eighteenth century, she presented Zebedee Marvyn as the sample of an individuality purely the result of New England society and education. He owned a large farm, which he worked with his own hands. He was a man past the middle of life, with a face deeply marked with the lines of energy and thought. His education had been merely that of the common schools and academies with which the states were thickly sown. Though toiling daily with his sons and the hired man, he kept an observant eye on the field of literature, and there was not a new publication heard of which he did not immediately find means to add to his yearly increasing stock of books. In particular was he a well-read and careful theologian in all the controversial tracts, sermons, and books with which New England abounded. There was scarce an office of public trust which had not at one time or another been filled by him. Mrs. Stowe records that the library of a well-taught young woman in New England at that time contained the *Spectator,* Paradise Lost, Shakespeare, Robinson Crusoe, the Bible, and the Works of Jonathan Edwards.

The Puritan was sensitive to the stirrings of Providence. The still, small voice of calm spoke through the earthquake, wind, and fire. He regarded the divine interposition in comforts, in health, in friends, in prosperity, in disappointments, in losses, and in pain. It would be difficult in all history to find a more robust faith and a more adamant Christian fortitude than that on which were laid the foundations of Puritan New England. Emerson was by no means blind to the faults of the Puritans and the commonwealth which they founded; but he appraised them as "great, grim, earnest men," who had "solemnized the heyday of their strength by the planting and liberating of America."

The Puritans—unlike the Pilgrims—did not come to America harboring abstractions of religious liberty. They risked their lives and sacrificed their property in order that they might worship according to what they conceived to be scriptural Christianity and establish a commonwealth fashioned after their own ideas. They welcomed only those recruits to their population who shunned infidelity, idolatry, and popery; neither should the godly be yoked by marrying "such as are wicked in this life or maintain damnable heresy." This practice was consistent with their idea that each congregation was a covenant, which implied that only persons of kindred spirit should be admitted into membership of the community. If an individual did not conform, he was at liberty to go elsewhere. They never dreamed that they were settling a colony in order to afford harbor for all sorts of persons who could not live comfortably elsewhere. There was land enough lying waste in the outlying wilderness for malcontents.

Among the malcontents in the Massachusetts Bay Colony, two have achieved enduring fame: Roger Williams and Anne Hutchinson.

Williams, an able and scholarly minister of sterling character, migrated to Massachusetts in 1631. His adversaries condemned him as a disagreeable and contentious person, unbalanced, indiscreet, and of poor judgment. However that may be, there is agreement that he was a quibbler, with a bent for controversy, and a genius for getting into hot water. He found certain ecclesiastical laws and regulations in Massachusetts no more palatable than were those of Archbishop Laud, by whom he was driven from England. Williams harbored separatistic principles and believed an established church to be sinful. He condemned compulsory church attendance and compulsory payments for its support. He denied the right of the authorities to inflict punishment for violations of the first four Commandments, especially observance of the Sabbath. He denied the title of the colony to its lands, arguing that the king had told a "solemn lie" in the charter by claiming the right to give title to lands that belonged to the Indians.

Williams proved to be a heavy liability to the authorities from several points of view, not least complications with the home government. Efforts to exact a promise of silence from the rebellious clergyman failed and he was sentenced to banishment to England—an early instance of the deportation of radicals to the country from which they emigrated. Before the sentence could be executed, however, Williams had taken to the wilderness, where he lived among friendly Indians until, in 1636, he came to Providence, Rhode Island, where he gathered to himself a few followers.

Williams was an unswerving advocate of freedom of conscience and of absolute non-interference by the state in matters pertaining to conscience; and the colony he founded embodied his conviction. Rhode Island was a primitive democracy which in an age of intolerance proved that a government could endure without religious regimentation. In word and deed Williams was the pioneer of religious freedom in America. He accepted the doctrines of the new Baptist sect and founded the first Baptist church in America. The radical Baptist tenet that infant baptism was unscriptural—and, therefore, unchristian—cast serious reflections on members of Puritan churches. In other words, the membership of Puritan congregations was unchristian. If this principle had been accepted, the civil government of the Massachusetts Bay would have fallen. From that point of view the Baptist teaching was "anarchistic."

Rhode Island became a "crank's paradise," New England's dumping ground for the disorderly and eccentric elements in her population. Williams disliked Quakers, some of whom in that day bore little resemblance to the calm, placid, and peaceful nonconformists of the

William Penn and John Woolman type; but in reply to complaints from Massachusetts about unruly neighbors who swarmed across her borders, Williams replied: "We have no law to punish any for declaring by words their minds concerning the ways and things of God."

Rhode Island furnished an asylum for a woman who was banished by the General Court of Massachusetts Bay as a "woman not fit for our society." And finally in 1638 her own church in Boston resorted to excommunication. The presiding officer announced the fate of Mrs. Anne Hutchinson as follows: "Therefore in the name of our Lord Jesus Christ and in the name of the Church I do not only pronounce you worthy to be cast out, but I do cast you out and in the name of Christ I do deliver you up to Satan, that you may no more learn to blaspheme, to seduce and to lie, and I do account you from this time forth to be a Heathen and a Publican and so to be held of all the brethren and sisters of this congregation and of others."

What was the offense which called forth these harsh judgments and sentences? Mrs. Hutchinson was doctrinally at variance with Calvinism and she rebelled against the legalism of the Puritan churches. In her home, which became a sort of round table, she showed her contempt for ministers and magistrates and dissected and analyzed sermons. She accepted the doctrine of predestination, but she obliterated the line of demarcation between justification and sanctification. She taught that through faith in Christ a person is freed not only from the consequences of sin but from sin itself, that is, a converted person has no sin, because Christ has taken away all sin. She professed to have immediate revelations from God. According to her doctrine of self-illumination, if a person had faith, the Divine Spirit would enter and he could do no wrong. It followed that Bible, priest, and church were unnecessary mediums, because each individual was a medium. The political and social consequences of Mrs. Hutchinson's Antinomianism (meaning against the law) were farreaching; if it had been accepted, New England would have become dotted with a multitude of sects and the law that only church members could exercise the right of suffrage would have been abandoned. It also brought to mind the orgies and excesses practiced at Wittenberg by the Zwickau prophets and by the followers of Thomas Münzer in Luther's lifetime. Moreover, Mrs. Hutchinson's ideas and practices were incompatible with the principles which guided the founders of New England, who were educated in the universities of England. Their ecclesiastical establishment rested on a learned clergy and a literate people.

The Puritans differed from the Church of England in that they confined baptism to believers and their "seed." The early New England Congregationalists maintained that only adult persons could be admitted to full membership in the church, after making public confession of religious experience and signing the covenant. Infants born to these members were baptized; but only upon profession of faith as adults were they admitted to full membership. If they failed to make such profession, they remained outside the fold, with the consequence that their children were denied the rite of baptism, since children shared in the covenant taken by their parents. Because of this provision, with the passing years the numbers standing outside church membership increased. The right of suffrage being included with church membership, the size of the non-voting population augmented, which in turn created dissatisfaction and unrest.

Within less than a man's lifetime, the conservative clergy in Massachusetts were compelled to deal with the mounting dissatisfaction. Finally the General Court of the colony called a General Synod of all the Massachusetts churches to meet in Boston in March, 1662. After extended discussions what was known as the Half-Way Covenant was adopted, but many congregations were reluctant to accept the radical change, which admitted to membership, albeit with some restrictions, those who had been excluded under the old system. There were clergymen then and in later years who could find no warrant in Scripture for the Half-Way Covenant and in no case would administer the ordinance of baptism to children, neither of whose parents was in full communion with the church. Jonathan Edwards was bitterly opposed to the Covenant.

A change with reference to ecclesiastical polity was indicative of a change in the spirit of New England churches and prophetic of even greater changes in the years to come—some of them far in the future. Massachusetts churches continued to abide by the plan of independent Congregationalism, which according to the Cambridge Platform of 1648 gave to synods a right merely to advise individual churches. In Connecticut the trend was in the direction of Presbyterianism. At the call of the legislature a synod meeting at Saybrook in 1708 drew up the Saybrook Platform which was semi-Presbyterian, or a rule by councils—away from the independency of early Congregationalism. According to this "consociation," churches were organized into county associations, ruled by a council of ministers and lay delegates, which was given disciplinary power over erring congregations, and supervision over the choice of new pastors. County associations sent delegates to an annual assembly which regulated the whole colony.

After the adoption of the Saybrook Platform, Connecticut Congregationalism listed heavily toward Presbyterianism; and within less than three-quarters of a century the names, Congregational and Presbyterian, were practically synonymous and were used interchangeably. This culminated in the Plan of Union in 1801, which has its own story.

The Great Awakening which shook the foundations of New England some thirty years after the adoption of the Saybrook Platform called forth condemnation of the "unconverted ministry" in the New England churches as sharp as those directed against Archbishop Laud by the founding fathers.

A student of the rise of modern democracy has made a concise summary of the first period of New England history in the following sentence: "The earliest Puritan colonies, at one and the same time, shared the character of a company of planters, a community of citizens, and a religious congregation."

FOUR

THE QUAKERS IN AMERICA

I F GEORGE FOX is the most important personality among the Quakers, John Woolman is the most lovable. "Get the Writings of John Woolman by heart; and love the early Quakers," wrote Charles Lamb. Of Woolman it has been said that he was a man who, in all the centuries since the advent of Christ, lived nearest the divine pattern. His religion was love; and his moral qualities were transferred to his writings. Of this tailor who wrote in a style of exquisite purity, it might be said, as was said of the Master whose teaching he followed: "Whence hath this man this wisdom, and these mighty works?" Of him the gentle Quaker poet Whittier wrote:

I am willing to own that in delineating a character of such moral and spiritual symmetry I have felt something like rebuke from my own words. I have been awed and solemnized by the presence of a serene and healthful spirit redeemed of the Lord from all selfishness, and I have been made thankful for the ability to recognize and the disposition to love him.

Visions, trances, and other abnormalities are usually attributed to religious ecstasy or to emotional strain under the spell of powerful revivalist preachers. But even a man with such a well-integrated personality as John Woolman, at the age of thirty-seven, recorded this strange experience:

In a short time I awoke; it was yet dark, and no appearance of day or moonshine, and as I opened my eyes I saw a light in my chamber, at the apparent distance of five feet, about nine inches in diameter, of a clear brightness, and near its center the most radiant. As I lay still looking upon it without any surprise, words were spoken to my inward ear, which filled my whole inward man. They were not the effect of thought, nor any conclusion in relation to the appearance, but as the language of the Holy One spoken in my mind. The words were, CERTAIN EVIDENCE OF DIVINE TRUTH. They were again repeated exactly in the same manner, and then the light disappeared.

John Woolman was born in Northampton, Burlington County, West Jersey, in 1720, thirty years after the death of George Fox. He died in 1772, about a century after Fox made his memorable visit to the American colonies, where he traveled extensively and gained recruits from Massachusetts to Carolina. Even before the arrival of William Penn in the colony of which he was the founder in 1682, the number of Quaker emigrants from the mother country was so great as to weaken the society in the country of its origin. In many places in colonial America, even at that early date, Quakerism was the dominating religious influence. During his visit to Rhode Island, Fox was present at a Quaker wedding in the home of a Friend who had formerly been governor of the colony. There were a goodly number present; and both Quakers and non-Quakers said they never saw so solemn an assembly on such an occasion, nor so comely an order.

The Quakers won an influential member when William Penn became a member of their society. As a student at Oxford this son of an admiral in the English navy was attracted to the society through the influence of a Quaker preacher. Expulsion from his home by his irate father did not swerve the young man from the straight and narrow road of the Quakers; he insisted on saying "thee" and "thou" and refused to remove his hat in the presence of persons who expected that courtesy. Penn's preference for the religion of the meek and lowly on one occasion sent him to the Tower of London and on another exacted a fine.

Upon the death of his father, Penn inherited his estate, which included a debt of sixteen thousand pounds owed to him by Charles II. This debt was paid to the satisfaction of Penn by granting to him a charter, in 1681, which gave proprietary rights to the colony which bears his name.

When Penn arrived in Pennsylvania in 1682, he found Swedes, Dutchmen, and Englishmen already settled within its boundaries and assured them that they would be governed by laws of their own making. In 1701 Penn issued his Charter of Privileges, which remained in force until 1776. It granted religious liberty to those who believed in God and confined office-holders to those who believed in Jesus Christ. The charter thereby excluded from its privileges Jews and "freethinkers"; but it exceeded the tolerance of other colonies, not excepting Rhode Island, by granting the right of suffrage and of holding office to Roman Catholics. No colony contained the medley of races, confessions, and creeds that were found in Pennsylvania. From England, Scotland, Wales, Ulster, France, Germany, and the Netherlands came emigrants seeking fortune, well-being, and religious freedom. Penn wrote brochures about the land of freedom, which were translated into Dutch, German, and French. He also traveled in the Rhine Valley and preached to the Mennonites who had many things in common with the Quakers.

Pennsylvania and Rhode Island were prototypes of the religious individualism, the multitude of sects, and the religious freedom that became characteristics of American society. With the exception of Rhode Island, Pennsylvania, and Delaware (which for a time was united with Pennsylvania), there was an established church in each of the thirteen colonies.

If the Quakers became important numerically and influential, the beginnings of Quakerism were tragic and inauspicious. The Quaker "invasion" of America began in July, 1656, with the arrival in the road before Boston of Mary Fisher and Ann Austin. Before they came ashore, the deputy governor sent officers aboard, who searched their trunks and chests and took away their books, after having commanded the women to be kept aboard. By order of the Council, the books were burned in the marketplace by the hangman. Later the deputy governor ordered the women brought ashore and had them committed to jail as Quakers, upon proof that one of them had addressed him as "thee" instead of "you." Pen, ink, and paper were taken away from them, and they were not permitted to have candle-light in the night. They were stripped naked in order to find out whether or not they were witches. After having been prisoners for about five weeks, the master of the vessel was compelled to carry them back to England.

William Sewel, the author of the pioneer *History of the Rise, Increase, and Progress of the Christian People Called Quakers*, which was first published in London in 1722, after relating these details, made the following comment: "Such was the entertainment the Quakers first met with at Boston, and that from a people, who pretended, that for conscience-sake, they had chosen the wilderness of America, before the well-cultivated old England."

In the years immediately following the deportation of these two women, their co-religionists who planted the "seed" in the New World met with the same furious persecution. Many were whipped, imprisoned, and mutilated, and a few were put to death. In October, 1658, an act of the General Court held at Boston provided for banishment of Quakers. They were said to be guilty of denying civil respect to equals and superiors, of withdrawing from church assemblies, of harboring tenets and practices opposite to the orthodox opinions of the godly, and of overthrowing the order established in church and state. In a sermon preached at Boston in 1658, Charles Chauncy, a member of the Harvard faculty, justified the treatment accorded Quakers in the following language: "Suppose you should catch six wolves in a trap, and ye cannot prove that they killed either sheep or lambs: and now you have them they will neither bark nor bite; yet they have the plain marks of wolves, and therefore ye knock them down."

From being bracketed with Unitarians, Deists, and infidels, by the beginning of the eighteenth century the Quakers emerged as valuable citizens, respected for their upright way of life and philanthropy. Strong men and women of Quaker stock became leaders in community and nation. Elizabeth Payson Prentiss records that when she arrived in New Bedford, Massachusetts, in 1845, as the wife of the recently ordained minister of the South Trinitarian church, New Bedford was known the world over as the most important center of the whale fishery; and it was also known for the fine social qualities of its people. Many of the original settlers of the town were Quakers, and its character had been largely shaped by their friendly influence. A charming simplicity marked the daily intercourse of life.

In his early teens, John Woolman recorded in his Journal his guiding faith and revealed the "seed" in the hearts of people who called themselves and others Friends:

I kept steadily to meetings; spent first-day afternoons chiefly in reading the Scriptures and other good books, and was early convinced in my mind that true religion consisted in an inward life, wherein the heart doth love and reverence God the Creator, and learns to exercise true justice and goodness, not only to all men, but also toward the brute creatures. . . . I found no narrowness respecting sects and opinions, but believed that sincere upright-hearted people, in every society, who truly love God, were accepted by him.

Throughout his life he had "many fresh and heavenly openings" and was taught "by renewed experience to labor for inward stillness; and at no time to seek for words, but to live in the spirit of truth, and utter that to the people which truth opened to us."

While he continued to work at his trade as a tailor, he attended meetings for worship and discipline; and he had "drawings" to visit Friends in the back settlements of Pennsylvania, Virginia, and New England. He refrained from speaking in meetings for many weeks together until he felt "that rise which prepares the creature to stand like a trumpet, through which the Lord speaks to his flock." "My mind was often tender," he wrote, "and I learned some profitable lessons."

At a yearly meeting in 1756, he felt a weight on his mind and stood up to clear himself of a burden which for some days had been increasing upon him.

Through the humbling dispensations of Divine Providence, men are sometimes fitted for his service. The messages of the prophet Jeremiah were so disagreeable to the people, and so adverse to the spirit they lived in, that he became the object of their reproach, and in the weakness of nature he thought of desisting from his prophetic office; but saith he, "His word was in my heart as a burning fire shut up in my bones; and I was weary with forbearing, and could not stay." I saw at this time that if I was honest in declaring that which truth opened in me, I could not please all men; and I labored to continue in the way of my duty, however disagreeable to my own inclination.

As a young man Woolman observed that at Christmas many people resorted to public houses to spend their time in drinking and vain sports, on which account he was much troubled. He saw that an humble man, "with the blessing of the Lord," might live on a little; and that where the heart was set on greatness, success in business did not satisfy the craving; but that commonly with an increase of wealth the desire of wealth increased. He admitted that trading in useful things was an honest employment, but he thought that those who were engaged in that employment needed to be well experienced in that precept which the prophet Jeremiah laid down for his scribe: "Seekest thou great things for thyself? seek them not."

Woolman believed that every degree of luxury had some connection with evil; he had seen that the liberal use of spirituous liquor and the custom of wearing too costly apparel led some people into great inconveniences. The spirit of lotteries was a spirit of selfishness. In his mature life, Woolman was convinced that if owners of great estates lived in that humility and plainness which belong to a Christian life and laid much easier rents and interests on their lands and money, so great a number of people might be employed in useful things that labor both for men and other creatures would be more agreeable and certain branches of business might be discontinued.

Even such a consecrated man as Woolman was torn between conformity and nonconformity and was vexed by the tyranny of public sentiment. He continued in the use of some things contrary to his judgment because of the "apprehension of being singular from beloved friends." But as the result of illness and meditation, he discontinued wearing dyed clothing and changeable modes of dress.

The French and Indian War (1755–1763) brought to Woolman trials and searchings of heart. In spite of the fact that several prominent Quakers favored paying taxes to provide money for the carrying on of war, there was in his mind a scruple which he could not get over. "I believed that there were some upright-hearted men who paid such taxes," he wrote, "yet could not see that their example was a sufficient reason for me to do so. . . . To refuse the active payment of a tax our Society generally paid was exceedingly disagreeable; but to do a thing contrary to my conscience appeared yet more dreadful." By refraining from fighting against invaders one does in some degree "feel that spirit in which our Redeemer gave his life for us." He felt that it required great self-denial and resignation of self to God to refuse to fight when wrongfully invaded, if by fighting there was a probability of overcoming the invaders.

Woolman lamented the changed attitude among the Quakers after toleration in the colonies was extended to their religion. He saw the danger of too much prosperity. "A carnal mind is gaining upon us," he said. By taking part in civic affairs and assisting in the prosecution of war, certain Friends were setting a bad example to their brethren and might "quench the tender movings of the Holy Spirit in their minds." "Thus, by small degrees, we might approach so near to fighting that the distinction would be little else than the name of a peaceable people," he said.

On his later journeys, Woolman "had many thoughts on the different circumstances of Friends" who inhabited Pennsylvania and Jersey from those who dwelt in Maryland, Virginia, and Carolina. Pennsylvania and Jersey were settled by Friends who had suffered persecution in England for their principles. They bought land of the Indians and taught their children to labor for their living. Few of this type of Quakers settled in the southern colonies. Woolman rejoiced, however, that by the faithful labors of traveling Friends in early times "there was considerable convincement among the inhabitants."

In 1742 while in the employ of a small storekeeper in New Jersey, who was a member of the Society of Friends, Woolman was requested to make out a bill of sale for a Negro woman. He complied with the request, but he told his employer in a friendly way that he could not write instruments by which fellow-creatures were made slaves without making trouble in his own mind. Woolman became an uncompromising opponent of slavery, so much so that on his visits to Quaker settlements his conscience troubled him when he accepted the hospitality of slaveholders. It did not seem right for him to save his money by kindness received from what appeared to him to be the gain of oppression. In his efforts to awaken the moral sense of Friends, Woolman found a zealous co-laborer in Anthony Benezet, a descendent of persecuted French Protestants.

In 1784, about a decade after the death of Woolman, the Yearly Meeting directed in cases where Friends continued to hold slaves, notwithstanding the advice and importunities of their friends, that the Monthly Meetings should disown them. This virtually put an end to slavery in the Society of Friends—far in advance of most religious denominations. Quakers, men and women, were active in the abolition movement and in anti-slavery societies; and literature published under the auspices of the Society of Friends laid bare the horrors of the African slave trade, and the part American citizens played in it, even after the traffic had been prohibited by law in 1808. The Quakers were a reading people and were well informed about the horrors of the foreign and domestic slave trade. This made them impatient with persons who were ignorant of, or indifferent to, the iniquities of the institution of slavery.

During the Civil War, through the individual efforts of Quakers and their Yearly Meetings, money and clothing were distributed to colored refugees. For example, at Alexandria, Virginia, a large apartment was set up as a workroom, where sewing machines were operated by refugees. Various articles were donated, such as garments of all kinds, piece goods, needles, shoes, schoolbooks, Bibles, and other books. The committee purchased blankets, woolen hosiery, sheeting, shirting, printed goods, bagging for straw beds, slates, and pencils.

In a letter addressed to the Representatives of the New York Yearly Meeting of Friends in 1864, Sarah Smith, a minister and member of the Indiana Yearly Meeting, formerly of Sheffield, England, reported on her work among the colored refugees near Vicksburg, Mississippi. At a meeting, which she attended, a colored minister arose and said:

> Brederen and sisters, we have had de blessed gospel preached dis day. We neber had de gospel in de South; it was all, "obey your masters"; and dey neber told us Jesus died for poor black man. Now, dis lady say, Jesus died for black and white; and we feel him here (putting his hand to his breast), we knows it is de gospel; for Jesus tell me he wash my sins away. I was de greater sinner man on de plantation, and Jesus touch my heart, and I tried to pray. I called for mercy. My Master heard me, and said he hab no praying niggers on his plantation; told de oberseer to give me five hundred lashes, but he could not whip de pray out of me. . . .

During the nineteenth century the Quakers gained a great reputation for philanthropy. They were prominent in reform movements and organizations to promote temperance, peace, women's rights, prison reform, establishment of institutions for the care of the indigent, the insane, and other unfortunates. There were Quakers who were not without misgivings over the association of their fellow-members with persons who stood outside their Society, even in philanthropic enterprises. They expressed criticism of Elizabeth Fry who was a leader in prison reform, because her association with people of importance stunted her spiritual growth and because the prominence and applause which her activity brought made her self-complacent. The War of American Independence had a demoralizing effect on the morals of young and old and caused many to renounce their religious principles. After the news of the battle of Lexington was broadcast from neighborhood to neighborhood, there was great enthusiasm for war, and many Quakers and Mennonites took part in military exercises.

Moreover, the effect of great revivals which swept the country after the turn of the century and the proselyting of rival churches was disconcerting to Quakers and created problems of keeping the growing generation in the faith. Rationalism was also making inroads; and with the loss of faith there was the inevitable indifference to meetings and increased immorality. The attempt on the part of some members of the Society to adopt evangelistic doctrines and methods was abortive— in a sense inconsistent with the fundamentals of Quakerism. In its origin Quakerism was a protest against the existing ecclesiastical system—theology and sacerdotalism. The Quaker way of salvation was individualistic, as against a mediating priesthood and forms and ceremonies.

At the beginning of the second decade of the nineteenth century occurred the greatest tragedy of Quaker history, according to Rufus M. Jones. In 1827–1828 the schism between two schools of thought divided the Society of Friends in America into two branches, and the schism proved to be permanent. The liberal element became known as "Hicksite," from Elias Hicks, who viewed with alarm the trend of events. He stressed the light within and minimized the value of human agencies in promoting the life of the spirit and inculcating morality. He leaned in the direction of quietism. His formal education was meager, but his mind was strong and alert. He did not believe that individuals could work out their own salvation by intellectualism. He was therefore leagues removed from "modernism" and Unitarianism— or salvation by character. Artificialities—human contrivances—could not work regeneration. For this reason he had doubts about the blessings and value of higher education and of Bible societies, which were springing up in many parts. He believed in spontaneous preaching— over against a "hireling ministry" and "studied preaching."

In common with many prophets of other times and places, Hicks did not adhere slavishly to the written word. He did not question the accuracy of the Bible; but he did not accept its authority in matters of faith and practice. He placed the emphasis on the inner light. His most radical departure from orthodoxy was the rejection of original sin. He did not question the fact of man's fall; but he taught that every soul at birth was as pure and undefiled as Adam was before his fall from grace. He did not worship Christ as the "Savior" in the Pauline Epistles. To Hicks, Christ was the spiritual revelation of God who is the inward light and spiritual guide in the souls of all men, without the aid of books or men.

Under the leadership of men like Stephen Grellet, Thomas Shillitoe, and Joseph John Gurney, the opponents of Hicks adopted the orthodox evangelical position. Lucretia Coffin Mott belonged to the Hicksite group. She was a tireless preacher and reformer. Hicks was instrumental in urging her to take up the cause of abolition. She was active in the American Anti-Slavery Society and was one of the organizers of the Philadelphia Female Anti-Slavery Society, of which she was president during most of its existence.

Only an author with the tender instincts of a Christian mother could have written the chapter on "The Quaker Settlement" in *Uncle Tom's Cabin*. Countless tears have stained the pages which describe the home of Simeon and Rachel Halliday, where Eliza and George and Harry found peace and safety in their flight from slave-catchers. Rachel Halliday might be fifty-five or sixty, "but hers was one of those faces that time seems to touch only to brighten and adorn."

The snowy *lisse* crape cap, made after the straight Quaker pattern; the plain white muslin handkerchief, lying in placid folds across her bosom; the drab shawl and dress, showed at once the community to which she belonged. . . . Her hair, partially silvered by age, was parted smoothly back from a high placid forehead, on which time had written no inscription, except peace on earth, good-will to men; and beneath shone a pair of large, clear, honest, loving brown eyes.

The little rocking chair in which she sat kept up a kind of "creechy-crawchy"; but old Simeon Halliday declared that it was as good as any music to him. For twenty years or more, nothing but loving words, and gentle moralities, and motherly kindness, had come from that chair. It was in this home that George Harris for the first time sat down on equal terms at any white man's table. Young Simeon learned that his father would willingly pay a fine or suffer imprisonment as a penalty for freedom's sake, nor would he permit young Simeon to speak evil of persons who voted for fugitive slave laws. "The Lord only gives us our worldly goods that we may do justice and mercy; if our rulers require a price for it, we must deliver it up," he said.

What a contrast between the Quakers in *Uncle Tom's Cabin* and the judgment expressed by Dr. Hopkins, the minister in Mrs. Stowe's novel *The Minister's Wooing:* "What a shame it is, what a scandal and disgrace to the Protestant religion, that Christians of America should openly practice and countenance this enslaving of the Africans."

FIVE

THE GREAT AWAKENING

THE year 1740 is associated with the Great Awakening; and the Great Awakening is associated with the name of Jonathan Edwards, the greatest American theologian and one of the three greatest American philosophers. The Great Awakening was not confined to a single year; neither was Jonathan Edwards the only great personality who took part in it. The great preacher and profound student sounded the call for the religious and moral revival by a series of sermons in which he called to repentance the churches which were losing hold on their members. The ministry was worldly and there was abroad in the land a moral laxity. In Europe the eighteenth century was losing its faith, preparing the way for the great upheaval known as the French Revolution. Rationalism and atheism were invading the American colonies.

The theme of the sermons preached by Edwards and his co-laborers was the "new birth"—the doctrine that when a man is born again a visible change is wrought in him. "Except a man be born again, he cannot see the kingdom of God," were the words of Christ addressed to Nicodemus. "The wind bloweth where it listeth, and thou hearest the sound thereof, but canst not tell whence it cometh, and whither it goeth; so is every one that is born of the Spirit." And Paul wrote that if any man be in Christ, he is a new creature: old things are passed away. Something new has come. Edwards preached on the Pauline doctrine of justification by faith, and he held fast to the Calvinist doctrine of election or adoption.

There was need for emphasis on this fundamental doctrine of the Reformation, because Arminianism had made great inroads on clergy and laity. Edwards preached weighty sermons based on historical research which called to mind the evils of the doctrine of good works, which caused men to put their trust in the merits of penances and veneration of relics and pilgrimages and forms and ceremonies. Arminianism was the doctrine which Archbishop Laud sought to introduce into the Church of England to confound the Puritans. History proclaims that when a priesthood attains to great power, bad men will be attracted into it and the church will become corrupt. "It is too evident to be denied," said Samuel Whitman in an election sermon in Connecticut in 1714, "that religion is on the wane among us. . . . Is not religion degenerating into an empty form?"

It has been pointed out that the Cambridge Platform gave way to the Half-Way Covenant which in turn led to the Saybrook Platform in Connecticut in 1708; that Massachusetts and Connecticut drifted in different directions, with the churches in the latter colony leaning in the direction of Presbyterianism.

The Presbyterian Church was divided into two parties. The "Old Side" party was made up of members mainly from Scotland and Ireland, who with few exceptions held that all baptized persons, not convicted of heresy or immorality, should be communicants. In other words, all baptized persons should be treated as regenerate who did not give evidence to the contrary. The "New Side" party was composed chiefly of men from New England, England, and Wales who believed that regeneration was a change which could be established by examination; and that if no such evidence was found, such persons should be treated as unregenerate and should be excluded from the ministry and the Lord's Supper. The effect of the Half-Way Covenant was to create two rolls of membership: one regenerate and in full communion; the other unregenerate and merely "owning the covenant." In the case of the second, vital religious experience was not a necessary qualification for church membership.

The effect of the Half-Way Covenant was to introduce Arminianism; and the effect of Arminianism was the agitation to restore evangelical doctrine and discipline. Jonathan Edwards was bitterly opposed to the Half-Way Covenant, and took an uncompromising position in opposition to the "Venerable Stoddard," his grandfather and predecessor in Northampton. In 1704 Stoddard avowed his belief that unregenerate persons ought to partake of the Lord's Supper: and in 1707 he published a sermon in defense of that doctrine. He maintained that the Lord's Supper was a means of regeneration and argued that it was impossible to distinguish the regenerate from the unregenerate. It was in opposition to Stoddard's teaching that Edwards preached the series of sermons on justification by faith and on the prevailing practice of admitting the unregenerate to membership. Edwards' doctrine spread rapidly and explains to a degree the system of revivals that swept periodically over the United States.

There was a terrible consistency in the preaching of Jonathan Edwards. The doctrine of eternal damnation was not glossed over, even to terrifying descriptions of the sufferings of the lost. In answer to critics who condemned him and other revivalist preachers for speaking terror to persons who were already emotionally upset, Edwards said that to blame a minister for declaring the truth to those who are under "awakenings" and not immediately administering comfort to them was like blaming a surgeon for not staying his hand when his patient shrinks and cries out in great anguish. The surgeon thrusts in his lance until he comes to the core of the wound, he said.

Moreover, Edwards contended that the revival should not be judged by human standards. He cited Isaiah (40:13) to instruct his critics how to judge the work of God's spirit: "Who hath directed the Spirit of the Lord, or being his counsellor, hath taught him." To judge *a priori*, he said, is a wrong way of judging the works of God. His judgments are a great deep. Who shall teach God knowledge, or enjoin Him in His way, or say unto Him, What dost Thou? God has made use of the weak and foolish things of the world to carry on His work. Some of the ministers employed were mere babes in age and standing, and some of them not so high in reputation, he said; "yet there was reason to think that it pleased God to make use of the infirmities of some . . . to chastise the deadness, earthly-mindedness, and vanity, found among ministers in the late times of declension and deadness, wherein wise virgins and foolish, ministers and people, have sunk into a deep sleep."

What raised a loud cry against some preachers was their frightening of children with talk of hell-fire and damnation. Here is a passage from a sermon addressed to children, preached by Gilbert Tennent in 1757. The title of the sermon was "Early Religion Recommended."

O consider, that you may never live till you grow big, for the most, by far, die when they are little, and this may be your case in a few days, in a few hours; haven't you seen coffins as short as yourselves, carried to the grave? And would it not be terrible for you to die unconverted, and to burn in hell forever? Your being young and little won't keep you from that bad place, and from the bad man, unless you be good yourselves before you die.

Edwards justified these sermons. Why should truth be concealed from children? he asked. All are by nature the children of wrath and heirs of hell—and everyone that has not been born again, whether he be young or old, is exposed every moment to eternal destruction. Edwards was sensitive to the dread words he spoke. He set apart special days of fasting in view of the doom of the lost, when he walked the floor, weeping and wringing his hands. It was the awful challenge of eternity, the thought of endless destiny, the hope in immortality, that inspired men to preach challenging sermons and to sacrifice the pleasures of life—and in many cases the refinements of civilized life—to seek out sinners, even if only one lost soul might be redeemed.

On July 8, 1741, Edwards preached his great sermon entitled "Sinners in the Hands of an Angry God" at Enfield, Massachusetts. His text was Deuteronomy 32:35: "Their foot shall slide in due time." Before the sermon was ended, the congregation was so bowed down with the conviction of its sin and danger, and there was such weeping, that the preacher was obliged to request silence before he could proceed. In 1740 George Whitefield spent several days with Edwards at Northampton and preached a number of times. Whitefield recorded that during his sermon "dear Mr. Edwards wept almost during the whole time of the exercise."

Edwards gave an account of Whitefield's visit. About the middle of the summer, he wrote, he called the young people who were communicants, from sixteen to twenty-six years, to his house, when many were so greatly affected that they fainted. In the summer and fall, the children in various parts of the town held religious meetings by themselves for prayer. It was about that time that there began to be cryings out in the meeting-house. It was a frequent thing to see a house full of outcries, faintings, convulsions, both with distress and with joy.

The following is an account of the revival at Plymouth, Massachusetts, by Nathanael Leonard, the pastor of the First Church:

After this, for some months together, you should scarcely see anybody at the taverns, unless they were strangers, travelers, or some come there upon necessary business. The children forsook their plays in the streets, and persons of all denominations, except a few, gave themselves to reading the Word of God, and other books of devotion, to meditation, prayer, conference, and other religious exercises, and refrained from their customary vices. And many that lived at a distance, being acquainted with this town in its former state, coming hither, beheld us now, with admiration, saying, Surely the fear of the Lord is in this place.

When abnormal "manifestations" began to assume the character of an epidemic, various explanations were ventured. Gilbert Tennent suggested that in primitive times some received the Word with joy. He argued that if persons after sorrow are overcome with joy and rapture, it was no wonder that divine things, which are of infinitely greater weight and consequence, produce strange things. Edwards said that a great deal of noise and tumult, darkness mixed with light, and evil with good, is always to be expected in the beginning of something glorious in the state of things in human society, or in the Church of God. God is pleased sometimes, in dealing forth spiritual blessings to his people, in some respects to exceed the capacity of the vessel in its present scantiness; so that he not only fills it, but makes their cup to run over; and pours out a blessing, sometimes in such a manner and measure that there is not room enough in it.

It was not only that persons were seized with jerks and convulsions; but there were phenomena even more strange and weird which gave countenance to a statement in a publication of the Humane Society of Massachusetts in 1788: "The boundary line between life and death, or the distinguishing signs of the latter, are objects to which the utmost efforts of the human capacity have never yet attained."

Edwards was particularly acquainted with many persons who had been the "subjects of the high and extraordinary transports of the present day"; and his contemporaries in the ministry related similar phenomena. Edwards knew a person who had more than once continued for five or six hours together, without interruption, in a clear and lively view of the infinite beauty and amiableness of Christ's person. To use the person's own expressions, the soul remained in a kind of heavenly elysium, "and did as it were swim in the rays of Christ's love, like a little mote swimming in the beams of the sun that comes in at the window. . . . The soul dwelt on high, was lost in God, and seemed almost to leave the body."

The case of William Tennent appears to be so remote from the realm of probability that one would not venture even to mention it were it not for the high standing of the author of a brief sketch of his life, published in 1810, by Elias Boudinot. William Tennent, a brother of Gilbert, was prominent in the revival of 1740 and a pastor of the Presbyterian Church at Freehold, New Jersey.

Tennent's intense application in preparing for the ministry affected his health to a degree that there was little hope for his life. He was conversing one morning with his brother, when he fainted and "died away." The neighborhood was invited to attend his funeral; but a doctor detected faint signs of life, and the funeral was postponed. No hope being entertained for his life, except by the doctor, the people again assembled to attend the funeral. Again the doctor obtained postponement; and after some time "the body, to the great alarm and astonishment of all present, opened its eyes, gave a dreadful groan, and sunk again into apparent death." Shortly a complete revival took place; but Tennent continued in so low and weak state for six weeks that there were grave doubts of final recovery. After about twelve months he was completely restored; but he was totally ignorant of every transaction of his life previous to his sickness. He was taught to read and to write as children are taught; and by degrees his recollection was restored. Tennent was reluctant to give any information about his perceptions when he was in the trance; but he did consent to give an account to Boudinot.

I found myself . . . under the direction of a superior Being, who ordered me to follow him. . . . I beheld at a distance an ineffable glory, the impression of which on my mind, it is impossible to communicate to mortal man. . . . I saw an innumerable host of happy beings, surrounding the inexpressible glory, in acts of adoration and joyous worship. . . . I heard things unutterable. I heard their songs and hallelujahs, of thanksgiving and praise, with unspeakable rapture. . . . The three days during which I had appeared lifeless, seemed to me not more than ten or twenty minutes.

The Great Awakening stirred up controversy concerning lay preaching, itinerant ministers, and the moral quality of contemporary clergymen. William and Gilbert Tennent were among the most outspoken critics of the ministry. William Tennent had a large part in the religious revival at the College of New Jersey (now Princeton University). In his famous Nottingham sermon on "The Danger of an Unconverted Ministry," he preached on Mark 6:34: "And Jesus, when he came out, saw much people." Tennent asked what was the cause of the great and compassionable commotion in the breast of Christ? It was because the people had no shepherd. They had great crowds of Pharisee teachers, orthodox and letter-learned, who were as good as none, in the Savior's judgment.

Gilbert Tennent was under fire because he cast reflections on "learned" ministers and seemed to prefer ignorant and itinerant preachers who appealed to the emotions. Tennent replied that he intended no contempt on the learning of ministers, but only signified his dislike at persons coming into the ministry who had no qualifications other than human learning. He admitted that he thought universities were corrupt in respect to religious principles and practices. In reply to the assertion that conversions were "mushrooms," Tennent cited sudden conversions in apostolic times: Paul, Zaccheus, Lydia, and the three thousand.

George Whitefield and James Davenport were among the most prominent itinerant ministers who offended the complacency of parish pastors and ruffled their dignity and threatened their prerogatives.

Whitefield was ordained in 1736 in Gloucester Cathedral, and immediately became known as a preacher of the "new birth" which aroused the ire of parish pastors who were jealous of him. Whitefield was out of his element at Oxford University, which resembled the other English universities in religious indifference and hostility and in the moral laxity of students and faculty. Whitefield was expected to join in the revels of his fellow students, and when he refused to conform was branded as an "odd fellow." Whitefield said he got more knowledge from reading the Bible in one month than he could ever have acquired from all the writings of men. This tireless preacher made a half-dozen or more visits to America and preached to multitudes on his travels from Georgia to New England. He remained within the fold of the Church of England, in spite of cold and unfriendly brethren who had taken holy orders in the same establishment; but he neither feared nor heeded ecclesiastical laws and regulations and ignored denominational barriers in building the kingdom of God in England and her colonies.

Whitefield made his first visit to the colonies in 1738, arriving at Savannah, Georgia, in May. He found prospects so discouraging that after a few months he returned to England, where he was greeted with a pastoral letter by the bishop of London warning clergy and people against him and his "irregular" methods. Pulpits of parish churches were closed to him. On subsequent visits to America he found the clergy of the Anglican Church generally unfriendly; but that mattered not. He found the doors of Congregational and Presbyterian churches open, and the great open spaces were suitable auditoriums for the carrying power of his voice. When he arrived at Philadelphia in November, 1739, his reputation preceded him, and multitudes from all denominations and from people without church affiliation assembled to hear him. In New York the minister of a Presbyterian church was the only member of the cloth who admitted him to his pulpit. After hearing Gilbert Tennent preach, Whitefield said he had never before heard such a searching sermon. "He convinced me," he said, "more and more, that we can preach the Gospel of Christ no further than we have experienced the power of it in our hearts." Whitefield preached at the Old South Church in Boston in the presence of ministers who joined the assembly. He said that the Lord enabled him to open his mouth boldly against unconverted ministers. "For I am truly persuaded," he said, "that the generality of preachers talk of an unknown and unfelt Christ; and the reasons why congregations have been so dead is, because they have dead men preaching to them. . . . For how can dead men beget children?"

In Cambridge, Whitefield visited Harvard, "the chief college for training up the sons of the prophets in all New England," and learned that it was not far superior to English universities in piety and true godliness. Tutors neglected to pray with and examine the hearts of their pupils. Discipline was at low ebb, and bad books were fashion-able.

A bold New England preacher fell under the influence of Whitefield and resolved to become an itinerant preacher. On some of his travels he was in company with Whitefield. This was James Davenport, a great-grandson of John Davenport, the celebrated minister of New Haven. In the streets of Boston he denounced the clergy with such vio-lence that he was imprisoned and adjudged insane; and in Connecti-cut he denounced as unconverted ministers those who were opposed to emotionalism and stirred up so much excitement that the General Assembly passed an act which designated as vagrants those who preached in a parish without the consent of the minister, or a majority of the church.

The character of the opposition to itinerant preachers and revi-valist methods during the Great Awakening reproduced reactions in other times and in other places from clergy clothed with greater power than frail human nature can carry gracefully. The invective poured forth against Whitefield, Davenport, the Tennents, and men of their spirit no more became the responsible stations of the "regular" clergy of the colonies than did the fulminations of the faculties of Harvard and Yale become the academic profession.

On July 5, 1740, Whitefield attended the Episcopal church in Charleston, South Carolina, when he heard a sermon full of venom directed against Methodists in general and Whitefield in particular. The following day an ecclesiastical writ was directed against White-field, who, however, continued preaching. At the annual convention of churches in the Province of Massachusetts Bay held at Boston on May 25, 1743, it was declared to be a heinous invasion of the ministerial office, offensive to God, and destructive of their churches for private persons of no education and but few attainments in knowledge and in the great doctrines of the Gospel, without any regular call, taking upon themselves to be preachers of the Word of God. The ordaining or separating of any persons to the work of the evangelical ministry at large, and without any relation to a regular charge, was looked upon as contrary to the Scriptures and directly opposite to their platform.

About two months later friends of the revival held another convention at Boston, and a statement signed by a long list of ministers was drawn up to counteract the previous statement. It declared that there had been a happy and remarkable revival of religion in many parts of the land, after a long time of decay and a withdrawal of the "Holy Spirit from his sanctuary among us." Never before had so many been brought under "soul concern" and making inquiry about the way of salvation. The revival was attended in many with unusual bodily effects. "But who can wonder, if at such times as this, Satan should intermingle himself, to hinder and blemish a work so directly contrary to the interests of his kingdom?" The statement, however, admitted the dangers and abuses of itinerant preachers and lay preaching.

The faculty of Harvard College, in a statement dated December 28, 1744, directed against George Whitefield, looked upon his going about in an itinerant way as utterly inconsistent with the peace and order of the churches of Christ. He was said to be acting either according to dreams or some sudden impulses and impressions on his mind, which he fondly imagined to be the Spirit of God. Referring to his "reproachful reflections" on Harvard College, he was branded as an "uncharitable, censorious, and slanderous man." His manner of preaching was said to be improper, because extempore preachers are of necessity less instructive, the greater part of the sermon being commonly "the same kind of harangue which they have often used before —so this is a most lazy manner of preaching." The declaration of the faculty of Yale College indorsed the "testimonies" of the Harvard faculty.

This appraisal by the academic minds in Puritan New England is redolent of a discourse entitled "The Error of Extempore Prayer and Preaching" by Thomas Sprat, who became bishop of Rochester in 1684, four years before the "Glorious Revolution." The bishop asserted that extempore praying was only praying by the fancy or the memory, not the spirit. The same was true in large measure of extempore preaching, he said; it was only a crafty management of the same phrases and observations which they had before composed and reserved in their memories. If you hear the preacher often, he continued, you will perceive, amidst all their extempore pretensions, they often travel in the same rounds, till they have trodden them bare enough.

The bishop thanked God that the Church of England neither required nor stood in need of any such enthusiastic spirit of preaching. Here the more advised and modest, the more prepared and deliberate a preacher is, the better he is furnished, by God's grace, to deliver effectually the church's solid sense, its fixed precepts, its unalterable doctrines.

The results of the Great Awakening were manifold, including sectarian bickering and spiritual deadness in some places and in some individuals, as the consequence of emotional contagion. Jonathan Edwards in appraising the effects of the revival, stressed the great alteration in the lives of young and old and a healthier moral atmosphere. In New England the Bible was held in greater esteem and was read more diligently. The Lord's Day was more religiously and strictly observed.

The most important development that grew out of the Great Awakening was a gradual democratization of religion by the weakening of denominational barriers and the undermining of the remnants of the power and authority of the clerical estate. It checked the recession from Protestantism which was a natural consequence of ecclesiastical establishments which to a degree resembled the state churches in Europe. The begowned clergymen in the New World could be as dictatorial and haughty as the men who had taken holy orders in the churches of the Old World. The fact that the minister regarded himself, and was regarded by others, as a sort of ruler within the boundaries of his parish tended to make him an indolent and incompetent pastor, not unlike the indifferent, pleasure-loving, and even immoral priest and minister in the Catholic and Protestant countries of Europe. This type of clergyman in the American colonies favored the use of church discipline to silence itinerant and lay preachers and to suppress separatists. Parish despotism was no more favorable to religious liberty than was despotism embracing a larger geographical unit. Unity at the expense of liberty of conscience is too great a price to pay. Freedom to preach and freedom to print are inseparable. Throughout the thirteen colonies the number of dissenters and sects multiplied, partly through the efforts of itinerant evangelists who ignored parish and sectional lines and partly by the invasion of immigrants from several countries of Europe, who brought with them a medley of Protestantism and a confusion of tongues—a veritable Babel of religions, languages, customs, and social and political heretics, beyond the ability of the orthodox to disperse.

Some of the results of the Great Awakening and contemporaneous events were not visible until after the dawn of the nineteenth century, when the repercussions of the American Revolution and of the French Revolution and the ideas that impelled these radical and heretical upheavals wrought miraculous events in the world of religion.

THE RISE OF METHODISM

THE Great Awakening in the American colonies coincided in point of time with the beginning of a great revival in England, which eventually assumed the proportions of a world movement in every English-speaking Protestant community—and in many Protestant and Catholic countries alien to the English language. The movement took strong hold in America in the same decade that the independence of the United States of America was recognized by Great Britain and unity found expression first in the Articles of Confederation and seven years later in the Constitution. Methodism was the name applied to this revival, which until the year following the formal recognition of American independence, in 1784, was a lay movement within the Church of England. It was at the "Christmas Conference" in Baltimore, 1784, that the Methodist Episcopal Church in the United States was organized. It was a religion and a church which made a strong appeal to a people moving from frontier to frontier during the next century. Methodism was carried to every frontier by itinerant ministers in the service of a church whose flexible government was smoothly adjusted to meet the changing conditions of a country growing numerically, geographically, and economically. In England, Methodism was the "poor man's religion." In America, Methodist ministers preached sermons that were understood by the plain people; and the sermons they heard and the hymns they sang brought cheer and hope to men and women on the frontier, just as the men and women—and children, too—in the mines and factories of England took new hold on life when Methodist exhorters emphasized the dignity of the human soul.

Methodism contained nothing new in doctrine. Its emphasis was on the practical side of life. The founder and great leader, John Wesley, wrote in his Journal on May 5, 1788, three years before his death and at the age of eighty-eight, the following thumbnail summary of the Methodist "faith":

There is no other religious Society under heaven which requires nothing of men in order to their admission to it, but a desire to save their souls. Look all around you, you cannot be admitted into the Church or Society of the Presbyterians, Anabaptists, Quakers, or any others, unless you hold the same opinions with them, and adhere to the same mode of worship. The Methodists alone do not insist on your holding this or that opinion, but they think and let think. Neither do they impose any particular mode of worship, but you may continue in your former manner, be it what it may.

John Wesley and his brother Charles were of the same spirit as George Whitefield, and their paths often crossed, in spite of disagreements and misunderstandings. When at the close of the year 1737, Whitefield embarked for Georgia, John and Charles Wesley had just returned to England after an absence of two years and four months in America where they undertook to teach Christianity to the Georgia Indians. They returned not only disheartened by their experiences; but John confided to his Journal that he had learned in America what he least of all expected, namely, that he who went to America to convert others was never himself converted to God. He wrote "I want that faith . . . which enables everyone that hath it to cry out, 'I live not; but Christ liveth in me; and the life which I now live, I live by faith in the Son of God, who loved me, and gave himself for me.' I want that faith that none can have without knowing that he hath it; for whosoever has it 'is freed from sin; the whole body of sin is destroyed' in him; he is freed from fear." Within a few days he preached in a London church on "If any man be in Christ, he is a new creature." He was afterward informed that many of the best people in the parish were so offended that he was not to preach there any more. With reference to two sermons which he preached at the end of the same month (February, 1738) he wrote: "I believe it pleased God to bless the first sermon most, because it gave most offense; being indeed an open defiance of that mystery of iniquity which the world calls *prudence*."

A minister who had taken holy orders in the Church of England and expressed such thoughts did not conform to the fox-hunting parson and absentee rector who gave the English clergy of the eighteenth century the reputation of being the idlest in the world. On many occasions Wesley's right to preach was challenged. In November, 1739, after having preached a sermon by invitation, a priest in the Church of England told Wesley that he could not preach in the afternoon. "Not," he said, "that you preach any false doctrines. I allow that all you have said is true; and it is the doctrine of the Church of England. But it is not guarded; it is dangerous; it may lead people into enthusiasm or despair." Clergy and laity condemned Wesley as "beside himself." This attitude was characteristic of conventional church members who did not want their complacency disturbed. As Wesley put it: "All religious people have such a quantity of righteousness, acquired by much painful exercise, and formed at last into current habits; which is their wealth, both for this world and the next." Even in the inception of the Methodist movement, when a little group of religiously-minded students at Oxford assembled for regular sessions of prayer, fasting, celebration of the sacrament of the Lord's Supper, and ministrations to the poor and unfortunate, they were derided and called "Bible moths," "sacramentarians," "holy club," "reforming company," and the like. Even the term "Methodist" was originally applied in derision.

In England and in other countries conventicle acts and ecclesiastical regulations sufficed to silence heretical preachers and to curb irregularities which endangered "pure doctrine." But George Whitefield set the example for men whose zeal for saving souls outran their reverence for ministerial dignity and respect for conventionality. The Conventicle Act forbade the holding of a religious service in a field if it were conducted "in other manner than according to the liturgy and practice of the Church of England." However, this act is no exception to the testimony of experience that a law which does not have the sanction of custom or of public sentiment is difficult, if not impossible, to enforce. Preaching on the highways and in the byways began partly because it was the only method of bringing the message of the Gospel to the rough and ignorant masses, and partly because the majority of churches were closed against the preachers.

On March 31, 1739, Wesley recorded in his Journal a meeting with Whitefield at Bristol. At first he could scarcely reconcile himself to

Whitefield's strange way of preaching in the fields. All his life, until very recently, he had been so tenacious of every point relating to decency and order that he should have thought the saving of souls almost a sin, if it had not been done in a church. Three days later he wrote that at four o'clock in the afternoon he "submitted to be more vile, and proclaimed in the highways the glad tidings of salvation." He spoke to three thousand people on the text "The Spirit of the Lord is upon me, because he hath anointed me to preach the Gospel to the poor." Some ten years later Wesley wondered "at those, who still talk of the indecency of field-preaching. The highest indecency is in St. Paul's Church, where a considerable part of the congregation are asleep, or talking, or looking about, not minding a word the preacher says."

The plain-spoken, sometimes unpolished, Methodist preachers appeared to be crude and boorish to the higher classes, who respected the refined and educated Church of England priest, even if they seldom, if ever, darkened the door of his church at the hour of worship. In the higher circles "everyone laughs if one talks of religion," said a distinguished French scholar who visited England in the early years of the eighteenth century. The historian, J. R. Green, says of this time that of the prominent statesmen, the greater part were unbelievers in any form of Christianity and were distinguished for the grossness and immorality of their lives. Purity and fidelity to the marriage vow were sneered out of fashion. It was frequently observed by Wesley that his preaching made little appeal to the rich and the educated. In fact his preaching and that of his collaborators stirred up passionate hatred in their opponents, and they were by no means confined to the upper classes. Wesley's Journal reveals disturbances by ruffians and by the rabble who tried to prevent him from preaching. The lives of the Methodist preachers were often in danger. They were mobbed, stoned, and covered with filth. On October 20, 1743, Wesley made the following entry in his Journal:

By how gentle degrees does God prepare us for his will! Two years ago a piece of brick grazed my shoulders. It was a year after that the stone struck me between the eyes. Last month I received one blow, and this evening two; one before we came to town, and one after we were just gone out. But both were as nothing, for though one man struck me on the mouth with such force that the blood gushed out immediately, I felt no more pain from either of the blows than if they had touched me with a straw.

The man who wrote this was not a fanatic, even though many of his converts and followers were. His voluminous writings reveal an orderly mind; his conduct was that of an industrious and disciplined man; his leadership was that of a statesman and masterly leader of men. Nevertheless he lived in a world of divine revelations. He was busy from early morning until late at night and traveled on horseback thousands of miles; and yet he set apart hours for fasting and prayer. At a love feast where about sixty of the brethren were present, about three o'clock in the morning, as they were continuing instant in prayer, the power of God came mightily upon them, so that many cried out for joy and fell to the ground. He sought and found God in every place; and when he lay down at night he could truly say: "Now I have lived a day."

Wesley talked with persons who had several times been in trances. They agreed that when they "went away" it was always at a time they were fullest of the love of God; that it came upon them in a moment, without previous notice, and took away all their senses and strength; that, with some exceptions, from the moment they were in another world they knew nothing of what was said or done by people around them. He visited a fifteen-year-old girl who was in a trance. Her face showed an unspeakable mixture of reverence and love, while silent tears rolled down her cheeks. "I do not know whether I ever saw a human face look so beautiful," wrote Wesley. "About seven o'clock her senses returned. I asked, 'Where have you been?' 'I have been with my Saviour.' 'In heaven or on earth?' 'I cannot tell; but I was in glory.' "

It has been said that Charles Wesley added sweetness to the Methodist revival by composing hymns which expressed the fiery convictions of its converts in lines so chaste and beautiful that the extravagant features disappeared. "Hymn-singing Methodists" came to be applied to Wesleyans in every land.

The memories of Charles Wesley and Isaac Watts are hallowed by a friendly disagreement among scholars as to which one merits the highest distinction among English writers of hymns. Their lives were in part contemporary. Watts died in 1748, forty years before Charles Wesley. The hymns of both men are included in hymnals published and used by almost every Christian denomination. A scholar in this field of religious history, David R. Breed, has made the following contrast: "Watts is more reverential; Wesley more loving. Watts is stronger; Wesley sweeter. Watts appeals profoundly to the intellect; Wesley takes hold of the heart. Watts will continue to sing for the Pauls and Peters of the Church; Wesley for the Thomases and the Johns."

John Wesley has been called the greatest religious leader produced by the British Isles during the eighteenth century; some historians have called him the greatest leader in Christendom since the era of the Protestant Reformation. Be that as it may, John Wesley and the movement he inspired and led occupies such a unique position and wrought such miraculous results throughout the Protestant world that in order to understand it one must seek out the formative influences. After he had passed the eighty-ninth milestone of his life, Wesley wrote the following remarkable entry in his Journal (April 12, 1789) at Dublin:

I met the Society and explained to them at large the original design of the Methodists, viz., Not to be a distinct party, but to stir up all parties, Christians or heathens, to worship God in spirit and in truth; but the Church of England in particular, to which they belonged from the beginning. With this view I have uniformly gone on for fifty years, never varying from the doctrine of the Church at all, nor from her discipline of choice, but of necessity. So, in the course of years, necessity was laid upon me. 1. To preach in the open air; 2. To pray extempore; 3. To form Societies; 4. To accept the assistance of Lay Preachers; and in a few instances, to use such means as occurred to prevent or remove evils that we either felt or feared.

Wesley's loyalty to the Church of England is explained in part by his belief in the necessity of institutional religion and the "means of grace." On his voyage to America and during his stay in the colonies, he made the acquaintance of the Moravian Brethren and as the result of frequent contacts with them learned to love and esteem them. His conversations with Peter Böhler about instantaneous conversion caused him to search the Scriptures, and particularly the Acts of the Apostles, where to his astonishment he found scarcely any other than such conversions, hardly any as slow as that of Paul who was three days in the pangs of the new birth. He even paid a visit to Herrnhut, but this type of pietism was too "free" to hold him. There were certain things in Herrnhutism which he could not reconcile with the Gospel of Christ, among them Antinomianism and the denial of the right of any man to be called "Rabbi, Master, Lord of your faith upon earth." These two points were a direct challenge to institutional religion, because mysticism places emphasis on the individual's direct relation with God, without the mediation of a priesthood.

In his later life Wesley read some of the writings of Swedenborg, and "began with huge prejudices in his favor, knowing him to be a pious man, one of strong understanding, of much learning." But he concluded that he was one of the "most ingenious, lively, and entertaining madmen that ever set pen to paper." About two years after his return from America Wesley read Luther's *Commentary on the Epistle to the Galatians* and found him shallow in his remarks on many passages and muddy and confused on almost all. He concluded that he was deeply tinctured with mysticism and therefore dangerously wrong. After completing a translation of Luther's *Life,* some eight years later, he lamented that the German reformer had no faithful friend who would rebuke him for his "rough, intractable spirit and bitter zeal for opinions, so greatly obstructive of the work of God."

Luther's absolute doctrine of justification by faith, and by faith alone, and his bold attacks on the doctrine of good works, were no more palatable to a man with Wesley's Arminianism than was Calvin's doctrine of predestination. Wesley's preaching was so slanted toward Arminianism that he was even accused of being a Jesuit in disguise.

Wesley drew up a formidable indictment of the doctrine of election. He denied that it was a doctrine of God, because it made void the ordinance of God to preach to save souls. It tended to destroy the comfort of religion, the happiness of Christianity. It had a tendency to destroy the zeal for good works and to overthrow Christian revelation, by making revelation contradict itself.

In his early twenties Wesley read Jeremy Taylor's *Rule and Exercises of Holy Living and Dying,* Thomas à Kempis's *Imitation of Christ,* and two books by William Law: *A Practical Treatise upon Christian Perfection* and *A Serious Call to a Devout and Holy Life.*

Of Law's books Wesley wrote that they convinced him, "more than ever, of the absolute impossibility of being half a Christian." Law is one of the great masters of English prose; and his books, which were published at the very beginning of the second quarter of the eighteenth century, made such a profound impression that they established their author as among the formative influences of the time. In spite of objections to certain statements, Wesley's indebtedness to Law was great. His objections to Law were fundamentally the same as his objections to the Moravians and to mystics in general, namely, that they had a false conception of church communion; that they believed in universal salvation; and that they were tainted with Antinomianism and quietism. Moreover, Law expressed admiration for Quakers as individuals and for their radiant life as it found expression in works of love and in silent communion with God. Wesley, on the other hand, could see no good in meetings based on silent worship. He also believed that the Quakers had departed from Christianity in their attitude toward the sacraments and the doctrine of justification by faith, neither could he accept the primacy of illumination over Holy Scripture.

As the title of one of his books suggests, Law formulated and discoursed on Christian perfectionism, which in one form or another has been professed by Christians as individuals or by men who have made it a tenet of their churches. Wesley and Methodists in general have been condemned by the "orthodox" for obliterating the line of demarcation between justification and sanctification and for teaching perfectionism. Perfectionism was not a Methodist "doctrine," but it is fact that individual Methodists taught it and preached it. Moreover, Arminianism has the flavor of legalism; and on that score Methodism has been attacked, particularly with reference to sumptuary laws—temperance, Sabbath observance, and the like. In church history, however, Christian perfectionism has taken on many shades of meaning.

In brief, William Law conceived Christian perfection to consist of nothing more than the right performance of necessary duties. He cited passages in Paul's Epistles to show that he that is born of God is possessed of a temper and principle that makes him utterly hate and labor to avoid all sin; he is said not to commit sin, in such a sense as a man may be said not to do that which is his constant care and principle to prevent being done. Nothing less than this great change of heart and mind can give anyone assurance that he is truly turned to God. There is but one term of salvation, that he that is in Christ is a new creature.

Christianity is not a school for the teaching of moral virtue, the polishing of our manners, or forming us to live a life of this world with decency and gentility. It is deeper and more divine in its design, and has much nobler ends than these; it implies an entire change of life, a dedication of ourselves, our souls and bodies unto God, in the strictest and highest sense of the words. . . . Death is not more certainly a separation of our souls from our bodies, than the Christian life is a separation of our souls from worldly tempers, vain indulgences, and unnecessary cares. . . . But how unlike are Christians and Christianity! It commands us to take no thought, saying, what shall we eat, or what shall we drink? Yet Christians are restless and laborious till they can eat in plate. It commands us to be indifferent about raiment; but Christians are full of care and concern to be clothed in purple and fine linen; it enjoins us to take no thought for the morrow, yet Christians think they have lived in vain, if they do not leave estates at their death.

Despite the fact that Wesley broke with Law on certain statements in his books, they were not far apart on Christian perfection. Wesley never contended for absolute perfection, nor did he believe that through faith in Christ a person is freed from sin, that is, that a converted person has no sin, because Christ has taken away all sin. He acknowledged that Christians are not perfect in knowledge and are not free from ignorance and mistakes, neither are they free from a thousand nameless defects, either in conversation or behavior.

The followers of Wesley numbered one hundred thousand at his death; and during the nineteenth century the number of Methodists in the countries of both hemispheres mounted into the millions. In the United States the Methodist Episcopal Church became the fastest growing Protestant denomination. But American Protestantism, no less than Protestantism in other countries, owes a special sense of gratitude to Methodism which leavened the whole lump. The American Methodists adopted the position on church government which John Wesley took. He believed that there was no one form of church government prescribed in Scripture. The visible church he defined as a congregation of the faithful, "in which the pure word of God is preached, and the Sacraments duly administered according to Christ's ordinance."

It was fortunate that the pioneers of Methodism in the New World were not convinced of the historicity of the apostolic succession and were not sticklers for liturgical conformity. Had they been of that school they would have learned that a frontier environment was not fruitful soil for planting stiff, formal, liturgical churches.

SEVEN

AMERICAN METHODISM

IN AMERICA, as in England, Methodism took its inception in the form of societies professing to belong to the Church of England; and the organization of a separate church under the name of the Methodist Episcopal Church was a product of the logic of events which culminated in the establishment of the United States of America. Before the Revolution no American bishop had been ordained on this side of the Atlantic Ocean. Americans who aspired to take holy orders had to travel to England to be ordained by an English bishop and to swear the oath of allegiance.

The Revolution placed the Church of England and the Methodists in great difficulties. The fact that Wesley publicly and aggressively took the side of the Mother Country in her contest with the colonies and the further fact that he did not realize that the colonists had no traditional attachment to the Church of England augmented the trials of the Methodists. The name itself had odious connotations; and in 1780 it was changed to the Protestant Episcopal Church—a change that removed some of the stigma of a ministry which was on the whole loyal to the Mother Country. Moreover, the Episcopal clergymen in the colonies and after independence did not like the Methodist societies any better than did their brethren in England. For this reason and others, the Methodists often found themselves without anyone to administer the sacraments to them. Wesley and his assistants insisted that the Methodists in the colonies receive the sacraments at the hands of the clergy of the Anglican Church; and throughout the Revolution they insisted that Methodists retain their relationship with the Mother Church. Holding these views, it is to the credit of Wesley that he sacrificed his own plans and acquiesced in the organization of a separate church.

The evolution of the Methodist Episcopal Church can be traced step by step, as its organization adapted itself to the needs of a growing church and an expanding country. On June 3, 1773, Thomas Rankin and George Shadford, Methodist preachers from England, landed at Philadelphia; and on July 4th of that year, Rankin, who was general assistant (Wesley's representative) called the first Methodist conference in America. The preachers who attended reported about eleven hundred members belonging to the several societies. Such conferences were held annually until 1784. Under instructions from Wesley, Rankin denied the request of the societies to have the sacraments administered by their own preachers, instead of by Anglican clergymen. Their places of worship were called "chapels" or "meeting-houses," never "churches." The dominating personality was Francis Asbury, who rose to this position by virtue of his administrative genius. He was born in England in 1745, and early in life became converted to Methodism. After some years of itinerant preaching, in 1771 he volunteered to go to America as a missionary. Asbury was not a willing subordinate, and on the eve of the Revolution was recalled to England, a summons which he ignored. After some uncertainty in his own mind as to the outcome of the war, he made his choice after he concluded that the rebellious colonies could not be reduced to submission.

In 1776 Wesley met Thomas Coke, an Oxford graduate who had become interested in Methodism. Coke's preaching became more evangelical and unconventional, and he was dismissed from the Church of England. Having drawn up a plan for the organization of the Methodist Church in the United States, at the beginning of September, 1784, Wesley ordained Richard Whatcoat and Thomas Vasey as presbyters for America and appointed Coke as the first superintendent. Several weeks later the three men embarked for the United States. Coke was the bearer of a letter written by John Wesley which read as follows:

To all to whom these presents shall come, John Wesley, late fellow of Lincoln College in Oxford, presbyter of the Church of England, sendeth greeting.

Whereas many of the people in the southern provinces of North America, who desire to continue under my care, and still adhere to the doctrine and discipline of the Church of England, are greatly distressed for want of ministers to administer the sacraments of baptism and the Lord's Supper, according to the usage of the same Church: and whereas there does not appear to be any other way of supplying them with ministers—

Know all men, that I, John Wesley, think myself to be providentially called at this time to set apart some persons for the work of the ministry in America. And therefore, under the protection of Almighty God and with a single eye to his glory, I have this day set apart as a superintendent, by the imposition of my hands and prayer, (being assisted by other ordained ministers) Thomas Coke, doctor of civil law, a presbyter of the Church of England, and a man whom I judge to be well qualified for that great work. And I do hereby recommend him to all whom it may concern, as a fit person to preside over the flock of Christ. In testimony whereof, I have hereunto set my hand and seal, this second day of September, in the year of our Lord one thousand seven hundred and eighty-four.

Shortly after Coke's arrival in America, he conferred with Asbury and explained to him Wesley's plan for the American church. Realizing that the trend in his church was away from Wesley, Asbury refused to exercise the duties of his office unless elected by the itinerant preachers. No time was lost, and the preachers met in Baltimore, where Wesley's letter was read. It was at this "Christmas Conference" that the Methodist Episcopal Church was organized under the joint superintendency of Coke and Asbury. Upon Asbury's refusal to accept Wesley's appointment as superintendent, the conference elected both Asbury and Coke to that office. Asbury was ordained deacon, elder, and superintendent on successive days. From that time until his death, some thirty years later, Asbury dominated American Methodism. From 1784 to 1803 Coke made nine voyages to America, and lived long enough to see that it would have been a mistake for the Methodists to continue their union with the Protestant Episcopal Church.

Immediately upon assuming the duties of his office as superintendent, Asbury proceeded to conduct himself after the fashion of a bishop by making arbitrary decisions and appointments—and not least by assuming the title "bishop," which was soon conferred upon him. However, Asbury was not without critics and adversaries, who contended that, by his letter, Wesley did not intend to invest Coke with the office of bishop, because the term "episcopal" was not used. In a letter written in 1791 to William White of Philadelphia, a bishop in the Protestant Episcopal Church, Coke stated that Wesley "did indeed solemnly invest me, as far as he had a right to do so, with episcopal authority." The qualifying clause was seized upon by the advocates of a more democratic government in the church as casting doubt on the right of Wesley to confer the office or title of bishop. Some extremists even averred that the title of bishop originated in the love of titles and distinction which is native in the human heart. Admitting that all too many members of the cloth of whatever denomination are inordinately greedy for honorary degrees and titles, it appears that Wesley, Coke, and the rank and file of Methodists regarded the office of bishop as purely administrative and not in the sense that Anglicans and Roman Catholics understand the term.

Especially resentful toward the display of authority on the part of ministers, and particularly antagonistic toward Asbury, was James O'Kelly, who was elected and ordained elder at the "Christmas Conference." At a General Conference held in 1792, O'Kelly enlisted a few followers in an attempt to limit the power of the bishops. Failing in the effort, the fiery and independent rebel seceded from the Methodist Episcopal Church and founded a sect which the members called Republican Methodists and later simply "Christians." It was congregational in polity and adopted the Scriptures as the only creed and rule of faith.

Not long after Asbury's death rebellion again flared up, when under the leadership of Alexander McCaine an effort was made to inject a larger degree of democracy in the government of the Methodist Episcopal Church. Like O'Kelly, McCaine contended that the existing government of the church never had the sanction of Wesley and that the episcopacy had been surreptitiously imposed on the Methodist societies. The General Conference of 1828 refused to adopt the proposed reforms, whereupon a number of churches split over the question; and in 1830 a convention of "Reformers" organized the Methodist Protestant Church.

At the "Christmas Conference" the "Articles of Religion," as given by Wesley in his "Abridged Form of Common Prayer," which he had prepared for the American church, were agreed upon and made the standard of doctrine. The "Articles" were selected from the Thirty-nine Articles of the Church of England. The "Form of

Discipline" was also agreed upon. It was similar to the form in use in the Methodist Society in England, except that it was more "episcopal" in construction.

By virtue of the fact that the "Christmas Conference" established an independent Methodist Episcopal Church, something entirely new was introduced into Methodism, namely, the governing conference, which decided all matters by majority vote. It was given power to elect deacons and elders and to admit men into the ministry and into membership in the conference. With the geographical expansion of Methodism, and as the number of preachers increased, the annual conferences were divided into sections. In 1792 the general conference came into existence.

The presiding elder was chosen and appointed by the bishop to act for him in looking after the interests of the churches within a given area and to preside at the quarterly conferences. With the dearth of preachers who were qualified to administer the sacraments, it became one of the functions of the presiding elder to discharge that sacred duty when he made his periodical visits in the district.

The local unit in the Methodist Episcopal Church was the class. Under the direction of a leader, the "believers" met frequently, usually in homes before the frontier community had the time and means to provide a meeting-house. The leader was responsible for the spiritual care of members of the class.

The rapid growth in membership of the Methodist Church has been attributed to the itinerant ministry and the circuit system. The circuit riders wrote a large chapter in the history of the West. There was a proverbial saying of bitterly cold days: "There is nothing out today but crows and Methodist preachers." On the frontier where population was sparse, a single circuit rider could serve a number of societies. At the General Conference of the Methodist Episcopal Church in Indianapolis in 1856 a lively discussion was precipitated by the proposal to extend the time of a minister's stay in a circuit or residence at a station. The committee to which the memorial had been referred reported that there was no evidence that any considerable number of people desired such alteration. An English Methodist who was a spectator at the conference reported that an American Methodist minister preached three or four times a week in the same church, so that within a period of two years he preached oftener to the same people than an English Methodist minister did ordinarily in three years.

The poverty of the itinerant ministers furnishes ample proof of their devotion and zeal, as it also proves how much can be accomplished with meager facilities and equipment. Many nights the itinerant had to camp out without fuel or food. His library was the Bible, hymnbook, and Book of Discipline. Peter Cartwright, one of the most colorful circuit riders, admitted that many of them could not conjugate a verb or parse a sentence, and murdered the King's English "almost every lick." "But there was Divine unction attended the word preached," he said, "and thousands fell under the mighty power of God." Bishop Asbury recorded in his Journal for the year 1806, when attending a western conference, that the brethren were in such want that he parted with his watch, his coat, and his shirt.

During that year Cartwright received about forty dollars; but many of the preachers did not receive half that amount. The preachers were not starved for want of food, he said, but they did not generally receive in a whole year money enough to get them a suit of clothes. What saved the day, he continued, was the fact that people and preachers dressed in homespun clothing, and the "good sisters" presented the preachers with clothing.

The camp meeting appeared as a frontier phenomenon in the closing years of the eighteenth century and the early years of the nineteenth century; and it soon became an important Methodist institution, though it was never officially recognized as such. It became one of the most important institutions of the frontier; and its technique was even appropriated in political campaigns. The West was a region of high religious voltage. The pioneers were individualistic, emotional, and often ignorant of the fundamentals of religion. Where the population was sparse, where distances were vast, where people lived close to nature, where church discipline was lax or entirely absent, where superstition crept in, the people developed special points of view in religion. Camp meetings were social gatherings and emotional outlets; and people came for miles and stayed for days to participate in them.

Historians have pointed out that the emotional excesses of camp meetings have been overstressed, and too little attention has been given to the conventional, routine work of churches and preachers, including the distribution of devotional books and tracts. Nevertheless, the camp meeting was only another form of revival meeting; and both forms were manifestations of democracy in church and state. The frontier democratized religion. Institutionalism yielded to spontaneity. The democratic American clergyman or preacher was in striking contrast with the educated, cultured, aristocratic pastor and priest in the established churches of Europe.

Saint, seeker, and sinner were subject to strange phenomena at these camp meetings, or protracted meetings, as they were sometimes called. Hundreds would lie for hours and sometimes for days in a state of insensibility. Another strange phenomenon was the "jerks." Men and women jerked backward and forward with such rapidity and violence that their bodies would bend so as to bring their heads near the floor, and the hair of women would crack like the lash of a whip. In some cases the "jerks" were so violent that the necks of the victims were broken. Peter Cartwright believed that the "jerks" were of the devil, not of the Holy Spirit.

More than one skeptic and scoffer came out of curiosity to camp meetings, determined not to yield to nervous excitability or to being frightened into religion. One "tough" came to Peter Cartwright's meeting prepared to drink the "damned jerks to death," if he were seized by them. In attempting to execute his resolution, his head jerked so violently that the whiskey bottle broke and severed an artery, causing death.

One of the most distinguished and loved of pioneer Methodist preachers, James Bradley Finley ("Father Finley"), set out to a camp meeting in Kentucky in 1801 determined not to yield to the spell of the hour. He recorded in his Autobiography that when he arrived at the meeting the scene was "awful beyond description." The vast sea of human beings—estimated by some to have numbered twenty-five thousand—seemed to be agitated as if by a storm. He counted seven ministers, all preaching at one time, some on stumps, others in wagons, and one standing on a fallen tree. His heart beat tumultuously, his knees trembled, his lip quivered. He became so weak and powerless that he found it necessary to sit down. A strange supernatural power seemed to pervade the entire mass of mind. "At one time I saw at least five hundred swept down in a moment, as if a battery of a thousand guns had been opened upon them, and then immediately followed shrieks and shouts that rent the very heavens. My hair rose up on my head, my whole frame trembled, the blood ran cold in my veins."

The conversions of Asbury, Cartwright, and Finley, and the hardships and rewards that came to them, were typical of hundreds and hundreds of circuit riders. Converted men became evangelists, who proclaimed the Gospel not only by the spoken word but also by their Christlike character and by their humble walk with God. They had spent their lives in the rough wilderness, these men of strong decisive character; their faces were deeply tanned, and their bodies were marked by exposure to the rays of the scorching sun. Many times they were forced to take shelter in smoking wigwams or in crude unfurnished log cabins and to make beds of gathered leaves. Their conversation and sermons betrayed their training in Nature's halls of learning—in deep woods and billowing prairies—and their familiarity with the vocabulary of the hunter, the trapper, and the canoeist. Like all true eloquence, theirs consisted of short, pungent words; it was bold, energetic, expressive, almost Indian in character. Their sermons, delivered in a blunt, clear, straightforward manner, revealed the daring spirit and decisive mind of the speaker. Within the compass of a brief discourse, words were used which owed their origin to circumstances peculiar to the United States: backwoods, canebrakes, corn shucking, dugout, snag; and odd expressions used in the West: to flash in the pan, to pull up stakes, to be a caution.

The people to whom Cartwright and Finley and the circuit riders in the first half of the nineteenth century preached were not tempted by the same snares of the devil that beguiled later generations. The Methodists of their day dressed plainly and wore no jewelry or ruffles. They walked long distances to attend preaching, prayer, and class meetings. They knew hymns by heart. Most churches had neither musical instruments nor chairs. James Gilruth, a Methodist preacher in the Ohio Conference, in 1830 recorded that he was much excited at learning that the bass viol had been introduced into his church. He vowed that he "would break this up or break down in attempting it." At a camp meeting in Kentucky in 1818 it was observed by Benjamin Lakin, a Methodist preacher, that many sinners were converted to God, and "many of the dressy ones . . . came down to cry for mercy and found the Lord." Upon returning from the meeting, one of the girl converts was found trimming off her ruffles. Lakin had never known a greater change in dress than had taken place in that neighborhood since the Lord began His work in it.

Either the equality of the frontier or jealousy in the human heart stirred up gossip and commotion at the display of jewelry. When a woman in Jericho, Warren County, North Carolina, in 1810, was threatened with discipline, her husband told the Methodist preacher that John Wesley was a man of too much good sense to make that a cause of discipline—of expulsion from the church. When he saw that the preacher was bent on expulsion, he requested that their names be taken off the class paper and that they be no longer be considered members.

It is easy to cite instances of excesses and absurdities, and even moral lapses, that accompanied camp meetings, and there were many "backsliders"; but it would be just as easy to name men and women who took on a new lease of life which gave them courage and poise in solving their problems and attending to their daily duties. When Peter Cartwright was in his sixteenth year he attended a wedding where there was drinking and dancing. After returning home, he fell to reflecting on the manner in which he had spent the day and evening. As he walked the floor with his guilty conscience, blood rushed to his head, his heart palpitated, and within a few minutes he became blind. He knelt with his mother to ask God's mercy; and then and there promised the Lord that if He would spare him, he would seek and serve Him. After a period of crisis and temptation, he was converted and found peace of mind at a camp meeting.

In retrospect, Cartwright admitted that in most of the Methodist revivals, many men and women of bad habits and ill repute professed religion and joined the church, and that this was often cited as a great objection to the meetings. In justification of revivals, Cartwright asserted that the economy of the church in saving souls was compared by Jesus Christ to a fisherman casting his net into the sea, and enclosing a multitude of fish, both good and bad. Whoever condemned the fisherman because his net gathered bad as well as good fish, he asked.

There were critics of Methodism who admitted that exigencies often occurred which rendered worship in the open air or in the woods commendable; but they protested against camp meetings because they afforded the mixed multitude opportunities to practice wickedness in its foulest forms. The meetings were generally held in remote places, it was alleged, where under cover of darkness the workers of iniquity hid themselves. These critics held steadfastly to the belief that true religion begins and is carried on by the Divine Spirit experienced in the heart and is distinct from the passions into which the preachers lashed the mind. They objected that the scenes at Pentecost could not be compared with the excesses of camp meetings. They asked what Wesley would have said if he could have attended some of the camp meetings, where the phenomena accounted by him to be the work of the devil were taken by his professed followers to be evidence of the power of God.

The western man was suspicious of the "expert," whether in government or in the church. The church satisfied the instinct of the pioneer to participate in activities of the community; and the emotionalism of the frontier kindled into the camp meeting, with the result that many preachers of limited education were commissioned. It was charged that small value was set on Christian education in the Methodist Church. A person professed conversion and was admitted to membership without being sufficiently grounded in the Bible and in the plan of salvation; and in this way the church was filled with ignorant members. It was also alleged that the constant change of ministers was a strong temptation in the way of the preacher to neglect the improvement of his mind, because he was at liberty to repeat at each successive change of circuit his stock of sermons. The Methodist fashion of "getting religion" brought irreverence and sensational preaching and wordy and unmeaning prayer. When the example of the disciples—a few illiterate fishermen—was adduced in favor of an unlearned ministry, it was objected that the argument did not take into account the fact that these fishermen had received, besides miraculous power and the inspiration of the Holy Spirit, three years of instruction from the lips of the Teacher sent from God.

After years of experience on the circuit, Peter Cartwright made the following argument in favor of the itinerant or traveling plan of ministerial operation, as the best and most scriptural mode of preaching the Gospel of Jesus Christ. Finding nothing contrary in the Scriptures, the Methodist Episcopal Church in her early organization saw proper to create a separate office, not order, of superintendent, or bishop. By the consent of the traveling preachers, the bishop appoints from year to year every traveling preacher in his field of labor. This saves a vast amount of time and trouble in the ministry, in running about and seeking to contract with congregations for specified time and stipulated amount of money. Moreover, it cuts off the temptation of selling the Gospel to the highest bidder, and giving the Gospel exclusively to the rich, and leaving the poor to perish without the means of salvation.

Again we shall appropriate the words of Peter Cartwright in stating the case for himself and his brethren.

For however education may be desirable, and however much the progress of this age may demand an improved ministry, especially an improved pulpit eloquence, I would rather have the gift of a devil-dislodging power than all the college lore or Biblical Institute knowledge that can be obtained from mortal man. When God wants great and learned men in the ministry, how easy it is for Him to overtake a learned sinner, and, as Saul of Tarsus, shake him a while over hell, then knock the scales from his eyes, and, without any previous theological training, send him out straightway to preach Jesus and the resurrection! When God calls any man to preach His Gospel, if he will not reason with flesh and blood, but do his duty and live faithful, my experience for it, God will qualify him for the work if he never saw a college.

Even at that early stage of American Methodism, Cartwright was fearful of having pewed churches, as membership expanded and communicants grew wealthy. The pew system, he said, must necessarily be offensive to the Lord's poor. He recalled that the Presbyterian and Calvinistic branches of the Protestant church used to contend for an educated ministry, for instrumental music, and for a congregational or stated salaried ministry. The Methodists universally opposed these ideas; and the illiterate Methodist preachers actually set the world on fire, while they were lighting their matches.

Perhaps a better perspective of this aspect of Methodism might be obtained if it were pointed out that a foreign student and observer of Methodism in 1856 listed a dozen Methodist periodicals, although there were undoubtedly other publications of one kind or another. Perhaps it is easy to take too seriously "recommended reading" for clergymen, as it is for undergraduates and postgraduates on the campuses of colleges and universities; but in 1827 the Illinois Methodist Conference recommended that candidates for the ministry should read a score of books. The list included the Bible, Wesley's *Notes*, and *Sermons*, Law's *Serious Call*, Clarke's *Commentaries*, Rollin's *Ancient History*, Mosheim's *Ecclesiastical History*, Locke's *On the Human Understanding*, and Morse's *Geography*.

EIGHT

THE EVE OF THE NINETEENTH CENTURY

A PROTESTANT established church is a contradiction in terms, because "Protestantism" implies the priesthood of the common man, the right of private judgment, and an open Bible. Protestantism cannot flourish except as a free church in a free state, which connotes a self-governing church independent of support from the civil government, but friendly to it and coöperative with it. During the American Revolution state governments displaced colonial governments, and during and after the Revolution privileged or established churches were abolished. The American Revolution, in a sense, ratified the distinctive character of American Christianity. The logic of events dictated a free-church system and its concomitant religious freedom. In contrast with the established churches in Europe, whether Catholic or Protestant, where the practice was to baptize all in infancy and to consider them as members of the church, unless excommunicated or convicted of certain crimes, the evangelical churches in America, with some exceptions, believed that there is such a thing as being born again and that only the converted or those "renewed by the spirit" can without sin partake of the Lord's Supper.

In the established churches of Europe admission to membership was mechanical. Children were taught certain fundamentals of the faith and doctrine prior to confirmation and admission to the Lord's Supper. There were even laws requiring men appointed to office under the state to qualify by receiving the Lord's Supper in the established church. Obviously, under such a system the eucharist must be open to all who have been baptized and confirmed; and it is equally obvious that the system is in harmony with the doctrine of baptismal regeneration, for if baptism is regeneration, all baptized persons should receive the Lord's Supper. It is clear that this doctrine of the sacraments was wholly at variance with the Cambridge Platform and with the teaching of "spiritual reformers" of various shades of Protestantism. They cried out against baptismal regeneration because they did not believe that baptism saved the soul and because they did believe that the preaching of it had an evil influence, just as belief in ceremony and veneration for altars, fonts, and churches was wrong. They laid it down without qualification that according to the Bible —the Book of the Protestants—a Christian must have a new heart and a right spirit, and that baptism could not give these. Robert Baird, the zealous Presbyterian minister, pioneer church historian, and author of a book on Religious Liberty in the United States, put it this way: The chief agency of the church is the presentation of the Gospel in all its fullness, in all proper ways, and on all suitable occasions, by a spiritually minded ministry, ordained and set apart for that work, combined with holy living and earnest prayer on the part of the members of the church.

Europeans, clergy and laity, did not understand the American system, because they were blinded by statistics of church membership, which proved that non-members were in the majority, or at least were in a formidable minority. Confronted by long philippics against the political and religious situation in the United States by state church prelates, dissenters countered by reading letters from friends and acquaintances who had immigrated to America and presented a different appraisal. They admitted that many people in the United States did not belong to church; but they asserted that in European countries there were a still greater number who in spirit and manner of life were abroad from the church, although counted members in statistics. Church membership in the United States, they argued, meant something. Even though church members were a minority, they were so zealous that they gave laws a Christian spirit. In other words, they leavened the whole lump.

This is attested by the fact that while eighteenth-century Europe was losing its faith, in America there was in proportion to the population a greater amount of true knowledge of the Gospel and godliness among both clergy and laity. It is true that contemporary clergymen lamented the spiritual decline in the half-century after the Great Awakening and discoursed on the demoralizing moral effects of the French and Indian War and the War of Independence, in conjunction with French infidelity and the iniquity of the French Revolution and the Reign of Terror. They bemoaned the alleged fact that the greater part of the churches had sunk into formalism; in many of them the necessity of being born again was ignored; and men without prayer and without faith claimed admission to Gospel ordinances on the so-called Half-Way Covenant. Contemporary sermons revealed the fear that the foundations of society were slipping, and they pointed to rationalism, infidelity, Jeffersonian Democracy, and the French Revolution and Napoleonic wars. There were lamentations over increased traveling, worldly labor and amusement on the Sabbath, increased consumption of liquor, neglect of family government and prayer, profanity, and dissensions within communities and within the country.

In every colony, with the exception of Rhode Island, Pennsylvania, and Delaware, there was an established church. In the southern colonies and in New York and New Jersey it was the Anglican or Episcopal Church that held the preferred position. The dissolute character of certain clergymen, notably Anglican priests, some of whom had been sent over from England, was a factor that contributed to the separation of church and state. Moreover, as has been pointed out, many Anglican clergymen were loyal to the British government and were hated and feared during and after the Revolution, as were the loyalists in general. The multitude of sects—notably Presbyterians and Baptists—made for religious diversity; and numerous petitions praying for religious freedom were adopted by them. In Virginia the leadership looking toward the disestablishment of the church came from three able and famous men. In 1768 Patrick Henry delivered an appeal for religious liberty before the bar of justice as the advocate for Baptists who were in trouble. James Madison, who was educated at Princeton, the center of Presbyterian influence and a fountain of revivalism, favored making the free exercise of religion a matter of right, not of toleration, and therefore advocated the disestablishment of the church. Thomas Jefferson, who as a youth had seen democracy in action in a Baptist church of his community, was a Deist (an "arch-infidel," some of his enemies called him). In his *Notes on the State of Virginia,* which he wrote in 1781–82, he indulged in severe strictures on the established church.

The bill of rights in the Virginia constitution—one of the first to be adopted—provided for religious freedom, although the clause was not made effective until 1785, when Jefferson formulated a motion, which Madison pushed through the legislature, putting an end to the established church.

In New England it was the Congregational Church that was established by law; and in no section of the country was the proposal to disestablish the church met with greater opposition. The Anglican Church in New England was, as has been said, a root out of dry ground. The soil, the climate, the atmosphere, the genius, and the history of the people were all against it. Its forms and ceremonies were associated with the persecution that drove the Puritans out of England. The oppressive colonial governors were Episcopalians; and in the Revolution the Episcopal Church was on the Tory side. But in the nature of the case a church established by law and working in close coöperation with the secular government of whatever creed or doctrine becomes dictatorial and abuses its power; and that is what happened to the Congregational Church in New England. The conduct of its ministry justified the sarcasm which said that the Puritans had left the Lords Bishops to be under the Lords Brethren.

Except in Connecticut, Massachusetts, and New Hampshire, every state had disestablished the church before the opening of the nineteenth century. New Hampshire retained her establishment until 1817; Connecticut until 1818; and Massachusetts until 1833. In justice to those states, however, it should be recalled that seven state constitutions required some sort of religious test in order to qualify for civil office; and in several states Catholics and Jews were under disabilities. It should also be mentioned in this connection that the year 1787 is a landmark which enriched the religious heritage of the American people. The Ordinance of 1787, sometimes called the Northwest Ordinance, which provided stages of government for the territory of the United States northwest of the Ohio River, guaranteed immunity from molestation to individuals regardless of their modes of worship or religious sentiments. Another landmark of no less importance is the First Amendment to the federal Constitution, ratified in 1791, which provided that "Congress shall make no law respecting an establishment of religion, or prohibiting the free exercise thereof."

It was not until the leaven of frontier democracy and the results of universal manhood suffrage—a frontier experiment—were felt in New England that her privileged churches gave way.

The religious history of Connecticut in the years following the American Revolution may be taken as fairly typical of New England, where Congregationalism was the religion established by law and where the established church held practically undisputed sway. In every village there was the meeting-house and the minister who was the object of profound respect as he marched down the street, wearing his cocked hat and carrying his gold-headed cane. Within a certain domain his word was law. Every householder was taxed for the support of the church; and law and custom demanded attendance at both Sunday services. Absentees could expect a call from the minister on the following Monday. For many years only members of churches were eligible to hold public office. The minister, with the support of substantial citizens, was quick to suppress sectarian meetings as likely to create discord in the village.

The first step away from the Congregational order was taken when every man was given the liberty of "signing off," as it was called, to any church of his own choice. This stimulated the growth of churches of many denominations, though it was still not good form to hold aloof from membership in some church. Having dealt a blow to the established church by giving equal rights to other denominations, the next step was to abolish all remnants of the intimate relations between church and state—to leave Christianity to itself and to establish religious freedom. Connecticut fell in line with the march of progress by giving to every man the liberty of going to church or of not going to church, of keeping the Sabbath or of not keeping the Sabbath, of supporting a minister or of not supporting him.

The state ratified the logic of the fundamental tenet of the Protestant Reformation—the right of private judgment; and joined with the people of the other states of the Union in proving that freedom of conscience is the best way of preserving religion and morals. American Christianity was equal to the test of separation of church and state, by drawing on the vast spiritual resources of the population. Any church or churchman who has ventured to ignore the line of demarcation between church and state has felt the righteous indignation of men and women who knew at what cost religious liberty was gained and the price the countries of Europe and Latin America have paid for rejecting it.

Timothy Dwight, president of Yale College, Lyman Beecher, prominent Congregational minister in Hartford, and other distinguished men of the state opposed separation; but most of them lived to see that their apprehensions were unfounded. Beecher made a handsome acknowledgement of his mistaken position:

For several days I suffered what no tongue can tell for the best thing that ever happened to the State of Connecticut. It cut the churches loose from dependence on state support. It threw them wholly on their own resources and on God. They say ministers have lost their influence; the fact is, they have gained. By voluntary efforts, societies, missions, and revivals, they exert a deeper influence than they ever could by queues, and shoe-buckles, and cocked hats, and gold-headed canes.

Timothy Dwight remained an unreconstructed clergyman. The horror of Jeffersonian Democracy and French infidelity and the rising tide of democracy confirmed that great teacher and able college president in his rigid Calvinism and staunch Federalism. The period from 1800 to 1815 was a "winter of discontent" for New England where it was believed that the election of Thomas Jefferson in 1800 meant the triumph of atheism. New England even talked of secession. Jefferson became the target of bitter propaganda broadcast by leading Federalists, who alleged that he was an infidel and in league with atheistic France. Clergymen used the pulpit to slander Jefferson and to discredit a republican form of government. And during the War of 1812 some of them took the part of Great Britain and opposed the prosecution of the war by the Madison administration.

In a sermon delivered before an audience which included the governor and lieutenant governor of Massachusetts, the council, and members of the legislature, in May, 1815, James Flint, a minister in Bridgewater, discoursed on the anxiety on the part of lovers of liberty at the conquests of Napoleon and paid tribute to the people of Eng-

land because they kept the tyrant at bay and never bowed the knee
to the great Baal. "We had to blush for our own country, that it had
taken no part in the triumphant cause of God and man," he said. "Our
country did take part in this cause, but it was against it. . . . Yes,
the exclusive republicans of America voluntarily added themselves
to the long list of degraded nations, who were by force leagued with
the infidel power of France against England." The speaker paid tribute to Spain and Russia for their part in the overthrow of Napoleon.
He deplored the attack upon Canada "as impolitic, as it was cruel and
wicked." It was to the honor of New England, he said, that by a large
majority of its inhabitants the measure was regarded in the light of
an unprovoked and murderous assault upon peaceable and unoffending
neighbors.

It would be unhistorical and unjust to omit mention of sermons
preached by clergymen which were the very opposite in spirit and in
content from those cited. A sermon by Solomon Aikin, a Congregational minister in Dracut, Massachusetts, in 1811 accused President
Adams and the Federalists of infringing neutral rights and of palliat-
ing and winking at every aggression from England and of making
every exertion to alienate the affections of citizens from France. The
Alien and Sedition acts, passed by a Federalist Congress, were condemned.

During the presidential campaign of 1800, in September, Abraham
Bishop delivered an oration in New Haven on the evening preceding
the public commencement in which he took the Connecticut clergy to
task. He referred to the fact that the Church of England and the
Roman Catholic Church in all Catholic countries had been employed
to support the government; but he counted on the good sense of all
Americans to repel the first attempts to bind them with ecclesiastical
fetters. They would say to the clergy: "Your business is to preach the
Gospel." The sheep would never thrive, he said, if the shepherd, instead of leading them to green pastures, constantly alarmed them with
the cry of wolves.

Timothy Dwight was powerfully disturbed by the events of the
second half of the eighteenth century. This son of a daughter of
Jonathan Edwards became president of Yale College in 1795, when
that institution was in a decline; its funds were low, the number of

students small, and their morals corrupt. During the score of years when he was president, Yale was visited with "five seasons of the special outpourings of the Spirit of God," when students made public profession of their faith. For about twelve years before assuming his duties at Yale, Dwight was pastor of a congregation in Greenfield, Connecticut, where he felt it his duty to oppose the lax discipline of the Half-Way Covenant and Arminianism that had been adopted. At Yale, in 1797 and 1801, respectively, he launched two thunderbolts against modern philosophy. The first was preached to the candidates for the Baccalaureate on "The Nature and Danger of Infidel Philosophy"; the second sermon was "A Discourse on Some Events of the Last Century."

In bold language Dwight exposed the loose patterns of conduct and opinion that followed in the wake of the French and Indian War and the War of Independence and the devastating effect of infidelity. He found in Scripture two great causes of infidelity: (1) The opposition of a heart which loves sin and dreads the punishment of it. (2) Philosophists, the authors of vain and deceitful philosophy, of science falsely so-called: scoffers walking after their own lusts. From the writings of St. John he concluded that Antichrist is he who denies that Jesus was come in the flesh, from which Dwight informed his hearers that the term could be applied to the "collective body of modern infidels."

He defended revivals against the strictures of men whose opinions of the subject were formed in the closet and not derived from facts or warranted by the Scriptures. Seasons of enthusiasm, he said, have often existed, and probably in every civilized country. In these seasons the human mind has not infrequently exhibited many kinds and degrees of weakness, error, and deformity; but Dwight asserted that nothing took place but that which sound philosophy must presuppose usually takes place in ardent minds. This did not prove, however, that nothing existed beyond enthusiasm. To infidels and libertines all religion is extravagance, enthusiasm, and superstition, he said, but no man of common candor could admit that impiety is an unhappy proof of real wisdom. The greatest danger, he argued, was a tendency in many persons toward what was called modern liberality, which was no other than indifference to truth and error, virtue and vice: more dangerous than the most contemptible enthusiasm or the most odious bigotry.

Timothy Dwight, in spite of a rather narrow outlook and an uncharitableness, not to say bigotry, on many counts lived up to the enlightened judgments and progress of his time. His contributions to education were notable. He was abreast of changes that were harbingers of epochal events in the nineteenth century, though he did not live to see much more than their inception. He was active in the organization and encouragement of the Connecticut Missionary Society, the Andover Theological Seminary, the American Board of Commissioners for Foreign Missions, the American Bible Society, the School for the Education of Heathen Youth, and the Connecticut Society for the Education of Young Men.

NINE

THE FRUIT OF REVIVALS

T HE nineteenth century in America produced a religious revival unprecedented in church history. Perhaps it would be more accurate to state that the century gave birth to a series of revivals, culminating, respectively, in 1800–02, 1857–58, and 1877–78; but in reality revivalism never ceased, though it may have flagged at times. In a letter dated at Lexington, Kentucky, on March 8, 1801, the writer commented on the great revival which took its inception at Cane Ridge, Bourbon County, Kentucky. In some churches, he wrote, the revival appeared like a fire that had long been confined, "bursting all its barriers, and spreading with a rapidity that is incredible." He said that the occasion justified the use of the language of sacred inspiration: "The flowers appear on the earth; the time of the singing of birds is come, and the voice of the turtle is heard in our land."

This great revival was marked by the emotional excesses that have been discussed in earlier chapters; and the number of meetings, their protracted character, and great crowds, numbering from twelve to twenty-five thousand, exceeded the great revivals of the previous century. Ministers from almost all denominations flocked in from far and near; and the thousands who heard them came on foot, on horseback, in wagons, and in carriages. Persons of all ages, children and graying men and women, clergy and laity, skeptics and church members, were struck down. Denominational lines were ignored. In the multitudes were Presbyterians, Methodists, and Baptists. The members of the first two churches were in full communion with each other; but the Baptists united only in the preaching.

Out of the great revival grew discord and schism; and individuals of independent natures and "come-outer" instincts led movements of secession which added to the medley of sects and denominations and set up religious experiment stations, some of which, in one form or another, have had enduring existence.

The Christian Church and the Disciples of Christ are names that suggest communions that grew out of the great revival. They emerged from a series of complications and schisms which united in denominations that acknowledged no name but "Christian" and no creed but the Bible. They were opposed to clericalism, because they placed the blame chiefly on the clergy for theological quibbles and denominational barriers that obscured primitive Christianity. They taught that in the Apostolic Church there was no essential difference between Christians. However, with the multiplication of congregations the need of some organization was felt; and clergymen were ordained. But the line between clergy and laity was not sharply drawn, and the laity were not prohibited from performing so-called ministerial acts. The organ question still divides the churches calling themselves "Christian," and was not peculiar to them. Zwingli and Calvin were opposed to organ music in churches, and pietists of various shades have taken the same position. It was not until after the middle of the nineteenth century that this question became really serious on the frontier, because organs were not available. It is reliably reported that a church in Indiana was constructed with doors and windows so narrow that an assembled organ could not be installed.

The genesis of the "Christian" movement need not be traced in detail. During the great revival, conservative and "New Light" factions in the Presbyterian Church came into conflict, which resulted in the withdrawal of Barton W. Stone and Richard McNemar and three other ministers from the Synod of Kentucky. These men of "unsound faith," as it was charged, formed a presbytery of their own in 1803, which was dissolved within a year, with the announcement that they would take the Bible as their only rule of faith and practice and take the name "Christian" instead of a denominational designation. Adherents of the new movement were called "New Lights" or "Stoneites."

A few years later a movement associated with Thomas and Alexander Campbell, father and son, took place in western Pennsylvania. Stone and the Campbells were alike in their dislike for creeds and confessions and in their plea for Christian union. The Campbells called their group Disciples of Christ; Stone's followers preferred the name Christian. They had fundamentals in common, but their disagreement was important enough to prevent organic union, though not coöperation. The difference between them was a matter of emphasis. This religion, which in its inception was a protest against denominationalism, synods, conferences, and creeds, was another spontaneous movement which sprang up on frontier soil. Peter Cartwright, who did not spare invective in attacking rival evangelists who belonged to households of faith other than his own, was especially critical of the Disciples of Christ and the Shakers. Because it adopted no standard of doctrine, Cartwright called the Christian Church a "trash heap." It adopted the mode of immersion, he said, "and directly there was a mighty controversy about the way to heaven, whether it was by water or by dry land."

Another religion which owed its inception and growth to revivals was the sect known as the Shakers. The "official name" was the Millennial Church, or the United Society of Believers. In the preface to a volume published at Albany, New York, in 1823, which presents a "summary view" of the church and a statement of its general principles, it was acknowledged that the United Society did not follow the example of any other religious denomination, because of the conviction that a uniform course of religious profession, joined to a lifeless stupidity in divine things, could not be well-pleasing in the sight of God, especially when blended with an ardent pursuit of worldly honor and glory.

The founder of the Shakers was born in England in 1736. She was Ann Lee, who never learned to read or write and who joined, in 1758, a society called the Shaking Quakers, because their indignation against sin in themselves caused them to shake. She was early the subject of religious impressions, was often favored with heavenly visions, and had the "gift of prophecy" manifested by "speaking with tongues." Through immediate revelation of Christ her influence over her followers was so great that she received the title Mother Ann. The exercises in their religious meetings were singing, dancing, shaking, turning, shouting, speaking with tongues, and prophesying. These "gifts" increased until the time of the organization of the Shaker Church in America in 1792. Previously, by a special revelation, Mother Ann was directed to go to America; and on May 19, 1774, with eight of her followers, she embarked for New York. She died on September 9, 1784, at the age of forty-eight years.

The Shakers knew that the scribes and Pharisees of their generation viewed their Society as made up of illiterate and contemptible individuals; but they took consolation in the fact that the primitive Christians were slandered by their heathen neighbors. After thirty-eight years' experience as a member of the United Society, Frederick William Evans, who was converted from agnosticism, wrote in his Autobiography that he had gained a degree of victory over self, which caused his peace to "flow as a river," and which filled him with sympathy for all "seekers after truth and righteousness."

In 1869 there were eighteen societies of Shakers, located in widely scattered places. One of the most important societies was at Mount Lebanon, New York, where the membership was augmented by a remarkable revival of religion in 1779. Many from various parts of the country, and of many denominations, adopted the faith. In 1838 occurred another revival, similar to the phenomenon known as Spiritualism which may be said to have taken its inception when members of the Fox family in Hydesville, New York, heard mysterious noises in March, 1848. There was a close kinship between Shakerism and Spiritualism.

Before the close of the nineteenth century, Shakerism had all but disappeared; but the sect constitutes another chapter in religious history to illustrate the freedom of the individual to "work out his own salvation" in America. The Shakers went to extremes in advocating celibacy as a substitute for poverty, famine, disease, and war, in exalting Mother Ann as the person through whom the Christ spirit was exhibited a second time, in adopting communism as a way of life, in millennial speculations, in rejecting the orthodox sacraments, and in disbelieving the inspiration of the Bible.

The first half of the century was a time of the flowering of the missionary spirit, when individual denominations and interdenominational establishments followed as best they could the march of population across the continent and brought the Gospel to heathen lands. There was a liberal leaven which softened sectarian rivalry and antagonism; but the great religious revivals, while they quickened the

spirit, also stimulated sectarianism and fomented schism. The influence of the laity and the increasing number of recruits to the ministry
of men whose education was meager and whose indoctrination was
superficial, made for looseness in doctrine and multiplication of sects.
Moreover, to the sects and churches indigenous to American soil, like
the Campbellites, Spiritualists, Mormons, and Millerites, was added
a score or more of foreign-language churches.

The revolutionary upheavals in Europe and in Latin America, and
the outpouring of emigrants who sought homes in the New World,
convinced members in all churches that the second coming of Christ
was imminent. William Miller, a sincere and honest farmer in Vermont, was so sure of the imminent crack of doom that he fixed the
year and the day of the month for the awful event. His study of the
Book of Daniel and Revelation made him so confident that he openly
proclaimed his theories and teachings, and thereby originated a new
sect known as Millerism and later called Adventism. Ten years in advance, he fixed the date of Christ's second coming on March 21, 1843.
Miller made extensive preaching tours and his writings were widely
read. Annual conferences of Millerites were held. As the day approached, believers abandoned their occupations; and at the dawn
of March 21st, crowds were assembled in open spaces and on hills to
await the coming of the Messiah.

Mormonism was born and developed in an atmosphere of "isms,"
in a time of intense missionary activity, when sects multiplied, when
humanitarian ideals took the form of abolitionism, equal rights for the
rich and the poor, for the black man as well as the white man, for
women as well as men. The achievement of the Mormons is that they
set down an Old Testament society in a desert area, where the cultivation of soil required community action. They established and made
workable a communistic theocratic state which attracted members
from every state in the Union and from several countries of Europe.
In a babel of tongues and types the church was the bond of union and
the instrument of community action. The Mormon Zion in Utah with
its great Tabernacle was something new and inviting to thousands who
heard about it through missionaries who were sent to the gentiles at
home and abroad and through newspapers and publications. The
Mormon elders and their missionaries were ambassadors of a religious

and social system that supplied the means of bringing converts to Zion in the New World.

A bureau of emigration was organized; and the bishops selected sites for the new colonies that were to receive converts from the older states of the East, and from Europe, Canada, and Hawaii. The missionaries were unusually successful in gaining converts in England, Denmark, Norway and Sweden. In these countries they reaped where others had sown. Mormon missionaries were sometimes mistaken for preachers of other denominations, sometimes American, much to their advantage. They usually worked among the poor and the ignorant and found the greatest responses from women. They appeared in various guises, sometimes even as beggars. They usually approached their prospects by talking about infant baptism and by making insinuations about the worldly character of the parish pastors, in contrast with the Mormon apostles who carried neither scrip nor purse. By stages the speaker would bring in the prophecies about the second coming of Christ—to put fear in the heart and to prompt the question of how to flee from the wrath to come. The answer would be to flee to the Zion in Utah, where there was an abundance of land to cultivate while awaiting the coming of the Lord. In Zion everyone was rich because wealth was equally distributed, and land, pasture, timber, and waterpower were at the free disposal of all.

The founder of Mormonism was Joseph Smith who was born in Vermont of people of shifting residence and Calvinistic views. When Joseph was eleven years old, he moved with his parents to Palmyra, New York, in an environment that produced newfangled ideas in religion and social philosophy. Like his semi-illiterate and superstitious neighbors, he developed special points of view and saw visions. Under the spell of these visions he became convinced that he was chosen of God to restore the Church of Christ on earth; and through an interview with an angel of the Lord he discovered the existence of plates of gold upon which was recorded the true history of the true Church of God. By means of another miracle Smith obtained magic spectacles which enabled him to read the plates. It was from these plates that the Book of Mormon was transcribed. This is in brief the traditional story of the origin of the Book of Mormon.

During the years when the Mormons were obtaining recruits and were suffering persecution at the hands of neighbors wherever their settlements were established, being finally compelled in 1846 to resort to mass migration to Utah, other individuals and groups, whether religious or secular, were also restless and floating. There were myriads of "fountains of knowledge and piety" in the Mississippi Valley founded by Christian families. The Great Valley also beckoned to the fleeing multitudes from Europe, the rich and the poor, the villain and the upright, the industrious and the indolent, to share its riches and to enjoy its free thought, its free press, its freedom of assembly, and its freedom to worship. The home missionary movements were created to give answer to the question that vitally concerned the sons and daughters of New England who established churches in the West: "Are they to be born in this free air, play with the children of freemen, read the language of Milton and Washington, have free access to the Bible, and remain timid slaves of men who deny the right of thinking?"

Lyman Beecher in a series of lectures, published in 1835 under the title *A Plea for the West*, exhorted his hearers to contribute money for the establishment of educational institutions to work among the immigrants whose coming was foretold in prophecy and portended the end of the world. He regarded the rapid and universal extension of civil and religious liberty as introductory to the triumph of universal Christianity; but he also knew from prophecy that revolutions and distress of nations would precede the introduction of the peaceful reign of Jesus Christ. When he first encountered the opinion of Jonathan Edwards that the Millennium would commence in America, he thought it chimerical; but all providential developments since, and all the existing signs of the times, lent it corroboration. This great preacher, who was called a thunderbolt by his contemporary clergymen, continued in the following prophetic vein:

What nation is blessed with such experimental knowledge of free institutions, with such facilities and resources of communication, obstructed by so few obstacles, as our own? There is not a nation upon earth which, in fifty years, can by all possible reformation place itself in circumstances so favorable as our own for the free and unembarrassed application of physical effort and pecuniary and moral power to evangelize the world. . . .

It is equally plain, that the religious and political destiny of our nation is to be decided in the West. There is the territory, and there will soon be the population, the wealth, and the political power. . . . The West is destined to be the great central power of the nation, and under heaven, must affect powerfully the cause of free institutions, and the liberty of the world. . . .

It is equally clear, that the conflict which is to decide the destiny of the West, will be a conflict of institutions for the education of her sons, for purposes of superstition, or evangelical light; of despotism, or liberty.

This chapter may be fittingly concluded by reference to the great revival of 1857–58, when it was estimated that not less than fifty thousand conversions occurred in a single week and not less than five hundred thousand souls were converted throughout the country. There had been nothing comparable to this religious emotion that swept the land during the hard times of that decade. It was mainly the work of laymen. Throughout the length and breadth of the Northern states men neglected their stores and offices to attend daily prayer meetings. At a prayer meeting in Boston, a man arose and said that his journey from Omaha to Boston was a continuous prayer meeting all the way. In this revival prayer was more important than preaching. The activity of men and women was manifested by personal visitation and the distribution of tracts. The *New York Tribune* published several extra editions filled with accounts of the revival in different parts of the country.

Charles G. Finney sensed that a divine influence pervaded the whole land. Slavery seemed to shut it out from the South. "The Spirit of God seemed to be grieved away from them," he said.

TEN

REVIVALISM: EXPONENTS AND CRITICS

R EVIVALISM has been a subject of acrimonious controversy both within and without the portals of the church. The disagreement has been concerned with doctrine and method. In general, the dividing line separates the Anglican, Lutheran, and Roman Catholic communions from the so-called Reformed churches. In other words, the liturgical churches, which also emphasize the sacramental side of religion, have usually held aloof from emotional religion. Liturgists have fondly and triumphantly cited St. Paul: "Let all things be done decently and in order." They were out of sympathy with evangelists who believed that progress and development in the churches were impossible without periodic excitements. Their sermons stressed "growth in grace." The issue was stated concisely and plainly by Charles Grandison Finney, the great revivalist whose doctrine leaned toward Christian perfection, and by Leonard Woods, a moderate Calvinist and professor in Andover Theological Seminary. Finney preached the doctrine that the Bible plainly asserts that regeneration is the work of man. Woods published an article under the title: "The Holy Ghost the Author of Regeneration," in which he sought to prove that regeneration is the work of God.

According to one "school," a sinner should be brought "under conviction" and remain under conviction for a long time—days, weeks, even years—until he found relief, that is, became truly converted. Finney, on the other hand, impressed upon the sinner the duty of instant surrender to God, instead of using the means of grace and praying for a new heart. He told him to give his heart to God and to enter at once upon a life of devotion to Christ, and warned him that if he remained long under conviction, he ran the risk of becoming self-righteous and resigned in a false hope. He made a plea for the use of what were called "new measures" and the casting aside of meaningless forms and outworn traditions. He spared neither clergy nor laity, and showed how what were considered essentials by a previous generation had fallen into disuse.

Formerly ministers even in America, he said, used to have a peculiar dress, after the fashion of soldiers. They wore a cocked hat, and bands instead of a cravat or stock, and small clothes, and a wig. Now, he said, a minister can go into the pulpit dressed like any other man. The church complained as much as if a divine institution had been given up. Many remnants of superstition still remained, however. Ministers still felt obliged to wear a black coat; and even in some Congregational churches in New England a minister would not be tolerated in the pulpit unless he had a flowing silk gown, with enormous sleeves. Will anyone pretend, he asked, that the cause of religion has been injured by giving these things up?

In regard to the order of public worship, the same difficulties were met in making every change, "because the church had felt as if God had established just the mode which they were used to." Finney cited the introduction and use of psalmbooks instead of following the custom, when books were scarce, of having the deacon stand before the pulpit and read off the psalm or hymn a line at a time, or two lines at a time, and then sing, and all the rest would join in. What an innovation and what a confusion when books were introduced and everyone sang from his own book! There was the same opposition to choirs, and to the use of pitch pipes and instrumental music. With reference to extempore prayer, he stated that in some parts of the church a man would not be tolerated if he prayed without having his prayerbook before him; and preaching without notes was equally obnoxious. He recalled the time when in the Congregational churches in New England a man or woman would be ashamed to be seen kneeling at a prayer meeting, for fear of being taken for a Methodist; and for a layman to pray in public was to interfere with the dignity and the authority of ministers. Serious apprehensions were entertained for the safety of Zion if women were allowed to assemble for prayer meetings. Missions, Sunday schools, Bible societies, and temperance societies were opposed as new measures not mentioned in the Bible. It is obvious that a man harboring these radical views was the target for asperity. This unique man was molded by unique experiences. He was an elemental man who braved the scorn of complacency, flouted orthodoxy, flew in the face of conventionality, and worked out his own salvation by hours and days of fasting and prayer.

Charles Grandison Finney, a tall, handsome fellow, fond of outdoor sports, was born on August 29, 1792, in Litchfield County, Connecticut. When he was about two years old, his father moved to Oneida County, New York, which was settled mostly by people from New England. His parents were not professing Christians, and among their neighbors there were few religious people. Before he attained the age of twenty-one, he attended few religious services. He was denied the privilege of attending college and took up the study of law. "I was almost as ignorant of religion as a heathen," he said. "I had very little regard to the Sabbath, and had no definite knowledge of religious truth." His study of law aroused interest in the Bible; and he was brought face to face with the question whether he would accept Christ as presented in the Gospel, or pursue a worldly course. His conversion to Christ came in 1821, when he was approaching his thirtieth year.

Finney's conversion came after months of prayer, weeping, and conflict. He would go into the woods for long periods of prayer. In his *Memoirs* he tells about seeing Jesus standing before him, just like any other person—so real was He. He wept aloud like a child. After his mind became calm enough to break off from the interview, he received a mighty baptism of the Holy Ghost. "I could feel the impression, like a wave of electricity, going through me. . . . It seemed like the very breath of God." In this state he was taught the doctrine of justification by faith as a present experience. As a young Christian he had many seasons of communing with God which could not be described in words. He soon found, he wrote, that it would not do to tell his brethren what was passing between the Lord and his soul because they could not understand it.

In 1822, shortly after his conversion, Finney put himself under the care of the Presbytery as a candidate for the ministry. Despite the urging of some ministers, he declined to study theology at Princeton because he could not accept the doctrine of election. His study of the Bible convinced him that the atonement was made for all mankind, not limited to a portion. Throughout his life he remained a New School Calvinist, with a tendency toward perfectionism. In the decade of the thirties he preached two sermons on Christian perfection in Broadway Tabernacle, New York. He was criticised so vehemently in his own Presbyterian Church that in 1836 he left the Presbytery, and his New York church became Congregational in polity. During the years of his presidency of Oberlin College, ecclesiastical bodies passed resolutions warning the churches against the influence of "Oberlin theology." Finney's predecessor at Oberlin, Asa Mahan, was also under fire because of "heresy." The two men had many things in common. Both were active participants in the great revivals from 1824 to 1832, when their methods were challenged by men no less influential than Lyman Beecher, who was reported as having said that Oberlin doctrines and influence were worse than those of Roman Catholics. Mahan emerged from the high Calvinistic tradition in which he was trained to the adoption of the doctrine of full moral freedom. In the later years of his life he preached to large congregations in England, advocating the doctrine of Christian perfection.

In the galaxy of great preachers before the Civil War, none was more powerful as a revivalist than Finney; and many of his brethren adopted his methods. In the first years of the thirties he delivered a series of lectures on revivals to members of his congregation in New York. They were delivered extemporaneously, taken down in longhand, published originally in the *New York Evangelist*, and then in a book entitled *Lectures on Revivals of Religion*. Twelve thousand copies of the volume were sold as fast as they could be printed. It was reprinted in England and France and translations were made in French, German, and Welsh. The lectures promoted revivals in England, Scotland, Wales, various places on the continent of Europe, in Nova Scotia, and in islands of the sea.

In the first years of his ministry while conducting a revival at Antwerp, New York, Finney had commenced to speak in the strain of direct application, when all at once an awful solemnity seemed to settle down upon the congregation, whereupon men and women began to fall from their seats and cry for mercy. Finney wrote that if he had had a sword in each hand, he could not have cut them off their seats as fast as they fell. Nearly the whole congregation was either on its knees or prostrate in less than two minutes after the first shock fell upon them.

Rather early in his ministry Finney made use of the "anxious seat" as a means of promoting revivals. He used this "new measure" because experience and observation taught him that, with the higher classes especially, the greatest obstacle to be overcome was their fear of being known as anxious inquirers. They were too proud to take a position that would reveal them to others as anxious for their souls. Finney learned soon after he began to call upon people to come forward to certain seats and offer themselves up to God while prayers were offered for them, that the Lord was aiming at the conversion of the highest classes of society: lawyers, physicians, and merchants.

While serving as pastor in New York City, he held "inquiry meetings" once or twice a week, and sometimes oftener, and every week a goodly number of conversions were reported. Whenever called upon to do so, members of the church would go out into the "highways and hedges" and bring people to hear the preaching.

These methods were appropriated by a number of able ministers who reported results similar to those observed by Finney—men like Lyman Beecher, John Todd, and Justin Edwards.

John Todd, who was a minister at Groton, Massachusetts, in the thirties, related that at the close of the meeting he called upon the impenitent, who had determined to make religion their chief concern, to rise. He then called upon those who were professors of religion to rise, if they would pray for them. Almost everybody in the congregation rose. The preacher then inquired what would become of those who continued to sit. Where would they go? While the congregation was thus standing, he called for the judgment hymn: "Oh, there will be mourning, before the judgment seat." While the hymn was sung slowly and solemnly, several who held their seats rose up.

Justin Edwards, who led a useful life as pastor, temperance worker, president of a theological seminary, laborer for the sanctification of the Sabbath, and zealous promoter of the work of the American Bible Society, was active in the revival in Boston and surrounding towns. In March, 1828, he wrote: "Boston appears to be more full of God than I have ever before known it." Edwards lamented that uneducated and ardent young men deprecated the value of education; and he proclaimed that it was wrong to state things that were not true for the purpose of awaking sinners; but his preaching assumed that children and persons of little learning and small abilities sometimes embraced the Gospel, appeared clearly to understand it, and deeply to feel its truths. "It is because the Holy Ghost can and does teach them as really as others," he said. "The truths of the Gospel are adapted to their condition, and exactly meet their wants."

The little child, when weeping over the wickedness of his own heart, in godly sorrow and true penitence, understands the doctrine as really as a man; and more so, unless the man has been taught it in the same way, by *feeling* it. . . . We see also the reason why some men, with the Bible in their hands, are "ever learning, and yet never come to the knowledge of the truth." They do not feel their *need* of the teaching of the Holy Ghost.

Two of the ablest men in the ministry and among the most power- ful revival preachers were Lyman Beecher and Asahel Nettleton; but they were also among the foremost critics of the methods of Finney and his school. John Todd said of these men that they were "the two great instruments in revivals such as I have never seen equaled. . . . Nettleton was one of the most remarkable men the world ever saw. . . . The Great Day alone can reveal the results of the life of Nettle- ton." Lyman Beecher described Nettleton's preaching as highly in- tellectual, as opposed to declamation or oratorical, pathetic appeals to imagination or to the emotions. It was discriminatingly doctrinal. As an example of his unsurpassed power of description, Beecher cited his sermon on the Deluge delivered one evening in a village a few miles north of Albany, New York. The crowded hall was filled with con- sternation, as if they heard the cries of the drowning, the bellowing of the cattle, and neighing of horses, amid darkness and desolation. The emotion rose to such a pitch that the floor seemed to tremble under the tones of his deep voice.

Nettleton's revivals usually commenced with the congregation confessing its sin. He introduced the doctrine of depravity, made direct assaults on the conscience, explained regeneration, cut off self- righteousness, and enforced immediate repentance and faith. Toward the close of the revival he had a set of sermons to guard sinners against dropping the subject. He gave personal attention and added a meeting of inquiry for all who were willing to attend. The effect of Nettleton's preaching, according to Beecher, was to put an end to opposition to revivals. His life spanned the years from 1783 to 1844.

It was in the midst of the revival in Utica, New York, in 1826, that Finney first heard of the opposition to his revivals that was springing up in the East. The controversy, which occasioned the calling of a convention or consultation at New Lebanon, New York, in 1827, on the subject of conducting revivals, was initiated by letters written by Lyman Beecher and Asahel Nettleton to prominent clergymen. These letters were published in 1828 under their names with the title *Letters on the "New Measures" in Conducting Revivals of Religion*.

Beecher and Nettleton were in agreement that the state of things in New England at the close of the Great Awakening was similar to the present. They referred to the "young itinerants" who denounced those settled ministers who would not go to all lengths with them. "Could Whitefield, and Edwards, and Brainard, and Davenport, now arise from the dead, I have no doubt they would exclaim, 'Young men, beware, beware!' " wrote Nettleton. Beecher traced out in the indiscretion of Davenport not only the suspension of the revival in Boston when he came to the city eighty years ago and began to denounce the ministers as unconverted men; but also the indelible prejudices against revivals which made old Calvinists formal and turned semi-Calvinists into Arminians, Arminians into Unitarians, and Unitarians into Universalists. Beecher stated that there were in Boston at the time he wrote orthodox churches in which there had not been for eighty years a common evening lecture, and could not be, owing to the extravagance of revivals which took place almost a century ago.

Some divinity students and others, in their attempts to imitate Finney, reminded Nettleton of the seven sons of Sceva at Corinth, exorcists, who undertook to imitate the Apostle Paul by driving out evil spirits, as recorded in the nineteenth chapter of the Acts of the Apostles. He asserted that Finney had been scarcely three years in the ministry and had had no time to look at the consequences of his preaching. He intimidated ministers who would not go to all lengths with him and denounced them as enemies of revivals. Nettleton had made the acquaintance of young ministers who had taken their stamp from Finney. "I am sorry to say," he wrote, "that the spirit which they manifest . . . appears to me to resemble anything rather than the 'wisdom which is from above,' or the 'fruits of the Spirit.'" The in-evitable consequence of their style of preaching, he said, would be to awaken in others the passion of anger, wrath, malice, envy, and evil speaking.

At the New Lebanon conference clergymen of outstanding repu-tation were present, including Beecher, Nettleton, and Finney. The opposition was pointed at Finney. According to Finney's *Memoirs,* the facts which came out at the conference did not sustain the charges that had been made in the published letters. Finney further alleges that Beecher's *Autobiography* gives a misleading account of revivals and of the relations between him and Finney. He cared little what Beecher and Nettleton were saying and doing about him, nor did he change his methods of conducting revivals. Finney's moral fibre and spirituality may be sensed by his recorded reaction to the opposition that was mounting against him before the New Lebanon meeting:

I shall never forget what a scene I passed through one day in my room. . . . The Lord showed me as in a vision what was before me. He drew so near to me, while I was engaged in prayer, that my flesh literally trembled on my bones. I shook from head to foot, under a full sense of the presence of God. At first, and for some time, it seemed more like being on the top of Sinai, amidst its full thunderings, than in the presence of the cross of Christ.

Never in my life . . . was I so awed and humbled before God as then. Nevertheless, instead of feeling like fleeing, I seemed drawn nearer and nearer to God. . . . After a season of great humiliation before him, there came a great lifting up. God assured me that he would be with me and uphold me; that no opposition should prevail against me; that I had noth-ing to do, in regard to all this matter, but to keep about my work, and wait for the salvation of God.

The sense of God's presence, and all that passed between God and my soul at that time, I can never describe. . . . I felt assured that all would come out right; that my true course was to leave everything to God, and to keep about my work.

The conference discussed the propriety of women taking part in social meetings. This was before the pioneers in the women's rights movement in the forties and fifties were met with violent prejudice against women's participation in public affairs. In a conference called to discuss the methods of conducting revival meetings, the scriptural soundness of permitting women to take part in public worship was the focal point of the argument. Beecher and Nettleton were in opposition, and stated their positions orally and in writing.

Beecher argued that female prayer in promiscuous assemblies for worship is expressly forbidden in the Scriptures. The Apostle Paul in speaking about the order of public assemblies of Christians and about prayer said: "I suffer not a woman to teach nor to usurp authority over the man; but to be in silence." Beecher further quoted St. Paul concerning the dress of women in public assemblies, namely, that they be clothed in modest apparel, with delicacy and sobriety. He cited I Corinthians 14:34: "Let your women keep silence in the churches; for it is not permitted unto them to speak." Beecher admitted that these texts taken from Paul's Epistle to the Corinthians had been explained away; but so had the proof texts which teach the divinity of Christ, the depravity of man, the reality of the atonement, and the necessity of regeneration. Anything can be explained away by those who are determined to obey their own will instead of the Bible, he said.

With reference to I Corinthians 11:3–16, which may be thought to imply that women did pray in public assemblies, Beecher answered that if they did pray, it must be supposed that it was under the special guidance of the Spirit; for none but the Lawgiver himself can make exception to his own laws. If women did pray, he argued, it was a case exempted from the general prohibition, by divine and not by human direction. "There is generally, and should be always, in the female character a softness and delicacy of feeling which shrinks from the notoriety of a public performance," he said. "It is the guard of female virtue, and invaluable in its soothing, civilizing influence on man; and a greater evil, next to the loss of conscience and chastity, could not befall the female sex, or the community at large, than to disrobe the female mind of those ornaments of sensibility, and clothe it with the rough texture of masculine fibre."

Nathan S. S. Beman of Troy, New York, replied that the practice of women taking part in public meetings was familiar to the apostles; and that in the eleventh chapter of I Corinthians the Apostle called to the attention of the churches the fact that Christian women had given a shock to eastern ideas by their practice of taking part in meetings without their veils. The Apostle did not reprove this practice, he said, but simply admonished them to wear their veils and they did so.

Nettleton was sorry to say that some young men had been considered as acting "amorously foolish" on this subject. He thought that the practice was "very taking with some real Christians"; but still more so with the hypocritical and disorganizing part of society. He predicted that the minister who introduced the practice of females praying in promiscuous assemblies, would ere long find to his sorrow that he had made an inlet into other denominations, and entailed an everlasting quarrel on those churches generally.

The strife over women's rights and woman suffrage was allayed in the first half of the twentieth century by appeasing moderate crusaders; but within the field of religion and ecclesiasticism the changes have been slow. The successful experiments in coeducation at Oberlin College and Antioch College, both church institutions in Ohio, were disconcerting to conservatives. Fanny Wright, an abolitionist and a freethinker in religion, attacked the conservatism of the churches and was denounced as the "Priestess of Beelzebub" and the "Red Harlot of Infidelity." Lucretia Mott was a preacher in the service of the Hicksite Quakers whose sermons had the flavor of the "modernistic" sermons of a later date. She discoursed on practical subjects such as temperance, peace, slavery, and women's rights, to the exclusion of dogma and doctrine.

Horace Bushnell, whose heterodoxy was anathema to many a New England clergyman, was entirely "orthodox" on the subject of woman suffrage, which in a book published a decade after the close of the Civil War, he derided as a "reform against nature" and supported his derision by arguments based on the Bible, history, biology, and psychology. Another New England clergyman of conservative views, John Todd, stated a few years after the Civil War that he would not interpose his veto on women speaking in church. He said he "would pull out the plug and let the waters out." They all know that it was done under protest and that nobody would be edified by it. He believed the practice to be unscriptural and against Scripture; yet there are some things "the Gospel bears with and winks at, till better light comes." He would make no proclamation of a change in the program, but "silently let the dear sisters ventilate."

It would be unhistorical to minimize the part women played in the religious life of family, church, community, and nation in the years before the Civil War. In this respect, as in many others, American churches set the example for the churches in other lands, partly because of the superior advantages American women enjoyed and partly because of the expanding activities of churches—Sunday schools, Bible classes, philanthropic societies, missionary societies, religious periodicals and publications. For example, in the decade of the thirties Elizabeth Payson Prentiss became a contributor to the *Youth's Companion*. This periodical was one of the first of its class to be published in the country and had a wide circulation among children throughout New England. Mrs. Prentiss was the author of many books and stories for children. Catharine E. Beecher, sister of the author of *Uncle Tom's Cabin*, was a prolific writer. Among her books were the following: *Appeal to the People, as the Authorized Interpreters of the Bible; Commonsense Applied to Religion, or the Bible and the People;* and *Religious Training of Children in the Family, School, and Church.*

It would be impossible to estimate the impact of Harriet Beecher Stowe's masterpiece and her other literary contributions on the moral and religious health of the American people—and of the people of almost every country of Europe. Little Eva in *Uncle Tom's Cabin* is the "most saintly child in American literature." Not without significance did the chapter entitled "The Little Evangelist" contrast Marie St. Clare "languidly holding in her hand an elegantly bound prayer-book," and Miss Ophelia, who had hunted up a small Methodist meeting and gone out with Tom, as driver, and Eva to attend it. And in Mrs. Stowe's recollections she revealed that the passage in *Uncle Tom's Cabin,* where Augustine St. Clare describes his mother's influence, is a reproduction of Mrs. Stowe's mother's influence in her family.

Mrs. Stowe's able biographer, Forrest Wilson, in *Crusader in Crinoline,* states that she could not countenance an abolition movement divorced from the Evangelical Christian Church, or one that was not as much a part of the church as missions and the Sunday school. In a tract published by the American Anti-Slavery Society, entitled "Two Altars; or Two Pictures in One," Mrs. Stowe contrasts "The Altar of Liberty, or 1776" with "The Altar of ——, or 1850." The first portrays a family in 1776: a mother who gave to her country her husband

and her children. The second "altar" portrays the happy family of a fugitive slave living in a northern city, who was arrested and returned to bondage.

Individualism was strong in the revival movement, which was one phase in the development of democracy. Finney himself was the personification of the practical and humanitarian side of life which was a part of the revival movement. After 1837 he devoted the major portion of his time to Oberlin College; and from 1851 to 1866 he was president of the institution. He continued to preach. He was an ardent temperance crusader and opposed the use of tobacco, tea, and coffee.

Revival meetings were instrumental in bringing comfort and happiness to relieve the monotony and isolation of the frontier settlements; and they enriched life for young and old everywhere at a time when amusements were few and means of communication difficult. There was inspiration in community singing, when thousands united in singing hymns and spiritual songs set to melodies that released the emotions. The contrast between the heavy solemnity of the hymns sung in the parish churches in Europe and the revivalist songs set to tunes with a "go" suggests the contrast between the architecture of the churches of Europe and that of the American churches. The American churches made use of the talents of the laity and emphasized the Sunday school, which enlisted the services of men and women, the educated and the uneducated, the laborer and the professional man and woman. In the American "meeting-house"—whether in a structure with a steeple, or in a schoolhouse, or under the trees, or on a street—men and women led religious services, offered prayers, and directed the singing.

The *Home Missionary,* a magazine published by the American Home Missionary Society, contains many communications and reports sent in by pastors serving foreign-language churches in the West, expressing enthusiasm for the "new measures" in American religion. A Norwegian Lutheran minister in Chicago in 1851 wrote that the religious practices peculiar to America were more and more appreciated among his people. The "new measures," he wrote, expand the mind; the heart is enriched in experience; and the divine life is strengthened. Prayer meetings, which were formerly ridiculed, are now well attended; our Sabbath school in English was laughed at; now it is well patronized by both parents and children. "I am happy to say that God's Spirit has evidently been with us, and is with us now," he wrote. "The old foundation of many, and their delusive hopes, such as baptismal regeneration, salvation secured by membership in the church according to a civil code, are vanishing."

ELEVEN

THE UNITARIAN MOVEMENT

IT WAS the dying wish of Increase Mather in 1722, after about three score and six years in the Gospel ministry, that the churches should stand fast in the faith and order of the Gospel which they had received. "And, therefore, from the suburbs of that glorious world into which I am now entering, I earnestly testify unto the rising generation that if they sinfully forsake the God, and the hope, and the religious ways of their pious ancestors, the glorious Lord will severely punish their apostasy, and be terrible from his holy places upon them."

When Lyman Beecher assumed his ministerial duties in Boston in 1826, a century after Mather laid down the pilgrim's staff, the churches of the metropolis of New England had repudiated the Calvinism of Jonathan Edwards and of his pupil and intimate friend, Samuel Hopkins, who carried the doctrine of election to even greater extremes. In the words of his famous daughter, Harriet Beecher Stowe, all the literary men of Massachusetts were Unitarians; all the trustees and professors of Harvard College were Unitarians; all the elite of wealth and fashion crowded Unitarian churches. Judges on the bench were Unitarians, giving decisions by which the peculiar features of church organization, so carefully ordained by the Pilgrim fathers, were nullified. The church, as consisting, according to their belief, in regenerate people, had been ignored, and all the power had passed into the hands of the congregation. This power had been used by the majorities to settle ministers of the fashionable and reigning type in many of the towns of eastern Massachusetts. The dominant majority entered at once into possession of churches and church property, leaving the orthodox minority to go out into schoolhouses or town halls, and build churches as best they could. Old foundations established by the Pilgrim fathers for the perpetuation and teaching of their own views in theology were seized upon and appropriated to the support of opposite views.

Beecher regarded Unitarianism as the deadly foe of human happiness, which would stop revivals and prevent conversion. When Charles G. Finney arrived in Boston to conduct evangelistic meetings, Beecher warned him that he could not use the methods he had used elsewhere, because Unitarianism had destroyed the foundations of Christianity, and the masses had no settled opinions. Every "lo here" or "lo there" found a hearing; and almost every conceivable form of error might get a footing.

By the beginning of the nineteenth century Unitarianism had infected many churches in New England, but there was only one professedly Unitarian church. This was King's Chapel in Boston. Under the leadership of the pastor, the members of the congregation participated in discussions about the doctrine of the Trinity, the upshot of which was the decision reached in 1785 to strike out of the order of service references to the Trinity. In the other churches Unitarianism was "boring from within." The ministers continued to use orthodox terminology and refrained from making a frontal attack on the old doctrine from their pulpits. They ignored rather than denied certain tenets of Calvinism. The cleavage between the liberals and the conservatives became more noticeable and wider when in 1805 Henry Ware, an avowed Unitarian, was elected by the Board of Fellows of Harvard College to the Hollis Professorship of Divinity.

This action was so revolting to the Trinitarians that they openly proclaimed that the university at Cambridge, with its professor of theology, had gone over to the open denial of the divinity of Christ, and that in Boston only one of the Congregational churches, the Old South, maintained the doctrine of the cross. The orthodox party founded, in 1808, Andover Theological Seminary as a "rampart for the truth." The orthodoxy of this institution was so offensive that the Legislature of Massachusetts hesitated for some time to grant it the power of holding sufficient funds. It was placed under the direction of the trustees of Phillips Academy and a board of visitors. All the while churches were dividing on the doctrine of the divinity of Christ, and new churches were set up by secessionists.

In a sense, Unitarianism was a part of the movement against eccle-

siastical authority which originally took the form of rebellion against
the theocracy founded by the Puritans. The position of the Unitarians
was stated in 1813 in a letter from William Ellery Channing and three
other ministers to Noah Worcester, inviting him to become editor of
the *Christian Disciple*. A publication was needed to show the great
mass of Christians the ground of Congregationalism, especially to
counteract an article in the *Panoplist,* an orthodox publication, recommending the immediate erection of ecclesiastical tribunals. The letter
stated that they were not precisely agreed as to the person or dignity
of Christ, nor did they wish the work to be devoted to any particular
view of that subject; rather did they desire to promote a spirit of
tolerance and charity on that and other difficult subjects. They were
opposed to the "peculiarities" of Calvinism, without censuring those
who embraced them. Their main objection to that system was that it
prostitutes the mind by teaching that men are naturally incapable of
discerning religious truth.

As editor of the *Christian Disciple* and of its successor the *Christian
Examiner,* Noah Worcester sought to show that the essential vitality
of Christianity does not lie in certain doctrines and dogmas; but that
every faithful, devout, and conscientious inquirer finds it. Editor and
contributors exposed and rebuked the "arrogance of sectarianism."

Samuel Worcester, a brother of Noah, was a rigid Hopkinsian Calvinist, who in 1815 became involved in a famous controversy with
William Ellery Channing—a controversy that marked a stage in the
schism within the Congregational churches and gave Channing the opportunity to state his position and clarify the points at issue. Prior to
that time the Unitarians were chary of disputing and defining, largely
because they deprecated theological minutiæ and terminology. It was
during this period that Channing matured into a great leader. The
measure of his ability and character is indicated by the term "Channing Unitarianism" which suggests a galaxy of intellectuals in religion,
literature, and humanism—Ralph Waldo Emerson, William Cullen
Bryant, Henry Wadsworth Longfellow, James Russell Lowell, and
Oliver Wendell Holmes, who acknowledged their indebtedness.

Channing was born in 1780 in Newport, Rhode Island, and early
manifested those traits of individualism and character which marked

him throughout his life, a life which ended in 1842. After graduating from Harvard College in 1798, he spent two years as a teacher in Virginia. Following a sojourn in his home in Newport, he took up the study of theology in Cambridge and in 1803 was ordained as minister in Boston, where he served the same congregation for almost two score years. As a boy, Channing had often listened to sermons preached by no less a person than Samuel Hopkins, the hero of Harriet Beecher Stowe's novel, *The Minister's Wooing*. Hopkinsian Calvinism, however, found stony soil in the young Channing. His theological studies were leavened with moderate Calvinism, but the doctrine of the Trinity was losing its hold. In the early years of his ministry this frail and modest man, who had little taste for polemics and controversy, was on good terms with his colleagues. He accepted the Bible as the guide of faith, and rejected creeds and dogmas. As late as 1815, as his *Remarks on the Rev. Dr. Worcester's Second Letter to Mr. Channing on American Unitarianism* proves, he opposed the organization of a new denomination.

Unitarians shudder, wrote Channing, when they hear that the ever-blessed God suffered and died on the cross. In not one solitary text in Scripture is the efficacy of Christ's death in obtaining forgiveness ascribed to His being the Supreme God; but in the broad sense the doctrine of the atonement is not rejected by Unitarians, he said. Some of the best works on the atonement have come from the pens of Unitarians. Channing denied the assertion that Unitarians disbelieve the doctrine of the Trinity because it is mysterious and because they prefer reason to revelation, human wisdom to the wisdom of God. They object to the Trinity because it is an unintelligible proposition, he said, but Unitarians never stop there. They always declare that Scripture with one voice disowns the Trinity, and that of all the fictions of theologians, the doctrine of three persons in one God has perhaps the least countenance from the Bible. Unitarians believe that no labored comments and no critical skill are required to teach common Christians the great truth that the Father alone is the Supreme God and that Jesus Christ is a derived and independent being. He stated that they dare not offer prayers to the Holy Ghost, because they found not one command or one example of such worship in the

Gospel of the Master. They read in Scripture such passages as these: "My Father is greater than I." "I can do nothing of myself." "My doctrine is not mine, but his who sent me."

If the mist of obscure phraseology were removed, Channing believed that Trinitarians would find that they had been wasting their hostility on a band of friends and brothers. "Whenever Trinitarians begin to explain themselves," he wrote, "we find that their three persons vanish into three undefinable somethings, and that God suffered for us on the cross by a figure or metaphysical fiction."

Channing sensed that the object of Worcester was to prepare the "orthodox" for separation from their Unitarian brethren; that they ought to refuse communion with Unitarians as Christians, to deny them the character and name of Christians—in a word, to disown them as brethren in Christ. Channing replied that to exclude from Christian fellowship men of upright lives on account of their opinions generates perpetual discord in the church. No two minds are perfectly accordant; shades of belief are infinitely diversified; every man discovers errors in the creed of his brother. The practice of denouncing the supposed errors of sincere professors of Christianity, he wrote, exalts to supremacy in the church men who have the least claim to influence. Humble, meek, and affectionate Christians are least disposed to make creeds for their brethren. Moreover, excluding men of apparent sincerity for their opinions entirely subverts free inquiry into the Scriptures. The multitude dare not think, and the thinking dare not speak. The right of private judgment may thus, in a Protestant country, be reduced to a nullity.

The system of excluding men for their opinions was, according to Channing, inconsistent with the great principles of Congregationalism, because the tribunal before which the offender is to be brought is the whole church, consisting partly of men in humble circumstances and of unimproved minds; partly of men engaged in active and pressing business; and partly of men of education, whose studies have been directed by law and medicine. Before this tribunal the most intricate points of theology are to be discussed and serious inquirers are to answer for opinions, which they have perhaps examined more laboriously and faithfully than all their judges. Since argument is insufficient to produce uniformity of opinion, recourse must be had to more powerful instruments of coercion—to ecclesiastical tribunals. Are our people prepared to submit to this most degrading form of vassalage? he asked.

Channing lamented that their long established Congregational form of church government was menaced by tribunals unknown to their churches and unknown to the Scriptures. He said it resolved itself into the old controversy—whether the clergy shall think for the laity, or prescribe to them their religion. Religion, when made a subject of debate, seems often to lose its empire over the heart and life. Fair dealing, uprightness, and truth are exchanged for the quibbling and arts of sophistry. The devotional feelings also decline in warmth and tenderness.

In spite of Channing's efforts to appease the orthodox Congregationalists and to avoid a schism that would leave a permanent mark in the form of a new denomination, it was not long before he determined to take the aggressive at the opportune moment. The conspicuous occasion for making public declaration of the Protestant principle of the right of private judgment, namely, the right of individuals to interpret the Bible in the light of their own religious knowledge and experience, was the ordination of Jared Sparks in Baltimore on May 5, 1819. By invitation Channing preached the ordination sermon before a distinguished congregation which included ministers from New England and other northern states. His famous "Baltimore Sermon" has also been called the "Magna Charta of Liberal Religion." It inaugurated a new epoch in American theological thought. It has been said that the sermon has never been surpassed as an intellectual interpretation of spiritual problems. Some idea of the immediate sensation it occasioned and of its enduring quality may be had by stating that within six weeks five editions were published, and for over a century edition after edition has appeared. Thousands of copies continue to be published yearly. The sermon not only precipitated the organization of the American Unitarian Association in 1825, but it injected into American Protestantism—and even into European Protestantism—an influence that lurked in homes, churches, communities, and states.

"Channing Unitarianism" was a religion of the intellect as distinguished from the emotional, hortatory, and stern religion of the revivalist. It placed great emphasis on the individual's responsibility, without eliminating the fatherhood of God and the unique character of Christ. Moreover, Channing's well-balanced intellect and sterling character, his God-fearing courage and conduct, made his name one to conjure with in causes which concerned the welfare and moral health of the people. It was the same inspired Channing who wrote and spoke in behalf of abolition, temperance, peace, and good faith in the conduct of domestic and foreign affairs.

The text for the "Baltimore Sermon" was taken from the fifth chapter of I Thessalonians: "Prove all things; hold fast that which is good." The preacher discoursed on the character of Calvinism which makes God unlovable, cruel, unjust, and partial, by teaching that God selects from "this corrupt mass" a number to be saved, and plucks them by a special influence from the common ruin. He admitted that this religious system did not produce all the harmful effects on character which might be anticipated. It is often counteracted by nature, conscience, common sense, by the general strain of Scripture, by the mild example and precepts of Christ, and by the many positive declarations of God's universal kindness and perfect equity. Channing believed that Jesus Christ was sent by the Father to effect a moral and spiritual deliverance of mankind; that is, to rescue men from sin and its consequences, and to bring them to a state of everlasting purity and happiness.

The idea that Christ's death has an influence in making God placable or merciful, in awakening his kindness toward men, was rejected. Channing maintained that Jesus, instead of calling forth in any way or degree the mercy of the Father, was sent by that mercy to be our Savior; and he asked for one text in the New Testament in which it is stated that God took human nature that He might make an infinite satisfaction to His own justice. The preacher also believed that this system was unfavorable to character, because it led men to think that Christ came to change God's mind, rather than their own; that the highest object of His mission was to avert punishment rather than to communicate holiness. We regard Him as a Savior, chiefly because He is the light, physician, and guide of the dark, diseased, and wandering mind.

The "Baltimore Sermon" loosed an avalanche of controversy. The picture which Channing had drawn of Calvinism was exaggerated and unjust, it was asserted. Professor Moses Stuart of Andover Theological Seminary confined his discussion to the doctrine of the Trinity and the dual nature of Christ, basing his argument on the New Testament. He asserted that if he had been correctly informed, "there are scarcely any of the younger preachers of Unitarian sentiments, in New England, who are not simple humanitarians."

An extended rebuttal was prepared by Samuel Miller, Professor of Ecclesiastical History and Church Government in Princeton Theological Seminary. His work was published in 1823 under the title *Letters on Unitarianism: Addressed to the Members of the First Presbyterian Church in the City of Baltimore*. He asserted that it was a matter of prejudice (not of fact) that the orthodox system was austere and repulsive and that it gave a gloomy and discouraging view of human nature. Is that system "gloomy" and "full of horrors" which directs the guilty and burdened mind to a Savior who is described by the inspiration of God as able to save to the uttermost, he asked. Like a faithful physician, it wounds but to heal. On account of the poverty of language, it was necessary to express ideas of Divine Simplicity by the term "unity." But before anyone undertakes to decide that a Trinity of Persons in God is inconsistent with Divine Unity, he said, he ought to be able to tell what Unity is. But nobody is able to do this. He argued that nobody can understand the mystery of the Trinity. He quoted Bishop Horne's *Discourse on the Trinity:* "If there be no Son of God, where is our redemption? If there be no Holy Spirit, where is our sanctification? Without both, where is our salvation?"

Miller asserted that Unitarians are of kindred spirit and faith with Arians and Socinians, and are not to be considered as Christians, in any scriptural sense of the word. Their preaching was to be avoided as blasphemy.

Avoid Unitarian publications, as you would a cup of poison; unless you are prepared and determined to go fully into the examination of the controversy. When you are urged to purchase or peruse them, ask yourselves, in the fear of God, "Am I in a situation to read on both sides of this dispute, to such an extent, and with such patience, as its importance demands?" If you cannot answer this question in the affirmative, turn away from the proposal with pious abhorrence. Life is too short to be wasted on trash, and the soul too precious to be made the sport of a series of fancied experiments in deadly poison.

One more unsurmountable objection to the Unitarian system, according to Miller, was that infidels everywhere prefer it to any other that bears the name Christian. It was not uncommon, he said, for Unitarians to boast that avowed Deists have greatly admired the discourses of distinguished Unitarian preachers; and he had been creditably informed of repeated instances of that kind in reference to Channing's "Baltimore Sermon." Unitarians use this as an argument that their system is so rational and so strongly commends itself to common sense that even infidels bow to its authority.

Two prominent theological professors participated in what was called the "Wood'n Ware Controversy" from 1820 to 1823. The participants were Henry Ware, whose election to a professorship at Harvard in 1805 aroused opposition from the orthodox party, and Leonard Woods, who in 1808 became the first Professor of Theology at Andover Theological Seminary. There were several exchanges between the two men. Woods occupied a doctrinal position somewhere between the Hopkinsian or extreme Calvinists and the Old Calvinists of more moderate views. The controversy was prompted by the appearance of Woods' *Letters to Unitarians* which, coming from a professor in a seminary which had been founded in protest against the Unitarian school at Harvard, naturally called forth a reply from Ware. His discourse was entitled *Letters Addressed to Trinitarians and Calvinists*.

Woods also crossed swords with Nathaniel W. Taylor, Professor of Didactic Theology at Yale whose theology and the debate over it played a part in disrupting the Presbyterian Church in 1837–38. Taylor assumed the duties of his professorship in 1822, and shortly Yale became as unpopular with the orthodox party as Harvard was in 1805. "New Haven Theology," with Arminian leanings, was anathema to Old School Calvinists who followed the example of brethren in Massachusetts by founding a theological seminary to counteract the effects of the "New Divinity." The "Andover" which was opened in 1834 bore the name Theological Institute of Connecticut which in 1865 was changed to Hartford Theological Seminary. Bennet Tyler was inducted into office as Professor of Theology and President, a position he held for thirty-three years, until 1857. His appointment was a recognition of his reputation as one of the ablest interpreters of the Old Theology and a recognized leader of the conservatives who were in opposition to Nathaniel Taylor.

Taylor's sermon preached at the Yale Commencement in 1828 loosed the fury. The professor's heresy concerned conversion. He affirmed that man is not born totally depraved, but with sinful inclinations. To induce a man to repent, appeal must be made to his natural desire for happiness, which Taylor called self-love. Regeneration will finally convert self-love into an unselfish love for God. Tyler, who had schooled himself in the character and methods of revivals by a sympathetic *Memoir of the Life and Character of Asahel Nettleton* and by a study of doctrine which produced *Letters on the Origin and Progress of New Haven Theology*, repudiated every negation advanced by the Unitarians and took sharp issue with Taylor's more optimistic Calvinism. Tyler believed in the absolute sovereignty of a perfect God, the total depravity of human nature, the substitutionary death of Christ, man's moral inability to repent, the elective grace of God, regeneration effected solely by the agency of the Holy Spirit, and the eternal punishment of the wicked.

The Taylor-Tyler dispute caused a serious rift in the Presbyterian Church, which down to the formal separation between the Old School and New School bodies, was the most influential denomination. The membership lists of the Baptist and Methodist Churches were longer; but by virtue of its efficient organization, its institutions of learning, its able ministers, and its political influence, the Presbyterian Church occupied a more important place in the American religious world. In the "Plan of Union" which was established in 1801, there were mixed congregations of Presbyterians and Congregationalists under ministers of either denomination. Although this arrangement had advantages for the Presbyterians, the Old School element resented the menace to orthodoxy through association with clergymen infected with the "New Haven Theology." Not even the zealous Lyman Beecher escaped suspicion. Beecher was on good terms with Nathaniel Taylor, and both men were in correspondence at the time they were under fire. Conservative Presbyterians assailed Beecher with formal charges of heresy, slander, and hypocrisy.

Beecher had left the pastorate of a Congregational church in Boston to become president of Lane Theological Seminary, which operated according to the Plan of Union. He was acquitted of the charges leveled at him, first, by the local Presbytery and, second, by the synod. His opponents then appealed to the General Assembly, and after three years of litigation the case was withdrawn. Coming in the middle of the decade of the thirties, the affair had a disastrous effect on Presbyterianism in the West, and was one of the contributory causes for the division of 1837–38. It also struck a crippling blow to Lane Theological Seminary, by reducing the enrollment and by alienating supporters in the congregations served by the institution.

The tension between the factions is illustrated by the experience of John Todd, who left a New England pastorate for a new field in Philadelphia. Todd occupied middle ground between Old School Presbyterianism and Taylorism, both of which he detested. At the dedication of his new church in Philadelphia in November, 1837, he preached a sermon on "Principles and Results of Congregationalism," which was a comparison of Congregationalism with other church systems. The opening of the splendid edifice brought the sectarian animosity to a climax; and the dedicatory sermon brought forth a howl of rage from Presbyterians, Episcopalians, and Unitarians.

Also disconcerting to the Old School was the founding of Union Theological Seminary in New York in 1836. This institution was unionistic and was independent of the General Assembly. This aggressive move on the part of the New School party was a factor in moving the faculty of Princeton Theological Seminary into the Old School camp.

The most prominent personality in the strife that immediately preceded the division of the Presbyterian Church was Albert Barnes who, in a sermon called "The Way of Salvation," delivered in February, 1829, before his congregation at Morristown, New Jersey, stated his agreement with the doctrinal position of Nathaniel Taylor and thus admitted that he was out of line with the Westminster Confession. The following year there was opposition to his installation as minister of the First Presbyterian Church of Philadelphia, the mother church of the denomination in the United States. Because of the prestige of the church, which was generally the place chosen for the meeting of the General Assembly, the Barnes case became a vital issue throughout the Presbyterian Church and revealed the cleavage between the "progressive" Calvinists of New England and the staunch Scotch-Irish. The Barnes case hung fire for several years and every year the factions drifted farther apart, with the Old School party favoring the termination of the Plan of Union and the establishment of strictly Presbyterian societies and foundations.

The crisis came in the General Assembly of 1837, when the Old School party had the votes necessary to expel the heretical synods and to sever connections with interdenominational societies. The New School party attempted to rescind the action of the General Assembly; but when their delegates presented their credentials at the meeting in 1838, the moderator refused to recognize them. The New School party had no course other than to organize a separate church, which eventually included almost one half of the membership of the church. The New School church had its strength mainly in the Northern states, whereas the great majority of presbyteries in the South were Old School.

With the exception of Channing's Baltimore Sermon, perhaps no product of the pen of a churchman aroused more immediate praise and condemnation than the publication in 1847 of a book by Horace Bushnell entitled *Christian Nurture*. Bushnell's views were so radical that during the many years he was pastor in Hartford, Connecticut, none of his Congregational brethren in the city would exchange pulpits with him or unite with him in promoting the cause of the churches. He was socially inclined and wished for an apostolic Christian fellowship, but with few exceptions, a cold and silent non-intercourse hedged about him. Because of what were regarded as dangerous tendencies in his treatise the Massachusetts Sabbath School Society suppressed the book.

Bushnell was ordained in 1833, when the debate between the Old School and the New School was at white heat. Like so many sensitive souls, Bushnell was attracted to the writings of Madame Guyon and Fenelon because of their devout fervor and unworldly standards. Most of all, however, he was influenced by Coleridge's *Aids to Reflection*. In his *Christian Nurture*, Bushnell rejected the view that only through conscious conversion could an individual become a member of a congregation—that only "true believers" who gave evidence of conversion could "testify." He held that a child in a Christian home should grow up a Christian and at the proper age be admitted to communicant membership, without having experienced a spiritual crisis followed by a dramatic conversion.

In a book published two years later, *God in Christ,* Bushnell gave even greater offense to the orthodox by expounding the "moral influence" theory of the atonement: that Christ's death on the cross revealed God's love and was not an atonement for the sins of the world or a reconciliation. He was interested in the spirit of religion rather than in efforts to reduce it to exact terms, and used words to suggest truth and experience—as symbols of thought understandable to the common man. His religion was tinged with mysticism, as against coldly intellectual processes and theological exegesis.

A few years before the publication of *Christian Nurture,* and before he was stigmatized as a dangerous heretic, Bushnell recorded that he was nearly convinced that his peculiarities of thinking would go down much better in the West than in the East, partly because Westerners were offended by nothing new, glued to no habits of thinking or not thinking, but ready to catch with eagerness at everything which seemed to be true. When he saw the houses, farms, churches, and schoolhouses in the Western Reserve, where they were "all alive," he was impressed by a most glorious exhibition of what it meant to be born of New England stock.

After the death of Channing in 1842, there was no man worthy of putting on his mantle of leadership, nor was there a successor capable of proclaiming Christian truth with his spiritual power and noble tolerance. Unitarians and Quakers are far apart on certain fundamentals, but they are alike in their attitude toward various forms of organized religion. Partly because they found no precepts in the Gospel requiring councils, synods, convocations, decrees, creeds, confessions, and other "adiaphora," neither Quakers nor Unitarians bound themselves together in closely knit and rigid organizations; and for that reason, among others, they did not vie with the adherents of other faiths in proselyting. At the beginning of the decade of 1860, there were relatively few Unitarian churches outside of New England. The American Unitarian Association was formed for the concentration of Unitarian efforts and the propagation of Unitarianism through the medium of books and tracts; but Unitarianism has been most effectively propagated by the unobtrusive infiltration of individuals into Trinitarian congregations.

Two able men rose to great influence after Channing's death, but they did not claim Channing as their progenitor, nor would Channing have claimed them as his spiritual offsprings.

Ralph Waldo Emerson was born in Boston in 1803, studied at Harvard, and in 1829 became pastor of a Unitarian congregation in Boston, where he remained only three years. He broke with the church when he became convinced that he could administer the Lord's Supper only if the elements of bread and wine were left out. That was too radical for Unitarians. His sermons were ethical rather than theological. In 1837 he delivered the Phi Beta Kappa oration at Harvard on "The American Scholar," which Oliver Wendell Holmes called "our intellectual declaration of independence." The following year in an address before the graduating class of the Divinity School at Cambridge he was even bolder. It was an indictment of the ministerial profession. He pictured the church as dead and helpless, with no place for scholars and prophets. He exhorted the divinity students to seek new revelations and to make the church a fit and comfortable place for originality and scholarship.

Emerson made his great contribution as an intellectual—as a philosopher and writer. He was associated with intellectuals in the Transcendental Club. His home in Concord was the mecca of intellectuals from all parts of the United States and of European savants as well. He discontinued preaching, but as a lecturer was in great demand.

Theodore Parker, who became famous both at home and abroad, moved even farther to the left than Emerson. He was born in 1810, attended Harvard, and became pastor of a church in the Boston area in 1837. Although Parker was not well acquainted with Channing, he had been influenced and inspired by him through the printed page and through personal contact. The soft-spoken and mild-mannered Channing was alarmed by the intemperate utterances and methods of Parker, who was also a member of the Transcendental Club. His radicalism was so offensive that Unitarian pulpits were closed to him. Friends provided other accommodations for his meetings; and in 1852 a new hall, the Melodeon, was opened; thereafter audiences of more than three thousand persons heard the great orator, perhaps next to Henry Ward Beecher of Brooklyn "the greatest pulpit orator of America."

Parker's sermon in 1841 on "The Transient and Permanent in the Christian Religion" shocked both Unitarians and Trinitarians. He made a plea for what he called common sense in religion. He crossed out all the miracles recorded in the New Testament; and the story of the birth of Jesus was compared with parallels drawn from Greek mythology. This sermon was an example of many that followed. On his visits to Europe he had seen Catholicism at firsthand. He was repelled by its superstitious practices and teachings; but he spared neither Trinitarians nor Unitarians within the Protestant fold. His epithets, applied to Calvinism, were similar to those hurled from liberal camps, except that they inflicted deeper wounds. He maintained that the Protestant compromise with Catholicism was untenable; and he sneered at the Unitarians because they believed in miracles and bowed to authority. He charged that Unitarianism had "not even the dignity of consistency."

Parker's untimely death in 1860, before he had reached the age of fifty, cut short a career which would have been even more influential and salutary if he had not laid himself open to charges that he was a Deist or a Pantheist. Even so, his fame and influence carried far. His voluminous writings found many readers in many lands. Like Channing and Emerson, his voice was raised in behalf of sound citizenship and moral integrity. He was a fearless defender of the right of free speech and spared no words in condemning persons who would silence prophets of a new order, whether it concerned Negro slavery or ecclesiastical despotism.

TWELVE

ANTI-MASONRY

WE HAVE seen how Unitarianism made inroads, at first imperceptibly, on the Congregational churches in and around Boston, until a succession of events, magnified by clashing personalities, ended in schism and divided congregations. We have also seen that in the minds of New England Federalists the triumph of Jeffersonian Republicanism in the political revolution of 1800 recalled the nightmare of the Reign of Terror in France. Congregational ministers branded Jefferson as the high priest of atheism, and preached sermons on the wrath to come with his advent; and President Dwight of Yale thundered against atheists and blasphemers who were undermining the foundations of Christianity. He proclaimed that Antichrist is he who denies the divinity of Christ.

The controversies and schisms that emerged from time to time, while clergymen debated the nature of Christ and the scriptural basis for the atonement, called forth such epithets as "Universalists," "Deists," "Socinians," and "Arians," to be applied to Unitarians. Under fire, sectarianism grew arrogant; and the Trinitarians were convinced that they were called upon to repair the rift in the walls of Zion. It behooved those who confessed their faith in Jesus, the Son of God, to guard the sheepfold lest thieves and robbers enter.

In the autumn of 1826 the kidnapping and disappearance of a hitherto unknown individual stirred up public indignation to such a pitch that churches and families were divided, and a political party was organized to give it expression. William Morgan, a native of Virginia and at the time a resident of Batavia, New York, prepared to publish a book that would betray the secrets of the Masonic order because he regarded Freemasonry as injurious to Christianity and dangerous to civil liberty. Before the book was published, Morgan disappeared, and a corpse found in the Niagara River was proof to many that he had met with foul play at the hands of the Masons. It was alleged that by their oaths, Freemasons were bound to seek the destruction of Morgan and to inflict upon him the penalty of those oaths. Masons were accused of shielding and defending the abductors; and it was alleged that lodges and chapters concealed the criminals and contributed money to protect them from justice. It was even stated publicly that Masonic newspapers, Masonic officers, and Masons of great respectability, including even ministers of the Gospel, justified the murder and declared that the victim had met his just deserts for violating his oaths. No less a person than Charles G. Finney made the statement that nothing could be done with the courts, with the sheriff, with the jurors, and with the witnesses, and that newspapers refused to publish information about the crime.

Finney was but the mouthpiece of many when he stated that Morgan was aware, as Masons generally were at that time, that nearly all the civil offices in the country were in the hands of Freemasons; that the press was completely under their control, and almost altogether in their hands; that Freemasons were exhorted not to enter into controversy with opposers of their order, for reasons that were obvious to well-informed persons. Finney charged that a Royal Arch Mason promises and swears that he will aid and assist a companion Royal Arch Mason who is in difficulty, whether he is right or wrong; that Masons never promise in their oaths to give pecuniary aid to individuals in need outside the Masons and their families. Finney insisted that if Masonic principles could not stand the light of day, they ought not to be tolerated. Everything else may be discussed, so why not Masonry, he asked.

Henry Dana Ward, the editor of the *Anti-Masonic Review* which was established in 1829, said that he and others who joined the Masons took the oath with an assurance that meant an institution organized by Zerubbabel and patronized by St. John and by the apostles of the Lord. Ward asserted that it was a lie that Masonry dates from the time of King Solomon. One method of refuting the ancient character of the order was to recite a chapter in the history of the Roman Catholic Church, and the enmity between Catholicism and Freemasonry. Where is the account of the church's conflict with ancient

Freemasonry, it was asked. The record is bare of any such conflict until 1738, when Freemasonry was about twenty years old. If the order is so ancient, why did not the war begin sooner, it was asked. Pursuing the argument, Ward declared that an oath to be faithful to ancient Freemasonry was precisely like the oath of a subject to an impostor prince, and was binding neither in the sight of God nor man.

Anti-Masonic literature was much taken up with efforts to combat the tactics of Masons who advertised the fact that men of distinguished attainments and exalted reputation in all walks of life were Masons. They were proud to claim as brothers Washington, Franklin, and Lafayette. Anti-Masons admitted that Masonry must have something to occupy the mind of a man of serious reflection; but they made a distinction between Masons as individuals and as members of the order, just as they did in the case of Jesuits. In both organizations the individual was lost in his capacity as a Jesuit and a Mason; and both orders began independent of politics, but later abused their power.

Finney asserted that the argument might have been used with great force in favor of idolatry in the time of Solomon and the prophets, when prophets, religious teachers, and great men of the nation lapsed into idolatry. Nearly all the learning and wealth and influence of the whole nation could be appealed to as rejecting Christ. Those who received him were but a few fishermen, with some of the lowest of the people. Anti-Masonic propaganda proclaimed that Masonic lodges admitted men of vilest character and retained in full fellowship the profligate, the abandoned, the worthless, the intemperate, and the profane, and did not expel men guilty of kidnapping, murder, and treason.

The editor of the *Anti-Masonic Review* thought that the "proposed handmaid of religion" had remarkable peculiarities. The members meet in the night in a room with but one entrance, where sits a trusty brother with a weapon of death in his hands, and where none may legally enter unless they have received the oath of secrecy which seals their lips upon every transaction happening within the door. "If Freemasonry has a grand object which is good, why hide the object?" he asked. "We might as soon expect to find thorns amidst clusters of grapes, as to find the barbarous oaths of Freemasonry growing out of any association humane, benevolent, or just: the penalties of its obligations better suit a company of banditti, than a society of Christians."

In consequence of the publication of Morgan's book and the excitement stirred up by the disappearance of the author, great numbers of Masons renounced the order. It has been stated that about two thousand lodges were suspended. Conventions of former Masons were called at which public confessions were made and resolutions were adopted. Signed renunciations by Masons were published, and among them were men of high standing and good reputation.

Charles G. Finney joined the Masons soon after he became twenty-one years of age. The lodge where he took his degrees was composed mostly of professed Christians; but when he came to join the lodge at Adams, New York, the master of the lodge was a Deist. Finney wrote that he was certain that there was no objection to a Deist becoming a member or master of a lodge, and that there were in that lodge some men who were as thoroughly irreligious as any men he had ever associated with anywhere. He belonged to the lodge at Adams nearly four years when he was converted to Christ and, after a severe struggle and earnest prayer, found that he could not consistently remain a member. Henry Dana Ward joined the Masons when he moved from Marietta to Athens, Ohio, and became a member of the faculty of Ohio University. Under pressure from faculty men who were Masons, he joined the lodge, he wrote. He was not impressed, and after three years became convinced that Freemasonry was a "cheat"; that it offered itself to many minds as a substitute for the religion of the Gospel. After the "abduction" of Morgan, both Ward and Finney stated openly that what had been published about Masonry was true.

The Anti-Masonic movement in the years immediately following the Morgan affair was both political and ecclesiastical. Among politicians and churchmen were men of ability and renown. John Todd, a prominent minister at Groton, Massachusetts, recorded in April, 1831, that the whole town was in a convulsion; that Anti-Masonry was exciting great attention; and that a lecture on the subject had been announced. Congregations were divided; ministers who renounced Freemasonry were locked out of their churches; members who retained their membership in lodges were expelled; public meetings were held; resolutions were adopted; and sermons were addressed to the explosive subject.

In 1829, for example, the New England Conference of the Methodist Episcopal Church resolved to have no connection with "speculative Freemasonry" and to consider any member who disregarded the resolution "as offending against the authority of the Conference." A Congregational Church in North Wrentham, Massachusetts, in 1830, made public the reason for withdrawing from their Masonic brethren and being formed into a separate church. As a Congregational church, the members considered it fully competent and authorized by the Lord Jesus Christ to decide its own cases of discipline; they neither knew nor acknowledged any higher authority, save the Head of the Church Himself. The Masonic order was condemned as a school of infidelity. "There is no system on earth so artfully contrived, and so completely fitted to make deists and atheists, as Freemasonry."

Years before the Morgan excitement, there was opposition to Freemasonry on the part of church members as individuals and on the part of certain denominations, especially from those whose membership was recruited from the pietists and from people in the lower levels of society—economically and "socially." In Pennsylvania, for example, political Anti-Masonry attracted voters with old-world backgrounds—Lutherans, Mennonites, United Brethren, and sectarians who had a long list of "unworldly" things. In Europe, Freemasonry was synonymous with the privileged classes, and in Protestant countries ecclesiastical dignitaries were "high-up Masons." Pietism and Puritanism took the form of protests against the worldliness of the clergy. Freemasonry in the United States was far more democratic; but at the time of the Anti-Masonic movement the Masons were of the wealthier and more influential classes. The Masons were strong in urban communities, whereas the Anti-Masons were more numerous in rural areas.

It was difficult for some, and impossible for others, to reconcile membership in a Masonic lodge with the high calling of the ministerial office. They asked how clergymen could take oaths inconsistent with the Christian religion and associate with Jews, Mohammedans, and skeptics of every grade—Universalists, Unitarians, and errorists—

who belonged to the Masonic order. They insisted that the morality which the Masonic order inculcates is not the morality of the Law and Gospel of God. Professor Moses Stuart of Andover Theological Seminary, who was appointed by the Suffolk Committee in Boston to inquire into the nature, principles, and tendency of Freemasonry, reported that he had found no evidence of the ancient character of the order. He continued:

> For a long time, I neither knew nor cared much about this subject. But recent attention to it has filled me with astonishment; and as to some things contained in it, with horror. The trifling with oaths, and with the awfulness of the ever blessed God, is a feature which I cannot contemplate but with deep distress.

A minister of wide reputation, Joel Parker, pastor of a Presbyterian Church in Rochester, New York, on a day of public fasting, December 4, 1828, named intemperance for the domestic sin; for the political crime, slavery; for the institution attired like an angel of light, Freemasonry. The minister asserted that the character of Freemasonry had not changed with the abduction of Morgan; but that crime excited attention to the principles of Masonry and produced investigations —precisely as thousands came out of the Catholic Church in consequence of Tetzel's imprudence in the sale of indulgences. Clergymen exhorted younger brethren in the ministry to stand fast in the liberty wherewith Christ had made them free and to shun the Masonic institution. The delegates to the Anti-Masonic Convention of Connecticut in 1830 resolved that they could not but view with horror the practice of clergymen submitting to be stripped, blindfolded, and haltered; and then swearing and appealing to Almighty God that they will keep the secrets of the fraternity, under revolting penalties; and perhaps the next day offering prayers and preaching the pure doctrines of Christianity which forbids taking the name of God in vain.

The religious strain in the membership and proceedings of the conventions of the Anti-Masonic party was pronounced. The roster of delegates to state and national conventions include the names of such celebrities as Noah Webster of New Haven, Leonard Bacon of Hartford, Amasa Walker of Boston, and William Lloyd Garrison of Boston.

Invited guests at the national convention at Baltimore in 1831 were Charles Carroll of Carrollton and Chief Justice John Marshall. Absence from the city prevented Carroll from accepting the invitation, but the famous jurist graced the occasion.

The Anti-Masonic Convention of Connecticut in 1830 heard a report of a committee which declared Freemasonry was opposed to the simplicity of Christianity and to truth. Its dreadful oaths trifled with life; and the order violated scriptural truths such as "Love your enemies" and "Be not unequally yoked together with unbelievers." The Anti-Masonic Convention of Massachusetts in 1832 resolved that Freemasonry in its nature is hostile to free government and injurious to religion and morality, "and in all respects unworthy to be permitted longer to exist among us."

The Anti-Masonic party did not long survive the election of 1832. It played a more important role as a local and state party than as a national party. However, it lingered on as a faction which complicated the problems of the major parties. Although the Anti-Masonic party was somewhat exceptional in the history of American political parties, in that religion played a major part in its inception and in shaping its policy, it was not a clerical party comparable to the experience of certain countries of Europe. The Anti-Masonic party attracted voters who believed that Freemasonry was a danger to Christianity, but they were not confined to a single ecclesiastical organization which was jealous of its preferred position or sought to gain control to promote its own interests.

Religion has exercised a powerful influence in American politics; but its influence has been indirect, in that party leaders and public servants have responded to that elusive thing called public opinion and have been chary of alienating the "church vote." The fact that local, state, and national political conventions invite clergymen of all denominations to invoke divine blessings on their proceedings and that Congress and state legislatures have chaplains, is eloquent evidence of the enduring heritage of the American people. There has never been an anti-clerical party in the United States because there has never been a clerical party. It is true that there were established churches in the colonies, and that in three states they persisted into the nineteenth century; but Protestant America has been quick to resent the encroachments or attempted encroachments by any church on the state and to insist that the principle of separation of church and state be respected and maintained. Fortunately, immigrants from Protestant countries of Europe, whose memories of established churches and of clericalism were fresh, were as intensely American on this issue as native-born citizens.

Anti-Masonry lost its potency as a political issue; but it persisted in the form of opposition to secret societies in certain churches and from individuals within and without the portals of churches. This opposition took the form of condemnation of secrecy, oaths, exclusiveness, and false claims; but it was also rooted in the fear that in the case of many the lodge would take the place of the church. The fact that burial services were conducted according to the ritual of secret orders was conclusive proof that the lodge was a competitor of the church. Then there was the ever-recurring argument that the associations with the heterogeneous membership of lodges would plant the seeds of heresy in the minds of church members and expose them to such worldly amusements as card-playing, the theater, social drinking, and attendance at Sunday sports and entertainments. The opposition to secrecy was extended even to such social and political organizations as the Grangers and the Farmers' Alliance. The editor of a Swedish Lutheran periodical in July, 1873, avowed that he had no objection to the agitation against the railroads; but he could not understand how anybody could indorse the secrecy of the Patrons of Husbandry. He deplored the fact that in America so many things were done through the instrumentality of secret societies. The editor's Americanization had not yet matured him into a "joiner."

The issue of secret societies not only fomented schism in congregations but it also prevented fellowship among the churches of the various denominations and raised barriers that separated synods and conferences professing the same doctrine. The Lutheran Church furnishes a classic example. The older, and therefore more "Americanized," synods, were inclined to be "liberal," whereas the synods whose membership was largely recruited from immigrants, excluded members of secret orders. In their efforts to solve this difficult problem, some synods rejected "disciplinary" measures in favor of "education." There were differences within the Baptist and Methodist churches. As early as September, 1816—ten years before the Morgan furore—a Methodist Conference, meeting at Louisville, Kentucky, resolved that they considered any traveling preacher joining with or associating with the Masons in their lodges as degrading, and advised preachers and members not to join or associate with Masonic lodges. And in 1825, also before the Morgan affair, the Illinois Conference of the Methodist Churches refused to elect a man as elder because he had joined the Masons.

In general the churches with a pietistic background, whose members were not richly blessed—or cursed—with worldly possessions and who had not qualified for admission to the upper level of the middle classes, were strait-laced on the question of secret societies; but with the rise in the economic scale of their members, the issue lost its potency. More than one pastor and deacon changed his mind about consigning Masons to perdition after seeing his son, a physician or prosperous business man, wearing the insignia of that order. With the passing years, mothers and fathers who had drained the cup of poverty and known the sting of class discrimination in their native countries across the Atlantic, beamed with pride when a son or daughter returned from college displaying the pin of a Greek letter society.

The Protestant Episcopal Church maintained a consistently "liberal" attitude toward fraternal orders. With the beginning of emigration from Sweden in the fifth decade of the nineteenth century, churchmen in the Episcopal church were hopeful of establishing closer relations between the Anglican Church, the Church of Sweden, the American Protestant Episcopal Church, and the Swedish Lutheran Church in the United States. They recognized the validity of the episcopate of the Church of Sweden and made overtures looking to the consecration of a bishop to preside over the Swedish Lutheran Church in the United States. However, the Anglican and Episcopalian dignitaries completely misunderstood the spirit of the Swedish immigrants. They were pietists, and the church they established in the United States bore little resemblance to the established church of Sweden. Not only was the church they founded Presbyterian and Congregational—not Episcopal—in polity, but members were disciplined for joining secret orders and indulging in the pleasures of the dance, the card table, and the theater.

John Wordsworth, Bishop of Salisbury, in 1910 delivered a series of lectures in the United States as part of the campaign to cultivate the goodwill of the Swedish Lutherans, both in America and in Sweden. He presented a judicious statement of the position of the Episcopalians with reference to secret societies. Membership in a professedly "infidel" society is one thing, he said, and is a justifiable cause for exclusion from church membership. But it is quite another thing, he continued, to include as "infidels" men who belong to such lodges as now exist in the British Isles and in Sweden, or to some benefit society which admits to its privileges men who are not of necessity Christians. The bishop admitted, however, that secret societies whose services partake of the character of a church, or a substitute for a church, come in for just criticism.

THIRTEEN

THE AMERICAN HOME MISSIONARY SOCIETY

THE application of steam power to transportation inaugurated the greatest migration in history. On rivers and canals in the Mississippi Valley steamboats were freighted with passengers and household gear and implements; and after 1840 the volume of traffic was enormously swelled by constantly increasing railroad mileage. Before the advent of the railroad, the homeseekers had left homes in the older states; but by the beginning of the fifth decade their numbers were augmented by emigrants from the British Isles, Germany, The Netherlands, Switzerland, and the Scandinavian countries. What had begun as a trickle in 1820 assumed the proportions of a stampede which carried with it hundreds of thousands of humble men and women who deserted their cottages in Europe in favor of a country whose fabulous riches and democracy had been described in letters written by friends and relatives who had gone before and had "struck it rich" in the western republic.

The grand experiment of the Mississippi Valley, in the light of the twentieth century, had scarcely begun in the first half of the nineteenth century; but it had already become the subject of prophecy. Albert Barnes of Philadelphia, the zealous promoter of home missions, in 1849 named the West as the battlefield of the world—the place where the destinies of the world were to be decided. And Lyman Beecher in 1835 predicted that at the close of the nineteenth century the Mississippi Valley would probably contain one hundred million people; and, when fully peopled, might accommodate three hundred million inhabitants.

The *Home Missionary,* the title of which reveals its field of interest,

commented editorially in July, 1851, on the great increase of the
population of the West as revealed in the Census of 1850:

> The day has come, when the numerical and political control of the coun-
> try is no longer unquestioned in the hands of that portion of the people
> who live amid well rooted and flourishing institutions, surrounded by
> churches and pastors and all the ripe and healthful organizations of settled
> society, such as schools, colleges and the prompt and efficient administra-
> tion of law. The scepter is passing away into the hands of a people strong
> in their impulses, conscious of their rapidly growing strength, and ambitious
> of using it; they are a people, too, comparatively undirected and unre-
> strained by the institutions of religion and education. With them, the noisy
> sectarian and the radical demagogue have equal chance for a hearing and
> an influence with those who represent the learning and experience of ages.

Writing in the fifth decade of the century, Robert Baird, a Presbyterian, paid a compliment to the Congregationalists by stating that
outside of New England they had never been zealous to propagate
their own peculiar forms and institutions. Rather than maintain their
own peculiarities at the expense of increased division in the household of faith, he said, the great majority of immigrants to other states
have chosen to unite with churches of the Presbyterian connection.
In his well-known sermon on home missions preached at the end of
the same decade, Albert Barnes, New School Presbyterian, asserted
that the American Home Missionary Society propagated the Calvinistic form of Christianity because in every community there were
minds likely to embrace that form. The more mind is elevated and
cultivated and brought into connection with colleges and schools, he
said, the more likely it would be to accept Calvinism.

Even before the religious leaders decided to concentrate their efforts
on the "Great West," whose waters find their way to the "Father of
Waters," the "arrogance of sectarianism" yielded to interdenominationalism by adopting the Plan of Union, which paved the way for
the organization of the American Home Missionary Society, twenty-
five years later.

The Plan of Union was adopted in May, 1801, by the General
Assembly of the Presbyterian Church, and in June of the same year
by the Congregational General Association of Connecticut. The Associations of Vermont, New Hampshire, Maine, and Massachusetts

lent support in one form or another. There were provisions in the Plan of Union which were intended to reduce denominational friction to a minimum in order to achieve the objective of promoting mutual forbearance on the part of missionaries to new settlements.

The missionary cause received a great impetus by the extensive missionary tours undertaken under the auspices of the Missionary Societies of Massachusetts and Connecticut, with the aid of the Philadelphia Bible Society and the Philadelphia Missionary Society. The first survey was made in 1812–13 by Samuel J. Mills, just out of Andover Theological Seminary, and by John D. Schermerhorn, of the Dutch Reformed Church. The report was published at Hartford, Connecticut, in 1814, under their names and with the title *Correct View of that Part of the United States which Lies West of the Alleghany Mountains*. The second journey was undertaken in 1814 by Mills and Daniel Smith. These men brought back information about the needs of the people in that area, and stressed the dearth of Bibles and devotional books.

The American Home Missionary Society was organized in 1826 by delegates from Presbyterian, Congregational, Associate Reformed, and Dutch Reformed churches; and it became at once the principal instrumentality through which the Plan of Union was put into operation in the West. Some of the existing missionary societies were auxiliaries to the larger organization. The reports of the American Home Missionary Society contain the names of auxiliary societies, officers, members, missionaries, extracts from correspondence, and names of churches subsidized.

The Fourth Annual Report of the American Home Missionary Society (1830) contains an optimistic statement pertaining to the success of the experiment of several denominations acting through a common organ. The experience of four years had convinced those who had watched the operation that it had not interfered with denominational preferences, it was reported. The ministers of each denomination were regarded as in good standing in all of the others. When the interest of the general cause seemed to require it, they passed from one denomination to the other, at the call of the churches. It had been made manifest, according to the report, that there had been no interference with ecclesiastical order; and no danger was to be apprehended to the purity and distinctiveness of the denominations engaged in the work.

Even as the report was written, there were indications that dissatisfaction was rising. The congregations composed partly of Presbyterians and partly of Congregationalists, and having a modified Presbyterian organization, were not satisfactory to Presbyterians, who alleged that errors of doctrine and improprieties of practice crept in. These difficulties augmented, until the open rupture between the Old School and the New School in 1837 practically terminated the Plan of Union and caused the withdrawal of the major portion of Presbyterian support from the American Home Missionary Society.

The growth and development of the American Home Missionary Society was remarkable—and equally remarkable was the Christian spirit which shaped its policy and directed its administration. A Swedish Lutheran pastor who served a number of congregations of immigrants in Illinois, paid a high tribute to the Society. He stated in 1859 before a session of the General Synod of the Lutheran Church that if the American Home Missionary Society had acted upon the principle of giving aid only to those who conformed to certain views, he would never have been able to preach the Gospel and to do what he had done among his countrymen. He was asked no questions as to what sect he belonged. It was a question only of building up the kingdom of Christ. Other pastors in similar circumstances offered testimony about the Christian excellence of the American brethren.

Albert Barnes stated what a missionary of the American Home Missionary Society "should be and usually is." He should be an educated man, having enjoyed the best advantages of literary and theological seminaries and possessing a library. He will aim to establish a library in every neighborhood; he will advocate temperance; he will appeal to the reason and the consciences of men; he will be a patron of benevolent institutions. He should be qualified to lead public opinion.

In appraising the work of the American Home Missionary Society, account must be taken of a host of men and women employed and supported by societies with the same objectives: tract societies, temperance societies, Bible societies, organizations to promote Sunday schools, and educational societies and foundations.

New England conceived of a literary education as synonymous with religious training founded on the Bible. The clergy exhorted their parishioners to pour money, missionaries, and teachers into the West, where so many of the pioneers were said to rejoice in the opportunity of detaching themselves from the Christian church. John Todd, minister at Northampton, Massachusetts, in 1835 stated that there were no less than twenty-three agents in New England begging for the Great West. Todd felt that if his country was ever saved and its institutions made permanent, New England, under God, must do it. As New England must lift and labor untiringly for generations to come, he said, it was highly desirable to have her distinctive character, her institutions, and her churches all move south and west, as fast as the providence of God opened the way. After he had transferred his labors to Pittsfield, he continued to be overrun with "agents from the West—poor, imprudent, and saucy."

In their zeal to enlist recruits for the soldiers of the cross and to open the pocketbooks of church members, reports and letters, sent in by home missionaries, presented a one-sided picture of conditions in the West. Albert Barnes admitted that reports from the West, written to influence the eastern mind, were as various as the points of view from which they contemplated it. One sees there only the evidence of a worldly spirit, and reports that all the institutions of learning and religion are forgotten and trampled down. Another sees only evidence that infidelity abounds. Another comes back with the report that Romanism is destined to prevail there. Another fears that the people are certain to lapse into barbarism. Another is struck with the countless numbers of emigrants there from the Old World, transplanting the institutions from foreign lands, corrupting and diluting the principles of liberty and constituting elements for the demagogue or the military chieftain.

Barnes, Beecher, Baird, and Bushnell agreed that emigration involves a tendency to social decline; that there must be a relapse toward barbarism, more or less protracted, more or less complete. "There is no literary atmosphere breathing through the forests or across the prairie," said Horace Bushnell in 1847. In contrasting the older sections of the country with the West, Barnes stated that in an older society it is comparatively easy to preserve the ascendancy of religion and to adhere to the lessons of virtue. For here is the sanctuary where we have been accustomed to worship from childhood; here is the Sabbath-bell, reminding us of the day of holy rest; here are our fathers' sepulchers, faithful though silent mementos of the value of the principles which they held, and of the worth of religion in life and death; here is the schoolhouse, a reminder of the lessons learned in early years. But in a new country, Barnes concluded, the power of these things is unknown.

In his *Plea for the West* Lyman Beecher avowed that the work of rearing the literary and religious institutions of the West could not be done by the West alone.

No people ever did, in the first generation, fell the forest, and construct roads, and rear the dwellings and public edifices, and provide the competent supply of schools and literary institutions. New England did not. Her colleges were endowed extensively by foreign munificence, and her churches of the first generation were supplied chiefly from the mother country. . . . The population of the great West . . . is assembled from all the states of the Union, and from all the nations of Europe, and is rushing in like the waters of the flood.

Beecher maintained that settlements in the West were so sparse that no homogeneous public sentiment could be formed to legislate immediately into being the requisite institutions. A nation was being born in a day, he said, and all the nurture of schools and literary institutions is needed to rear it up to a glorious and unperverted manhood.

In reply to the question how the requisite supply of teachers for the sons and daughters of the West could be raised up, Beecher said it could be accomplished by the instrumentality of a learned and pious ministry, educated in the West. "Schools wane, invariably, in those towns where the evangelical ministry is neglected, and the Sabbath is profaned, and the tavern supplants the worship of God," he wrote. "Thrift and knowledge in such places go out, while vice and irreligion come in." No opinion is more false, he continued, than that mediocrity of talent and learning will suffice for the West. There is not a place on earth where piety, talent, learning, argument, and popular eloquence are more highly appreciated.

Notwithstanding, the eloquent preacher warned of the dangers from "uneducated mind," which was augmenting by the rapid influx of foreign immigrants, the greater part of whom were unacquainted with American institutions, unaccustomed to self-government, inaccessible to education, and easily accessible to prepossession, inveterate credulity, and intrigue, embodied by sinister design. He feared that the foreign-born population might at no distant day equal, and even outnumber, the native population in the West. Beecher harbored the suspicion that emigration was rolling its broad tide at the bidding of the powers of Europe hostile to free institutions, and associated with the Holy Alliance, to arrest and put them down. "Is this a vain fear?" he asked. "Are not the continental powers alarmed at the march of liberal opinions, and associated to put them down? By fleets and armies they cannot do it. But do they therefore sleep on their heaving earth and tottering thrones? Has Metternich yet to form an acquaintance with history?"

Robert Baird discerned the signs of the times in a more favorable light. Writing in the decade of the fifties, he judged that there was far less infidelity among the American population, especially in the Middle and Southern States, than there was a half-century earlier; but in New England and in the portions of the West settled from New England, there was a considerable amount of a "subtile infidelity, the legitimate fruit of Universalism and Unitarianism" on the one hand, and of a certain fanaticism on the other, which led men to reject Christianity, because the Bible and the churches "will not speak as they think they should do" on temperance, slavery, and other kindred topics.

Albert Barnes took courage in the thought that no organization of infidelity could vie with the Bible Society, the Tract Society, and the Sunday School Union in circulating books. No amount of wealth embarked in such a "book concern" could give a distribution of Paine and Volney equal to that which could be given to *Pilgrim's Progress* and Baxter's *Saints' Everlasting Rest*. He also pointed out that settlers in the West had removed themselves from false religion and bad principles of government, and that the hardships and experiences of emigrants had made them strong, self-reliant, generous, hospitable, and respectful of clergymen and women.

In the two decades preceding the Civil War, Americans in all parts of the country were fearful of "alien ideas" imported in the minds of emigrants from Europe. They believed that foreign infidelity was blended with Socialism and "Red Republicanism," which had manifested itself in the revolutionary disturbances which rocked the countries of Europe in 1848 and in the years immediately following. Of all "forms of error," however, Roman Catholicism was by far the most formidable, because of the number of its adherents, its organization, wealth, influence, and the "worldly and unscrupulous policy" of its hierarchy. To a large extent the "foreign mind" in the West was said to have little sympathy with the principles of the Protestant faith.

Barnes's Home Missionary Sermon was reassuring, however. He had no fear that Roman Catholicism was destined to be the prevailing religion of the West, and he listed the reasons for his optimism. The Roman Catholic priesthood was not indigenous to the American environment. A clergy, to have power in this land, must be of the people; must have a large share of American feeling; must enter into all our notions of civil liberty and mental freedom. He posed this question: "What man will point to an elementary book in education, in morals, in jurisprudence, in history, in theology, in exposition of the Scriptures, from the multitude of the Catholic priesthood in this land, that is adapted to mould the American mind?"

Catholic schools and colleges were inferior because they were taught by foreign nuns and Jesuits who were incapable of giving a correct history of the country and who could not teach sciences without exposing their faith and morals to imminent danger. He posed the following question: "Where is there a Jesuit institution in the United States, or a Roman Catholic institution anywhere, that dares to give its pupils a true history, or a true account of the condition of North and South America; or that dares to go back and trace the history of New England and Mexico?" He cited the obvious and palpable mistakes which Roman Catholics were making in their attempts to spread their religion. They build magnificent and costly cathedrals, erect convents, fit up public places of worship in a manner adapted to make an impression on the outward senses of mankind. Protestants, on the other hand, send out living teachers of religion, distribute books and tracts, and seek to rear the temples of religion in the hearts of men. Finally, Barnes was not fearful of Catholics because they were not increasing nearly as fast as Protestants.

Barnes cited the number of colleges and schools that had been established in the West. He rejoiced that that vast territory was better supplied with colleges than New England was a hundred years after the landing of the Pilgrims. Among the societies and organizations active in promoting education in the West, were three societies founded in New England in the decade of the forties. The Society for the Promotion of Collegiate and Theological Education at the West assisted five prominent institutions: Western Reserve, Illinois, Wabash, and Marietta Colleges, and Lane Theological Seminary. Other institutions received aid from time to time. The Board of National Popular Education, as the name indicates, promoted popular education. Miss Catharine Beecher was active in this. The Ladies' Society for the Promotion of Education at the West provided salaries and transportation for teachers, who were expected to teach for at least two years.

The famous "Iowa band" of home missionaries is illustrative of the zeal and methods of the Congregationalists. In October, 1843, ten students from Andover Theological Seminary began their journey westward with the inspiration to plant the seeds of Congregationalism. They founded Iowa College at Davenport, which was later moved to Grinnell. This town was founded by Josiah Grinnell, one of many Vermonters who deserted New England for the West. For a time he was a colporteur in the service of the American Tract Society. In 1854 he purchased six thousand acres of land in Iowa and with three associates founded the town which bears his name. His plans for Grinnell University were underway when it was absorbed by Iowa College.

The reports, letters, journals, and autobiographies written by home missionaries collectively constitute a colorful and important chapter in social history—a genetic history of religion as a spiritual and cultural force. The experiences of clergymen, lay preachers, colporteurs, and missionaries, by whatever designation, differ as to details and with reference to time and place; but whether in the service of one denomination or the other or ministering to native-born or foreign-born, they were quickly overpowered by the environment and either adapted themselves to it or abandoned their calling.

The career of Flavel Bascom is typical, and he has given an extended account of it in an autobiography consisting of two hundred and seventy-three manuscript pages. The value of the autobiography is enhanced by the fact that it is based on a diary.

Bascom graduated from Yale in 1821, and from 1831 to 1833 was tutor at that college. In 1833 he accepted a commission from the American Home Missionary Society to preach the Gospel in Illinois. His salary was five hundred dollars a year. He furnished his own horse and buggy and charged his traveling expenses to the society. The hospitality of the pioneers and the fabulously low hotel rates reduced his expenses to an almost unbelievable sum. His accommodations at home and his labors abroad were unfavorable to habits of study, even if the required books had been available. He learned that customs and tastes of the people did not require written sermons, nor elaborate preparations. The man who could get up and talk with the utmost freedom and fluency was listened to with the greatest admiration, without regard to the soundness of his logic or the literary polish of his style.

In Putnam County, Illinois, Bascom preached in a Presbyterian meeting-house which was made of logs and consisted of an old and a new part. In the old part the seats were made of rough slabs, and in the new part, which had no floor, the sleepers were used for seats. The pulpit was made by setting two posts in the ground about four feet apart, and on the top of these was nailed a board to support a Bible and hymnbook. Behind the pulpit was a seat for the preacher, which was made by boring two holes in one of the logs and inserting two pins on which a board was placed. This structure, wrote Bascom, was far in advance of many houses in which he subsequently preached the Gospel. Men, women, and children in about equal numbers, and a "good supply of dogs," made up the congregation; and the preacher and the singers were not the only ones whose voices were heard in the assembly.

The missionaries in the service of the American Home Missionary Society had scant respect for their competitors professing the Baptist and Methodist faiths. They dismissed them as ignorant and incompetent. Flavel Bascom, referring to a sermon by a preacher of the early pioneer sort, said that the speaker, having stated the text, never referred to it again, but commenced an indiscriminate quotation of passages from Genesis to Revelation and back again, with apparently no connection between them except that some word in one verse would serve as a catchword to remind him of another. Thus he went "bellowing and blowing through the Bible," shedding no more light upon the passages quoted than the "roar of artillery does upon the Declaration of Independence."

The disrespect between Congregationalists and Presbyterians, on the one side, and Baptists and Methodists, on the other side, was mutual. Some Baptists were under the influence of Daniel Parker, who opposed any outside organizations and a paid ministry. One Baptist was reported as having said that "Judas was the first preacher to receive pay." Peter Cartwright was especially critical of young missionaries sent out "to civilize and Christianize the poor heathen of the West." He said that they were generally "tolerably well furnished with old manuscript sermons"; but this way of reading sermons was out of fashion in the West. The great mass of the people wanted a preacher who could mount a stump, a block, or an old log, or stand in the bed of a wagon, and without note or manuscript quote, expound or apply the Word of God to the hearts and consciences of the people. Despite the fruits of the efforts of the pioneer Methodist preachers, as evidenced by churches, missionary societies, and hundreds of traveling and local preachers, the newly-fledged missionaries wrote back to the old states wailings and lamentations over the wastes and the destitute condition of the West.

Cartwright singled out a "fresh, green, live Yankee from down East," who had regularly graduated, had his diploma, was regularly called by the American Home Missionary Society to visit the far-off West—a perfect moral waste, in his view of the subject. Having been taught to believe that Methodist preachers were nothing but a poor, illiterate set of ignoramuses, he longed for an opportunity to display his superior tact and talent and throw "us poor upstart preachers in the West, especially Methodist preachers, into the shades of everlasting darkness."

A Methodist preacher in those days, when he felt that God had called him to preach, instead of hunting up a college or biblical institute, hunted up a hardy pony or a horse, and some traveling apparatus. With his library always at hand, namely, Bible, Hymn Book, and Discipline, he started, and, with a text that never wore out nor grew stale, he cried, "Behold the Lamb of God, that taketh away the sins of the world!"

In spite of misunderstandings, rivalries, and jealousies, rooted in the clashing of personalities and creeds, differences in cultural and racial backgrounds, and disagreements over slavery, temperance, Sabbath observance, and the like, the frontier exhibited unity in the midst of diversity and remarkable tolerance in the midst of intolerance. There was a spirit of give and take—a form of Christian excellence—which leveled barriers and blotted out traditions rooted in more stratified societies. On the other hand, there was good sense in the remark of a deacon in Illinois in 1840 who opposed the proposal that Christians should disband their organizations and join a new sect called "Unionists" because he did not believe in "being united all to pieces." The home missionary who preached to a Presbyterian congregation in Bloomington, Illinois, refrained from revealing his background because the word "Congregationalism" was fraught with heresy.

The circumstances of the ordination of Flavel Bascom are illustrative and eloquent of the spontaneity of the frontier and of the elemental character of the Christian church. After having been licensed to preach for two years, Bascom applied for ordination in order that he might regularly administer the ordinances of the Gospel. A council of Congregational churches and pastors could not be convened for the purpose, because the only Congregational church existing in Illinois in 1833 had been organized in Northampton, Massachusetts, and was without a pastor. Bascom, therefore, sought ordination by a Presbytery. At the appointed time, with three ministers present, the Presbytery was organized and proceeded to examine Bascom and another candidate. Although both men were New School in theology and were brought up under the instruction of Nathaniel W. Taylor, the exponent of "New Haven Theology," while a majority of the Presbytery was Old School, no objection against ordination was raised.

When Bascom became pastor of a Presbyterian church in Chicago, the membership was recruited from all of the New England and Middle States, from several Western and Southern States, as well as from England, Ireland, Scotland, and Wales. In church polity they were Presbyterians and Congregationalists; in theology some were extreme Old School and some were ultra New School. On questions of reform there were radical differences. While all claimed liberty for their own opinions, they were tolerant of the opinions of others. A church or congregation of that pattern in contemporary Europe would have been unthinkable. A home missionary in Lyons, Iowa, in an address delivered in 1862 was a sound historian when he said: "The Great Valley already disproves the theory that the descendants of Puritan and Cavalier, Old World men and New, cannot mingle and make one."

The very poverty of the frontier and its meager facilities and accommodations made for forbearance and coöperation. For example, in the center of Pleasant Grove, Illinois, was a log schoolhouse, in which preaching was appointed at twelve o'clock on every Sunday, when Baptists, Methodists, and Cumberland Presbyterians held services in rotation. If any other denomination wanted to be heard, they were permitted to "put in a sermon" after the stated preacher had finished and before the meeting broke up.

The reports and correspondence of many agents in the service of the American Home Missionary Society appear to be harsh and uncharitable in judging the foreign-language churches. It is not without significance, however, that among the immigrants themselves, laymen and clergymen, the fundamental difference between the churches of their native countries and the American churches was quickly recognized and admitted. In contrast with the friendly, democratic American pastor, the pastor and priest in the established churches were stiff, aloof, and formal. As one emigrant put it in a letter to his relatives in the Old Country, in America the shepherds seek out the sheep, whereas in Europe the sheep must seek the shepherds. The pastors who sought to recruit members for their congregations among their foreign-born countrymen admitted that it was difficult to appeal to them because their membership in the state church was nominal and they scoffed at repentance and grace. A home missionary in Michigan Territory expected to find recent immigrants from Scotland more punctual in attendance on religious ordinances; but he had been unable to get them together, except a few, once a month at a prayer meeting. Only one Scotchman had been persuaded to subscribe to a temperance pledge. The Scotchmen wanted the liberty to drink when they had a mind to. At Lockport, Illinois, a home missionary found a large number of Roman Catholics who swore, drank and would receive few Bibles.

An editorial in the *Home Missionary*, published by the Executive

Committee of the American Home Missionary Society, dated January, 1851, presents a thumbnail summary of the problem of giving missionary aid to the foreign-born:

The increasing influx of Germans into our country . . . has been every year more and more under the attention of philanthropic and Christian men. A very slight acquaintance satisfies the evangelical enquirer that the majority of this class have not been educated in notions sufficiently strict in respect to experimental piety. The incompleteness of the Reformation in many parts of Germany—varying from Romanism as little as possible lest it should too much shock the prejudices of the multitude; the alliance of the church with the state; and competitive with the Papists in hierarchical orders and ceremonial display, have all tended to render religion an affair of forms. The German Reformed and Lutheran churches of this country, we have been accustomed to regard as having a higher standard of qualifications for their members than is discoverable in the case of recent emigrants.

The American churches thought they could proselyte among the German and Scandinavian Lutherans because the use of foreign languages would keep them apart from Protestant churches and make for cleavage in the population of communities and nation, and also because their "sacramental superstition" and mechanical way of admitting members suggested semi-Romanism. With the increase of emigration from Germany and Norway and Sweden in the twenty years before the Civil War, the Lutheran Church in the United States became divided into American Lutherans, or "New Lutherans," and "Old Lutherans," who were recent immigrants. The American Lutherans argued that since Lutheranism in the various countries of Europe had acquired a distinctive flavor, the Lutheran Church in America should adapt itself to the genius of American institutions and society. The editor of the *Lutheran Observer*, the organ of the American Lutheran party, in an editorial published on September 19, 1851, stated that the ministers and members of the "Old Lutheran" party were nearly all from Europe, learned for the most part, but bigoted and semi-Romanist. The editor lamented their exclusiveness and sacramental superstition.

The American Home Missionary Society gave financial aid to foreign-language churches on most generous terms; and the clergymen who were recipients of such aid wrote grateful acknowledgements and admitted that without it they could not have accomplished so much for their countrymen. One of the first Swedish Lutheran ministers, Lars Paul Esbjörn, who was ordained in the Church of Sweden, in 1850 wrote to a missionary society in Sweden that he had been granted aid by the American Home Missionary Society and that until a Lutheran synod was organized in Illinois, he would be under the supervision of the Congregational Church. Although Lutheran doctrine and Congregational doctrine differed, he wrote, it was agreed that he should preach the Gospel and administer the sacraments and conduct services and enforce discipline as a Lutheran clergyman. He feared that his enemies, both in the United States and in Sweden, would spread the report that he had left the Lutheran Church in favor of Calvinism. The further circumstance that he would accept only "believing" members for his congregations—something new to many Swedes—would no doubt occasion polemical writings in the Old Country, he suspected.

Although the division of the Presbyterian Church into "New School" and "Old School," dealt a crippling blow to the noble experiment in Christian unity and fellowship, the Congregational Church continued to carry the burden of the American Home Missionary Society and on the same liberal terms that had prevailed during the years when the Plan of Union was in operation. The Home Missionary Society continued the policy of building up the Kingdom of God in the spirit of the Sermon on the Mount. And the Congregational Church, instead of thinking primarily of building a huge ecclesiastical structure and augmenting its own membership, was willing to lose its life in order that other communions might find theirs.

The experiment of the American Home Missionary Society has not ceased, neither has the grand experiment of the Mississippi Valley been fully appraised. The results may be revealed in their fullness in generations to come. "The completed culture of two hundred years cannot be set down in two decades by the Mississippi, any more than the magnificent sweep and swing of a Connecticut elm can be put down full-grown upon a prairie." Thus spoke the Rev. Samuel C. Bartlett of Chicago at the forty-fifth annual meeting of the American Home Missionary Society in 1871.

FOURTEEN

THE AMERICAN TRACT SOCIETY

WITHIN less than a score of years the religious life of the American people flowered into five great experiments in interdenominationalism which gave to American Christianity a unique status and grew out of the experience of the people and the genius of their institutions. In 1810 was founded the American Board of Commissioners for Foreign Missions; in 1816, the American Bible Society; in 1824, the American Sunday School Union; in 1825, the American Tract Society; in 1826, the American Home Missionary Society. These organizations and their auxiliaries, by emphasizing the ecumenical character of Christianity and by ignoring or minimizing the barriers of doctrine and polity which set them apart, solved certain problems of individual denominations and developed a spirit of fraternity which was prophetic of even greater undertakings. In general the objectives of these organizations were identical; and the successes and achievements of one worked to the advantage of the others. If proof were needed, it would be sufficient to cite the fact that many names of members in the societies were identical.

The American Tract Society was peculiarly American in its inception, in its methods, and in its recognition of the priesthood of the common man by levying on the time, efforts, and talents of laymen. It was essentially a laymen's missionary movement borne on the wings of the colporteur system, in which individual Christian effort and example were augmented by the miracle of the printing press. The American Tract Society was the answer to the challenge of the frontier; and the system of colportage was peculiarly adapted to frontier conditions.

Characteristically, the organizers of the American Tract Society searched the Scriptures to justify the colporteur system. They learned that the system existed substantially in the days of the apostles, when the disciples went everywhere preaching and "holding forth the word of life" in fireside conversation and social prayer. "The providence of God has since furnished an auxiliary to these labors in the printed volume and awakening tract; but the spirit and kind of effort are identical with that of primitive Christianity." In the vast and sparsely populated territory in the West the number of evangelical preachers was small in proportion to the population. Unlike the early settlement of New England, where motives of piety and safety led the colonists to cluster together in villages, the settlers in the forests and on the prairies of the West planted their families wherever land was most productive, irrespective of social, educational, or religious considerations. Instead of being of one faith, the same new township might contain single representatives of all creeds of Christendom, or the majority might have no faith. There was no homogeneousness, and no possibility of sustaining the ministry of a particular order. It was obvious that some laborer like the colporteur must penetrate the forests—must climb the mountains—must scour the prairies—and leave behind him such testimony for God as Baxter or Doddridge had borne.

In further justification of colportage, the publications of the American Tract Society cited the fact that Republican institutions are based on the theory of the ability of the people to govern themselves and presuppose the existence of intelligence and virtue. Primary schools, colleges, academies, and seminaries must be multiplied; and until such time as they can be put into operation, colporteurs go to all the people. Under a system which tolerates all religions—and none are privileged—truth and error are left to their own resources. Shall the defense and propagation of the Gospel be considered a matter of professional duty, when in all other subjects men are accustomed to influence the opinions and conduct of their fellow men? In the United States there were no barriers to the universal diffusion of the Gospel. There were no police, no censorship of the press, no established hierarchies to cramp the free and elastic spirit of Christianity and prescribe forms of its manifestations.

The power of Christian love and faith, asserting itself in direct personal contact, could not be frustrated by threats of excommunication and discipline from exponents of cocksure orthodoxy or priests clothed in the authority of holy orders. In the kingdoms from which most of the emigrants from Europe came, religion was an affair of the state and was supported by taxation—not by voluntary sacrifice, as in the United States. They could not be expected to make efforts in their adopted country to erect churches and support pastors. "A cold, dead formalism holds the place of vital godliness even with many nominal Protestants; and the very idea of a spiritual faith, manifesting its power in a prayerful, holy life, is a thing almost unknown among them. Experimental religion is regarded as fanaticism." The movement of awakening and reform must be commenced at the fireside and in the family; and the work must be done, to a great extent, by the press and by individual Christian example and effort.

It was admitted that thousands of foreign immigrants were destitute of evangelical ministers, churches, Sabbath and day schools, Bibles, religious books, and were still exemplary Christians, and that Roman Catholicism was a political threat and a menace to spirituality by substituting unmeaning ceremonies and idolatrous rites for holiness of heart and life; "yet God has gracious designs of mercy in thus bringing into the arms of American Christians millions of immortal beings."

The Address of the Executive Committee of the American Tract Society to the Christian Public was Tract No. 1. It was stated that the world at large, the adjacent states of South America, the islands of the West Indies, and the United States, in particular, presented a vast and inviting field for the exertions of a society combining the efforts of the whole Christian community. The country had a population of more than eleven million, four million of whom were children. Under the operation of the system of common schools, aided by the influence of the Sunday schools, it would be comparatively easy to extend the power of moral and religious instruction through the medium of tracts to these nurseries of the church and the state. "Should God smile upon the Society, it would speak to the remote corners of the globe."

It is obvious that the only difficulty in forming a Tract Society . . . lies in the doctrinal character of the Tracts to be circulated. On this subject the most full and liberal provision is made in the Constitution of the American Tract Society. The different denominations composing the Publishing Committee come to their work with the solemn and honest stipulation to be each the protector of his own peculiarities; and in this labor of mercy to publish and distribute such Tracts only as shall inculcate those great doctrines in which they all harmonize. Man's native sinfulness—the purity and obligation of the law of God—the true and proper divinity of our Lord Jesus Christ—the necessity and reality of his atonement and sacrifice—the efficiency of the Holy Spirit in the work of renovation—the free and full offers of the Gospel, and the duty of men to accept it—the necessity of personal holiness—as well as an everlasting state of rewards and punishments beyond the grave—these are doctrines dear to our hearts, and constitute the basis of our union. . . . If in any instance we should hesitate about the terms in which any truth should be expressed, we may always be relieved of our embarrassment by resorting to the terms of the Bible, and adopting the very language of the spirit of all truth.

The time setting of the formation of the American Tract Society is revealed in a paragraph of the tract stating that New York City was chosen for the center of its operations because its port was in communication with foreign ports and every part of the interior; and when the canals under construction were completed, there would be direct inland water communication between New York and every village of note in the country west of the Alleghany Mountains. "We live . . . at an eventful period of the world. The purposes of God's mercy appear to be rapidly unfolding, and rapidly and surely advancing toward their final issue. New scenes are already opening upon the world and upon the Church; and the 'enterprise to be achieved is the conversion of the world to its Redeeming God and King.' "

The American Tract Society was deeply indebted to the London Religious Tract Society, which was instituted in 1799. It was the parent of all other tract societies, whether in Europe or in America; and it was generous in granting permission to reprint its publications and in giving the benefit of its example and coöperation. During the first twenty-five years of its existence it published about fifty-eight million tracts and probably accomplished more than all other religious tract societies combined. Its tracts circulated "from the shores of the Baltic to the Cape of Good Hope, through the whole of Europe and India, and were pressing upon the inhabitants of China." There were a number of auxiliary societies in Great Britain. For example, the

Church of England Tract Society, which was established at Bristol in 1811, had auxiliaries in different parts of England and Ireland and in several of the British colonies.

The influence of the consecrated life and efforts of Hannah More (1745–1833) counted heavily in the early years of the London Religious Tract Society and of the American Tract Society. The irreligious spirit of the French Revolution, the misery and wretched moral condition of the English masses—and the indifference of the bishops and clergy of the Church to the hungry souls—aroused her to action. Of good family and education, her sensitive nature and fine-grained character revolted against the ungodly habits and immoralities of the age. She saw the fashion of the world with its pomps and artificialities passing away. In her first book, which appeared anonymously, she spoke with truth and directness. It bore the title *Thoughts on the Importance of the Great to General Society.*

Her strict observance of the Sabbath as a day of rest from society and from worldly occupations and as a day of religious improvement brought the charge that she taught Calvinism, sympathized with the Methodists and encouraged dissenters. Though attached to the Church of England, her creed was summarized in the following statement: "Bible Christianity is what I love, that does not insist upon opinions indifferent in themselves—a Christianity practical and pure, which teaches holiness, humility, repentance, and faith in Christ." The strictness of her *Practical Piety* was criticised by some of her friends. Her reply was "The Gospel is strict; the cutting off a right hand, or the plucking out of a right eye, though only used as metaphors and illustrations, is surely more strict than anything I have ever said." In comparing the influence of Samuel Johnson and Joseph Addison, as moralists and Christians, with Baxter and Doddridge, she stated that it is only the distinguishing doctrines of the Bible, urged by those who have felt their power that can have any permanent influence upon the life and conscience of others.

The necessity of furnishing the masses with the right sort of reading in order to promote temperance, economy, social stability, and moral improvement impelled Hannah More and her friends to publish monthly the tracts of the "Cheap Repository." Miss More's most famous tract "The Shepherd of Salisbury Plain" appeared originally

in the pages of the "Cheap Repository," and was published as Tract
No. 10 of the American Tract Society. *Hannah More's Repository
Tracts* in eight volumes were published by the American Tract
Society.

Out of these activities grew the London Religious Tract Society,
and very soon its activity was broadened by translating tracts into
other languages and by devising means of distributing them. In 1815
began a new series of children's books, ornamented with many en-
gravings; and in 1824 began the publication of two monthlies: the
Tract Magazine and *Child's Companion*. The example of the London
society prompted the publication of the *American Tract Magazine*,
in 1825, a bi-monthly at fifty cents per year, sent gratuitously to
auxiliaries which made yearly remittances to augment the society's
funds.

The genesis of the American Tract Society stems from New England, although societies for the promotion of Christian knowledge
sprang up in other parts of the country. At a meeting held in Boston
on May 23, 1814, the New England Tract Society was organized and
a constitution was adopted. It continued under this name until June,
1823, when it became the American Tract Society. With the view of
forming a more national tract society by uniting the principal tract
societies of the country, in the autumn of 1824 negotiations were
entered into between the American Tract Society and the Religious
Tract Society in New York. Having raised the necessary sum of
money to erect a house for the new society, and after many conferences, a merger was effected on May 11, 1825. The American Tract
Society in Boston became a branch of the national society whose
headquarters were in New York, with branches and auxiliaries in the
principal cities and towns of the country. The stereotypes and plates
of the Boston society were transferred to New York; and the tracts
which had been published by the New England Tract Society were
listed by the American Tract Society and numbered continuously.
One of the most active auxiliaries to the American Tract Society was
the Boston Ladies' Association for Evangelizing the West. Its tracts
and reports were published by the American Tract Society. As the
name indicates, the tracts and the work of the colporteurs were
pointed to the West, and more especially to the German population.

Among the one hundred colporteurs in the service of the association in the early forties twenty-eight were German and French.

The output of the American Tract Society was tremendous and was indicative of the generous support, financial and otherwise, that was immediately enlisted. Moreover, the American Tract Society co-operated with temperance, Bible, missionary, and Sabbath societies in printing and circulating their literature. Missionaries in the Sandwich Islands requested a supply of tracts to be distributed by them to the crews of whaling vessels and of other ships. During and after the Civil War the American Tract Society worked together with other organizations in setting up schools and churches for colored refugees.

The publications of the American Tract Society included religious and devotional books, biographies, histories, tracts and periodicals. Volumes of approved excellence included Bunyan's *Pilgrim's Progress,* Baxter's *Saints' Rest,* Doddridge's *Rise and Progress of Religion in the Soul,* D'Aubigne's *History of the Reformation,* and Flavel's *Redemption.* It proposed to place its Evangelical Family Library of fifteen volumes or its Christian Library of forty-five volumes in many households. A sampling of the tracts, bound in the first seven volumes under the title *Publications of the American Tract Society* (which already numbered two hundred twenty-six), reveals the following titles: "The Dairyman's Daughter," by Rev. Legh Richmond; "Family Worship," by Rev. Philip Doddridge; "Remember the Sabbath to Keep it Holy," by Sir Matthew Hale; "The Evils of Excessive Drinking," by Benjamin Rush, M.D.; "Divine Songs for Children," by Isaac Watts; "The Sabbath A Blessing to Mankind"; "The Ruinous Consequences of Gambling"; "The Seventh Commandment," by Rev. Timothy Dwight; "The Conversion of President Edwards"; "Universalism"; "Theatrical Exhibitions."

In the nineteenth century almanacs occupied a prominent place in homes and were diligently read and referred to by young and old. In 1820 the New England Tract Society began the publication of the *Christian Almanac.* After the consolidation of the societies it continued to be published by the American Tract Society. When John Todd was invited to become the editor of the *Christian Almanac* for 1826, he considered it a good opportunity to speak to a half million of immortal beings.

The *Sabbath Manual* was published coöperatively by the American Tract Society and the American and Foreign Sabbath Union which was organized in Boston in April, 1843. The manual was prepared by Justin Edwards who was a tireless worker in the service of temperance, Sabbath, and Bible societies. By the end of 1850 one million, one hundred and seventy-five thousand copies of the *Sabbath Manual* had been printed. Translations had been made into German, French, and Spanish. Money had been appropriated for the distribution of the publication to immigrants at Buffalo, Pittsburgh, and other great thoroughfares, and for missionaries, clergymen, and others, exclusive of grants by their colporteurs.

Justin Edwards traveled extensively and made contacts with leaders in many walks of life by personal interviews and by attending conventions, conferences, and public meetings. When at Montgomery, Alabama, he wrote to the American Tract Society on January 21, 1848:

The *Sabbath Manual* I find in many families; and in view of what I see, I have often wished that the *Temperance Manual* had gone with it; for rum, whiskey, and brandy drinkers will break the Sabbath, and Sabbath-breakers will neglect the Bible, and neglecters of the Bible will disobey God.

My ears have often been greeted with the encomiums which have been bestowed in different places on the colporteurs who passed that way, and my heart delighted to hear it so often repeated, in widely distant sections of country, "I presume the one who came along here, was *one of the best of them.*" Thousands will bless God for ever for the colporteur, who left his home and wandered far over mountain and vale, through forest and flood, to visit the parent and the child, to sell them good books, if they could buy, and if not, to give them, especially that book of books the Bible.

The calling of the colporteur was identical with that of the itinerant preacher or circuit rider, and their experiences were similar. Before the Civil War, the ordinary salary of a colporteur was one hundred and fifty dollars a year. In some cases a larger sum was allowed, and in others the salary was less. The society paid the traveling expenses of the colporteur—and sometimes they were unbelievably low. A certain colporteur spent an entire year in Kentucky and expended for meals, lodging, and horse-keeping only fifty cents. The hospitality of the Kentuckians matched the zeal of the colporteur who went "about doing good." In the absence of preachers, the colporteur brought to the settlers in the remote parts of the country the master-pieces of such preachers as Baxter, Bunyan, Doddridge, Flavel, and Paul.

Hundreds of thousands of emigrants from Europe had occasion for expressing gratitude to the American Tract Society and the American Bible Society for kind words and friendly advice and as-sistance when "a word fitly spoken is like apples of gold in pictures of silver." Upon the arrival of an emigrant ship their agents were on hand to extend words of welcome and a helping hand. They were invited to join in a session of prayer on deck and assured of Christian fellowship in the churches of their adopted country. They were presented with copies of the Bible with the compliments of the American Bible Society and with tracts and brief books of Daily Devotions in their native languages, published and distributed by the American Tract Society.

The children were not forgotten. One little book which was in frequent demand at the depositaries of the American Tract Society in schoolhouses and churches and in country stores was *Little Meg's Children*, by the "Author of *Jessica's First Prayer, The Children of Claverly*, etc." It was a story about motherless children in a wretched tenement in the east end of London, "more than a mile from St. Paul's Cathedral." The death of the mother left Little Meg, ten years old, in charge of two younger children, while the father, a sailor, was on a long voyage. To boys and girls who knew the peace, quiet, and solitude of the West, with its vast distances, its billowing prairies and deep forests, the security of homes, in spite of frugality, the hospitality of the frontier, the dismal home and surroundings of Little Meg and her children, must have seemed strange. The pathetic story told about the prostitute who befriended Little Meg, drunken men and women, screaming children, and the din and tumult of the crowded city. The theme of the story was God's protecting care for deserted children.

The most serious criticism of the American Tract Society came from abolitionists and anti-slavery crusaders. Harriet Beecher Stowe

rebuked the American Tract Society for its alleged pro-slavery attitude. The gravamen of the indictment was stated in a pamphlet entitled *The Unanimous Remonstrance of the Fourth Congregational
Church of Hartford, Connecticut, Against the Policy of the American
Tract Society on the Subject of Slavery.*

The pamphlet referred to criticism of the American Tract Society
in the religious press and in resolutions adopted by individual congregations and larger units. Typical of the criticisms was the action of
the General Association (Congregational) of Iowa in 1853, which
alleged that anti-slavery sentiments had been expunged from publications of the American Tract Society and of the American Sunday
School Union. It charged that it had been the deliberate policy of
the Tract Society not to utter a direct condemnation of the "most
giant iniquity of our land."

The *Remonstrance* dealt with the contention of some that the
American Tract Society simply expressed no opinion on the subject
of slavery, but contented itself with preaching the Gospel, leaving to
anti-slavery societies the work of opposing slavery. Why not in
like manner leave to temperance societies the work of opposing intemperance, was the reply.

It also dealt with the comparison with the American Bible Society,
which took no official position on slavery. In rebuttal it was stated
that the Bible Society had for its single object the publication and
distribution of the Bible without note or comment, and sought to
proclaim truth in no other way. The Tract Society, on the other hand,
inculcated specific moral and religious truths or the application of
the general doctrines and precepts of the Bible to the circumstances
of men.

In behalf of the Tract Society it was argued that if its publications
condemned slavery, its agents and publications would be excluded
from the South. The *Remonstrance* posed the following question:
"Is it Christian, or is it Jesuitical—is it like Paul, or is it like
Ignatius Loyola—to consent to suppress part of the Gospel in order
to preach the remainder?" If that principle were carried out, it was
stated, it would lead missionaries to China to avoid condemning the
use of opium; missionaries to India to be silent with reference to

caste; missionaries to Turkey to refrain from attacking polygamy, lest the rulers of the people should expel them from the country. It would also enjoin silence respecting polygamy for fear that colporteurs sent to Utah Territory would be driven out.

The First Article of the Constitution of the American Tract Society prohibited the circulation of works which did not meet the approbation of all evangelical Christians. It was argued that, by publishing anti-slavery literature, that article would be violated. The *Remonstrance* contended that the clause in question referred only to a doctrinal difference and to sentiments of denominations, rather than to individuals. It cited tracts which discussed practical questions on which "evangelical Christians" differed among themselves as individuals—tracts against the manufacture, sale, and use of intoxicating drinks. Not all "evangelical Christians" were agreed on that question. There was not a denomination represented in the American Tract Society that did not contain ministers and members who used liquors and defended the practice from the Bible. Moreover, the pamphlet cited the fact that "evangelical Christians" of Great Britain, France, Germany, and Switzerland did not give their adhesion to the doctrine that total abstinence was a Christian duty. Tracts against dancing as a social amusement had been published. Were all evangelical Christians agreed on that view? Ask the Episcopal brethren. In similar fashion the pamphlet raised questions with reference to card-playing and other forms of gambling, Sabbath-breaking, attendance at the opera and theater, and novel-reading—all of which had been condemned in tracts.

Finally the *Remonstrance* contained this telling paragraph:

And are you not mistaken in supposing that by simply preaching the evangelical doctrine and general principle of rights, you are sapping the whole system of slavery, and preparing the way for ultimate emancipation? Are you not aware that the Southern Church of all denominations now claims that the Bible is the best defence of slavery? . . . But has it ever occurred to you, that some such act as the expulsion of your agents and the exclusion of your publications from the South for opposition to slavery, may be the very best thing which is needed to usher in the dawn of freedom?

The American Tract Society, in common with the various branches of organized Christianity and their individual members, faced the dilemma of slavery which Henry Clay sententiously declared was "a curse to the master and a wrong to the slave." It divided churches; it split political parties; it plunged the country into a bloody Civil War.

FIFTEEN

THE AMERICAN BIBLE SOCIETY

IT HAS been said that the substitution of the book for the church was the essence of the Protestant Revolt. Nevertheless, in countries where Protestantism became the established religion, pietists and puritans, who trusted to the inspired pages of the Bible for the bread of life, felt that the clergy stood between them and the voice of God. Paradoxically, in some countries where biblical teaching was the basis of the established church it was rare to find a Bible in homes; and some pastors used the prayerbook to an even greater extent than the Bible. Enforcement of conventicle acts or some other disciplinary measure was invoked against persons who met in homes or in secluded places to read the Bible. In England and in America family worship was as important in the lives of individuals as worship in the meeting-house. It came down from parent to child with the large family Bible, where births, deaths, and marriages were recorded. The Bible was regarded with deepest reverence. In sermons and religious literature it was said to have been "transmitted from heaven."

The experiences of an eleven-year-old school girl who lived in Canandaigua, New York, as recorded in the Diary of Caroline Cowles Richards, 1852–1872, were not unique. "Before I go to school every morning I read three chapters in the Bible," she wrote. "I read three every day and five on Sunday and that takes me through the Bible in a year." In response to roll call in school, every scholar recited a Bible verse. She recorded that one morning her grandfather gave her ten cents for learning the Forty-sixth Psalm and promised to give her a dollar for reading the Bible through in a year. Her grandmother knew the Bible "from Genesis to Revelation excepting the 'begats' and the hard names."

Indicative of the importance of the Bible in the life of the American people were the measures taken by the Second Continental Congress and by the Congress under the Articles of Confederation. In 1777 in response to a memorial on the subject of Bible distribution, Congress appointed a committee which reported in favor of appropriating money to defray the expense of importing twenty thousand copies of the English Bible from Holland, England, or elsewhere. The report was adopted and the importation ordered. In 1781 Robert Aitkin, a printer in Philadelphia, in view of the scarcity of Bibles caused by the exigency of war, petitioned Congress to patronize his proposed edition of the Bible. The petition was referred to a committee of three, which in due time, on September 1, 1782, reported that "Mr. Aitkin has, at great expense, now finished an American edition of the Holy Scriptures in English; that the committee have from time to time attended to his progress in the work; that they also recommended it to the two chaplains of Congress to examine and to give their opinion of the execution." After the chaplains had reported their approbation, Congress resolved that it "highly approve the pious and laudable undertaking of Mr. Aitkin . . . and recommend this edition of the Bible to the inhabitants of the United States, and hereby authorize him to publish this recommendation in the manner he shall think proper."

In the previous chapter it was stated that the organization of the American Bible Society on May 11, 1816, was one of five great experiments in interdenominationalism. By unanimously adopting the constitution, the different religious denominations met on the broad platform of the Bible, "where names, sects, and parties fall." At the time of the meeting, there were already in existence state and local Bible societies—female societies, young men's societies, collegiate societies. As in the case of the American Tract Society, the American Bible Society was indebted to a similar organization in Great Britain. This was the British and Foreign Bible Society, which was instituted in 1804 and owed its origin to the London Religious Tract Society. Within thirty years after its organization, the British and Foreign Bible Society had more than two hundred and fifty auxiliaries, three hundred and fifty branches, and fifteen hundred associations; and it had printed or had granted aid to print or reprint the Scriptures or portions of them in one hundred and fifty-eight languages. In making acknowledgement of its debt to the British and Foreign Bible Society, the American Bible Society used the following language in its First Annual Report (1817):

> God has been pleased to make the people of Great Britain the instrument of forming, maturing, cherishing, and constantly and substantially aiding Bible societies, not only within her own territories, but throughout the world. . . . To honor those whom God honors, is both a Christian privilege and duty. Of the founders and patrons of the British and Foreign Bible Society—a Society preeminent in the felicity of the design and the grandeur of its plans—when they are gone down to the grave, posterity will say, in the language of an eminent statesman and orator of antiquity, "Bestowing their lives on the public, they have every one received a praise that will never decay, a sepulcher that will always be most illustrious."

In addition to the example and aid furnished by the British and Foreign Bible Society and by Bible societies in the United States, the foreign missionary spirit, which a few years earlier brought forth the Foreign Missionary Society, prepared the way for the American Bible Society. In 1815 a plan for the organization of a national society originated with the New Jersey Bible Society and was sent to sister societies. In 1816 the managers of the New York Bible Society adopted resolutions favoring the project, and they were transmitted to Elias Boudinot, president of the New Jersey Bible Society. The upshot was the publication of a notice in periodicals calling a meeting in New York.

Probably the major credit for the consummation of these plans belongs to Samuel J. Mills, whose heart was on fire for foreign missions and who had made extensive missionary tours to the West in 1812–13 and in 1814. This man, undistinguished in personal appearance but greatly distinguished by profound wisdom and industry and executive ability and love for God and man, within a short span of life took the lead in forming Bible societies in Pennsylvania, Ohio, Indiana, Illinois, Tennessee, Mississippi, and Louisiana, and was a leading instrument in instituting the American Board of Commissioners for Foreign Missions, the United Foreign Missionary Society, and the African School. Through his personal contacts with thousands of influential men of the nation, and by his addresses before ecclesiastical bodies, he paved the way for the convention that organized the American Bible Society. Lyman Beecher, president of Lane Theological Seminary at Cincinnati, Ohio, was secretary of the convention and wrote as follows: "We came to the meeting in great weakness, humility, and prayer, feeling the difficulties in combining all denominations, and feeling, every one, the necessity of keeping his heart and tongue, and walking very softly, lest a spark of unhallowed fire falling on a train, it should explode."

By the constitution of the American Bible Society its managers were, in the circulating of the Holy Scriptures, restricted to such copies as were "without note or comment"; and in the English language to the "version in common use." Its sole objective was the universal circulation of the Scriptures among all nations, irrespective of country, caste, or color; and it could not venture beyond its appropriate sphere to coalesce with tract, peace, education, Sunday school, colonization or anti-slavery societies—or any other society that might compromise its catholicity and unity.

The founders of the American Bible Society and its first officers were connected with the leading evangelical churches, such as the Protestant Episcopal Church, the Presbyterian, the Dutch Reformed, the Methodist Episcopal, and the Society of Friends. Many prominent men were enrolled as members and officers—John Jay, John Quincy Adams, Daniel Webster, Bushrod Washington, Felix Grundy, Charles Cotesworth Pinckney, De Witt Clinton, Daniel D. Tompkins, Francis Scott Key, Theodore Frelinghuysen, John Jacob Astor, to mention a few. Presidents and faculty members of colleges and universities were active members—among them were presidents of Yale, Brown, Amherst, Princeton, and Rutgers. Members of young men's Bible societies in cities and in colleges and universities were active in the work of distributing Bibles. The number of auxiliaries connected with the American Bible Society increased from year to year, until about thirty years after its foundation, there were about twelve hundred auxiliaries and twenty-five hundred branches located in all states and territories of the United States. Through local societies Bibles were distributed to destitute families. Systematic efforts were made to place the Bible in every family that was without a copy.

Women banded themselves into associations to promote the cause and enlisted in the self-denying work of visiting the poor and the ignorant in their homes in order to awaken interest in reading the Bible. In some congregations committees were chosen to divide cities into sections, each of which was assigned to a "team" of women. Grants for the purchase of Bibles and Testaments to be distributed among boatmen and passengers and emigrants from Europe by the "boatmen's preacher" at Utica, New York, were made jointly by the Oneida County Bible Society and by the American Seamen's Friend Society.

Local Bible societies and auxiliary societies were on the alert for new opportunities. In 1835, for example, the Bible Society of Pittsburgh called to the attention of the Board of Managers of the American Bible Society the problem of supplying the population of the West with the Scriptures—a population rapidly augmenting by emigrants from various countries of Europe. A special grant of money was made to the French and Foreign Bible Society to distribute Bibles at the Port of Havre de Grace. The chaplain, stationed at the port, wrote that the German emigrants seemed surprised and gratified to receive German Bibles and Testaments. It was evidently a new thing under the sun, he wrote. "I tell them that in America every one has his Bible, and that American Christians wish every one who comes to the country to have one."

Among the medley of Protestant denominations there was practically no opposition to the Authorized Version, the translation of the Bible which was printed and distributed by the American Bible Society. The conspicuous exception was the Baptist Church, which prior to 1835 had coöperated with the national society. Baptist missionaries in India wanted the American Bible Society to give aid in the publication of the "Bengalee Scriptures," which translated the Greek word for "baptize" to the word meaning "immerse." The Board of Managers replied that if the request were granted, the translation of the Scriptures would exclude missionaries of other denominations. "It is not competent for the American Bible Society to assume any sectarian attitude favoring the denominational views of any particular church, either at home or abroad," was the statement. The Baptist Church then seceded from the Bible Society and organized the American and Foreign Baptist Bible Society; but a considerable portion of the Baptist denomination remained in the older society.

The principles on which the British and Foreign Bible Society was formed excluded the circulation of the Apocrypha; but in view of revolutionary changes in the countries of Europe and of Latin America, and in recognition of the fact that Roman Catholics preferred the Catholic version of the Bible, which contained the apocryphal books, it was decided to depart from the orthodox procedure. Immediately the lawfulness of circulating the "uninspired relic" was challenged and a long and anxious discussion followed, with the result that the British and Foreign Bible Society resolved henceforth to distribute in all languages the "sacred canon" exclusively.

Following the example of its great British prototype, the Managers of the American Bible Society procured plates for the Catholic Bible to be distributed among the peoples of the new Latin American republics. Again following its example, the American society considered the propriety of distributing the Catholic Bible. They sought the advice of the "wise and prudent," and found among them a difference of opinion. "To perpetuate that harmony which now so happily prevails among their auxiliaries, and to prevent an evil which has shaken the mighty society of England, as with the heavings of an earthquake, your board has with great unanimity resolved, that no book containing the Apocrypha shall henceforth be issued from your Depository." Thus read the Twelfth Annual Report of the American Bible Society (1828).

The Managers made efforts to ascertain how far the Protestant version of the Bible could be circulated in Spanish America, and the information was not encouraging. However, the Managers anticipated great moral changes in the emancipated nations of that hemisphere, following in the train of their political reform and the progess of free inquiry. With an unshackled press and the multiplication of schools, it was believed that the time was not distant when the Ruler of Nations would cause the Catholic version of the Scriptures to be analyzed, its spurious parts to be rejected, and the inspired portions to be circulated widely.

On his visit to New Orleans in 1814, Samuel J. Mills learned that the French inhabitants of that city were happy to receive the New Testament in their native language. The Roman Catholic bishop would have no part in the distribution of the copies; but he interposed no objection, because he preferred to have the Protestant version in the possession of the people rather than to have them remain entirely ignorant of the Sacred Scriptures. In 1821, however, a letter from the secretary of the Louisiana Bible Society contained the information that the Catholic priests in the state had not concurred willingly in circulating the Protestant version of the New Testament which had been sent out; but they would cheerfully aid in the distribution of De Sacy's French version. Few among the Spanish inhabitants could read, but those who could were willing to accept the Catholic Spanish New Testament of Father Scio, which had been "most properly printed for their use" by the American Bible Society.

A letter to the American Bible Society from John C. Brigham, dated at Valparaiso, Chile, in 1825, stated that the time had come when the priests, though they might not encourage, would not forbid the people to read the Bible. Priests had repeatedly told him that the people ought to read the Scriptures. And in the following year came a letter addressed to the assistant secretary of the American Bible Society from a Catholic priest in Cuba thanking him for Bibles and New Testaments which had been sent to him. The priest promised to do all he could to introduce the Bible in the schools.

An agent of the British and Foreign Bible Society in 1825 wrote from Bogota, Colombia, about the organization of a Bible Society in that city. The project was discussed in meetings held in the chapel of the university, which was the principal Dominican convent in the city. The rector of the university and the prior of the convent were warm friends and supporters of the movement. Priests and academic men were on both sides, but the motion to organize the society was carried unanimously.

The same agent reported from Mexico in 1828 that for the first time in his tour and residence in Spanish America he met with open opposition and a formal attempt to prohibit the sale of the Scriptures. Writers of articles in newspapers impugned the free use of the Scriptures by all classes without note or comment; and they also protested against what they called a mutilated Bible—without the Apocrypha. Other articles in the same papers recommended the reading of the Scriptures in their "unadorned, uncommented simplicity and force." With one exception the articles on both sides of the question were written by priests. In one city the agent dined twice in a Dominican convent and was kindly treated by the friars, some of whom bought Bibles.

In the Thirteenth Annual Report of the American Bible Society (1829) it was reported that in one diocese in Mexico an ecclesiastical decree had been issued against the sale or distribution of any Bible unless accompanied by the Catholic notes. In the preamble of the decree it was stated that "Bible societies (meaning the British and Foreign and the American) were endeavoring to propagate the lamentable sentiments of the Protestant sects; namely, that the only rule of faith is the Bible, interpreted by each one according to his own judgment; a principle directly opposed to that laid down by the holy Council of Trent, by which it was determined that the living voice of the church should settle the meaning of the Scriptures."

The revolutions of 1848, which were directed against Metternich and his satellites and which put the pope in flight and exile, gave hope to the supporters of the American Bible Society that eventually the Bible, without note or comment, might be placed in the hands of every individual of "our ruined race." In France, in the states of Italy, and even in "intolerant Austria" the way had been prepared for putting the Bible in the hands of the people without effective opposition from the "bigoted tools of a corrupt priesthood."

The American Bible Society was the instrument of Protestantism in which the laity, appropriately, assumed the major role in bringing the Gospel to people of every race and creed, Christian and non-Christian, in every land. It was a powerful leaven. In her novel *The Minister's Wooing*, first published in 1859, Harriet Beecher Stowe put her own words into the mouth of Madame de Frontignac, a Roman Catholic, who said to Mary whom she found reading the Bible: "That is a beautiful book, and to read it all by one's self must be lovely. I cannot understand why it should be dangerous; it has not injured you."

SIXTEEN

THE AMERICAN SUNDAY SCHOOL UNION

THE inception of the American Sunday school dates from the closing years of the eighteenth century, when Robert Raikes of Gloucester, England, established the first Sunday school that suggests the institution that became an integral part of American Christianity. From meager beginnings on the eve of the nineteenth century, by the beginning of the third decade the number of Sunday schools had increased to the extent that associations for promoting and supporting them had taken form in a number of cities, and a publication program had already been launched. As in the case of the American Bible Society and the American Tract Society and their prototypes and auxiliaries, the American Sunday school was indebted to England for example, inspiration, and aid. The London Religious Tract Society and the American Sunday School Union coöperated in a common effort to propagate the doctrines of a common salvation in the same language by publishing identical manuscripts. The Sunday School Union, which was established in London in 1803, set the example by publishing lessons, primers, hymnbooks, tracts, catechisms, and instructions for teachers.

The organization of a national society which became known as the American Sunday School Union was effected in May, 1824, a year which marked the seventh anniversary of the Philadelphia Sunday and Adult School Union which, after it had transferred its funds, books, and other publications to the new organization, ceased to exist. Previously, in 1820, the Religious Tract Society of Philadelphia, which was instituted in 1815, had transferred its publications—printing and sale—to the Philadelphia Sunday and Adult School Union.

The establishment of the American Sunday School Union marked another achievement in the field of popular education and it registered another triumph of religious toleration over sectarianism and sacerdotalism and excessive orthodoxy. It was a laymen's movement, and as such made a contribution to democracy in education, secular and religious. By constitutional provision no clergyman could ever be an officer or manager of the society. The union embraced Baptists, Episcopalians, Methodists, Presbyterians, Moravians, Dutch Reformed, Congregationalists, Lutherans, Friends, German Reformed, and others.

The first grand principle of our association is Union—that as a society we recognize the existence of various evangelical denominations only so far as to avoid their points of difference—that there is no representation of them, as such, in our body, nor of us, in theirs. . . . By this cooperation nothing is relinquished, nothing is ever modified which pertains to denominational peculiarities. . . . It is only in their modification that conflicting opinions arise. We are in no sense opposed to denominational associations; nor do we see anything in this to excite hostility or alarm.

In line with this official statement of policy, the American Sunday School Union sponsored an ambitious publication policy. The publications were militantly Protestant and contained nothing incompatible with the various creeds of evangelical churches, which made it possible to set up schools in communities where no single denomination was strong enough to support a school but where several denominations were represented. The success of the experiment in union among Christians is indicated in the Eighth Annual Report of the American Sunday School Union (1832). Professor S. S. Schmucker of Gettysburg Theological Seminary, an institution of the General Synod of the Lutheran Church, offered a resolution expressing confidence in the principles and efficiency of the American Sunday School Union. It was seconded by a minister of the Moravian Church.

Men in many walks of life and of wide experience taught Sunday school classes. Men who had attained high distinction in community, state, and nation gave of their time to instruct children, youths, and adults. Among them were governors, members of Congress and of state legislatures, judges, lawyers, mayors, presidents of colleges and universities, and professors. Chief Justice Marshall served as vice-president of the American Sunday School Union. William Henry Harrison for several years taught a class in a humble Sunday school; and the Sunday before he left Ohio for Washington to become President of the United States, he met his Bible class as usual. The list of vice-presidents of the American Sunday School Union in 1832–33 contained the names of Arthur Tappan of New York, Timothy Dwight of New Haven, Gerrit Smith of Petersborough, New York, Theodore Frelinghuysen of New Jersey, William Wirt of Baltimore, Felix Grundy of Nashville, James G. Birney of Alabama, and John McLean, Associate Justice of the Supreme Court.

Supplementary to, or a part of, the Sunday schools, were the Bible classes which were usually taught by the pastor of the congregation and sometimes by a qualified layman. Robert Baird, who wrote in 1855, knew of pastors in country churches who had no fewer than five hundred persons in one Bible class. In some churches there were separate classes for men and women.

Sunday schools furnished excellent opportunities for women to serve churches, communities, and the nation. The early years of the American Sunday School Union produced several publications in the interest of mothers. Among them were the *Mother's Magazine*, published monthly in New York, and the *Christian Family Magazine and Children's Journal*, also published in New York. Then there were Maternal Societies which met once a week or fortnightly for the purpose of conversing on the subject of bringing up children, for the reading of appropriate literature, and for Bible reading and devotions.

At the meeting of the American Sunday School Union in Boston, on May 29, 1844, the Reverend Joel Parker of Philadelphia discoursed on the "safe and useful action" afforded women by the operations of the society. He lamented that in the great increase of lay action in the church, women had sometimes been drawn into improper positions and induced to hope for usefulness in addressing popular assemblies. The Sunday school, he said, gives woman an opportunity for exerting her heaven-born influence in a way altogether congenial to her character and to the condition in which God has placed her. She has a stronger sympathy with the children than the other sex. The speaker alluded to the fact that the Roman Catholic Church had established religious houses to call forth female influence; but he avowed that the Sunday school was better than a nunnery as a means of directing female influence. Through the Sunday school thousands of Protestant women had taken the veil and had the happiness of instilling religious instruction into the minds of children.

Parker's tribute to women and his appraisal of their "proper" sphere of usefulness was prompted by the increasing number of women who spoke plainly about their rights and urged their sisters to join with them in demanding equal rights with men. Some of them rejected Paul's admonition that women should keep silence and argued that if the apostle had lived in their day, instead of eighteen hundred years earlier, he would have given proper recognition to women's ability.

Four years before Parker's address, Horace Bushnell, whose heresy on scriptural doctrine was offensive to his brethren in the Congregational ministry in Hartford, preached an "orthodox" sermon on American politics. He was led to inquire what part was proper to the women of the land in political strifes. It was worth noticing, he said, that of the two women most conspicuous in the history of the Lord's trial scene, Pilate's wife, who stayed at home, gave him some sound advice which it had been well for him to follow; while the busy maid who went out made an apostle lie and swear as vilely as the worst man could. Bushnell thought it would not take many years of rough publicity to make ladies mere women and abolish the delicate respect which men yielded to them. He said he would have remained silent on the subject but for the revolution which was beginning to appear in the manners of the female sex in certain sections of the country. "Perhaps I am unreasonably anxious," he said, "but if that revolution is to go on as it has begun, it will certainly destroy some of the most precious and best influences we have left. Do save us one half of society free of the broils and bruises and arts of demagogy. . . . God made the woman to be a help for man, not to be a wrestler with him. . . . But if to all our present powers of strife and faction we are to add a race of factious women, there will not be left enough of feeling and rest to make life tolerable or allow virtue to breathe."

The American Sunday School Union immediately embarked on an ambitious publication program; and in keeping with the instructions to its missionaries and agents to avoid all controversy and partiality to any denomination, it was stipulated that the Committee of Publication should consist of twelve members from at least four different denominations, and not more than three members from any one denomination.

In addition to periodical literature, scores of cheap little tracts and books, from eight to fifty pages in size, were prepared for young people. A *Sunday-School Hymn Book* was an early publication; and shortly after the Civil War appeared the *Scholar's Budget of Stories and Anecdotes*. This volume of one hundred and twenty-eight pages contained articles, poems, and stories reprinted from the *Youth's Companion, Blackwood's Magazine, New York Observer, Christian Witness, Sabbath School Treasury, Sunday School Friend, Sabbath School Messenger, Sunday School Journal, Mothers' Journal, Christian Intelligencer, The Presbyterian,* and *Religious Souvenir*. Some of the books were translated into German and French, and donations of books were made to missionaries in countries like India, Palestine, Burma, and the Hawaiian Islands.

The major objective of the American Sunday School Union was to place the open Bible in the hands of the rising generation. In the words of a speaker at the meeting of the Union in 1844, the Bible was opened wide in the broad sunlight, so that all mankind might decide for themselves what the Lord required them to believe and do. The American Bible Society donated thousands of copies of the Scriptures to the Union for purposes of gratuitous distribution; and at an early meeting the Board of Managers resolved to obtain the necessary supply of Bibles and Testaments from the Bible Society.

By a resolution adopted in May, 1830, the American Sunday School Union became pledged to direct its efforts chiefly to the establishment of Sunday schools in the Mississippi Valley. The appraisal of conditions in that vast territory, and the statement of problems confronting the churches and missionaries, were identical with appraisals and statements presented to the American Home Missionary Society and the American Tract Society. In 1833 the Report made to the Board by the Committee on Missions and Agencies stressed the state of education in the West as another argument for continuing to prosecute the work of the American Sunday School Union. The Report stated that with the exception of Ohio, where an excellent system of common schools had recently been commenced, nothing deserving notice had been attempted by legislative authority to promote education in common schools, excepting to lay the foundation, in some cases, of school funds. It lamented the fact that tens of thousands had grown up, and tens of thousands were growing up, without knowing how to read. The report recommended that Sunday schools be established as widely as possible in order to remedy the evil in some measure. Sunday schools would give to hundreds of adults the opportunity of learning to read, and the libraries connected with them would exert a wholesome influence upon parents and children by stimulating an appetite for reading and by diffusing knowledge.

Within a period of three years after the adoption of the resolution had pointed to its activity in the West, more than four thousand Sunday schools were instituted. Through the generosity of a few citizens of Albany, New York, four thousand copies of the *Temperance Recorder*, a periodical published by the New York Temperance Society, were made available for gratuitous circulation. During the years many reports from the West showed how the American Sunday School Union stepped in to establish Sunday schools before there was a settled ministry and congregations to support them.

On the delicate subject of slavery the missionaries and agents of the American Sunday School Union were instructed to abstain from all remarks. This may explain in part why the Board received from various sources calls to vigorous activity in the South. The Union responded in 1833 by resolving to endeavor to plant and to sustain for five years Sunday schools in every neighborhood, where they were desired by the people, within the boundaries of Maryland, Virginia, North Carolina, South Carolina, Georgia, Alabama, the District of Columbia, and the Territory of Utah. The new states and territories of the South were included in the resolution pertaining to the field in the West.

The "union principle" in the American Sunday School Union called forth high praise from clergymen in diverse denominations; but there were also churchmen who reflected the attitude of priests and pastors in the established churches of Europe who distrusted the competence of laymen to give instruction in the fundamentals of the Christian religion without clerical supervision and censorship. For a number of reasons, the development of Sunday schools in Europe lagged far behind the movement in the United States.

In 1855 an article in the *Episcopal Recorder* leveled the charge against the American Sunday School Union that by its "taboo" of certain doctrinal distinctions, it compromised the doctrine of the Protestant Episcopal Church. The writer was disturbed because the Board of Publications was made up of twelve laymen and no clergyman; he was of the conviction that laymen who had no theological training lacked judgment in dealing with theological questions. They would not show proper respect for doctrinal differences, he wrote. He was aggrieved because the American Sunday School Union was controlled by churches which did not have proper respect for "holy orders" and the Episcopal tradition.

The great revival that swept over the country in 1857 and 1858 gave a great impulse to the Sunday school. At the close of the century the enrollment in Sunday schools was over twelve million, almost one half of the Sunday school population of the world. The success of the Sunday schools is one obvious result of a free-church system in which the survival of churches hinged upon their success in attracting to their folds the youth of the land, whereas in the countries of Europe children were born into membership of the established churches.

The free-church people in Europe heard how much the Sunday school had done for the American children; and in many parishes they set up schools patterned after those in America. Sunday school papers and literature were filled with stories about the wonderful land in the West; and many tracts were translations of the publications of the American Sunday School Union. Many of the children who read these tracts and papers were later to seek their fortunes in the American Republic, so eloquently described in letters from America as the "Land of Canaan."

SEVENTEEN

THE OBSERVANCE OF THE SABBATH

A COMPETENT student of his own time wrote in 1855 that there was no subject on which American Christians were more happily united than that of the proper observance of the Sabbath. He found that every state in the Union had made laws in favor of proper observance of the Lord's day, because the whole economy proceeded on the principle that America was a Christian country and because the courts had pronounced Christianity to be "part and parcel of the laws of the Land." He said that he uttered the language of every American Christian when he said: "Woe to America when it ceases to be a Sabbath respecting land."

The testimony of two famous contemporaries of Robert Baird, who wrote these words, may be cited in corroboration. Harriet Beecher Stowe wrote that there was something almost preternatural in the sense of stillness and utter repose which the Sabbath day brought with it in those early days. The absolute rest from earthly employment, the withholding even of conversation from temporal things, marked it off from other days. "To the truly devout the effect was something the same as if the time had been spent in heaven."

Horace Bushnell who, like Mrs. Stowe, spent his early life in Connecticut, related that when he was a lad he was dispatched one wintry Saturday afternoon to bring home a few bushels of apples engaged of a farmer a mile distant. The careful and exact man looked first at the clock, then out of the window at the sun, and turning to him said that he could not measure out the apples in time, that Saturday, for him to get home before sundown. Therefore, he would have to come again on Monday. Those were the days when men's lives went by their consciences, as their clocks did by the sun, said Bushnell. "It is more than respectable—it is sublime." The New England Sabbath always began at sunset on Saturday night and ended at the next sunset; and the school tasks and sewing and secular reading, which were as strictly prohibited on Saturday evening as on Sunday, were allowed on Sunday evening.

Horace Bushnell's letter written to his wife from Cuba in February, 1855, presents a striking contrast: "You can hardly imagine anything more desolate than a Sunday here on this island. . . . Work, work all day and night; no church, no religion visible by any sign but tithing. How different from the hallowed peace and the almost heavenly riches of our own Christian Sabbath!"

Among the first tracts published by the American Tract Society were those bearing the following titles: "On the Lord's Day"; "Remember the Sabbath Day, to Keep it Holy"; "The Sabbath a Blessing to Mankind." These tracts taught that a Sabbath well spent was followed by a prosperous week; for it is the "blessing of the Lord that maketh rich." "And has not God frequently manifested his anger against Sabbath breakers? How many have perished in the midst of their amusements, and have been suddenly called to the bar of God while engaged in actual rebellion against him!" Blot out the Sabbath, and no longer will the salutary lessons of the Bible lead ungodly men to repentance and salvation.

Educators, clergymen, lawyers, and businessmen stressed the instructional side of the Sabbath through preaching and Bible-reading. Mark Hopkins, president of Williams College, in a sermon before the American and Foreign Sabbath Union in May, 1847, stated that the Sabbath is God's institution for training the moral nature of man. It has an important bearing on the purity of the public conscience, he said. "It is his appointed school day for the race. It is very much from its recognition of the Christian Sabbath, that our government is known as a Christian government."

Home missionaries and colporteurs reported that profanity and immorality were prevalent on the frontier and that there was lack of respect for the Sabbath. For example, a missionary wrote from Trumbull County, Ohio, in 1808 to the Connecticut Missionary Society that the due observance of the Sabbath was a subject upon which he had frequently insisted, both in public and private; and Peter Cartwright, during the period of his residence in the Green River country in southern Kentucky, found that Sunday was a day set apart for hunting, fishing, horse-racing, card-playing, balls, dances, and all kinds of jollity and mirth.

On the other hand, there are records to show that there were Sabbatarians on the frontier. The records of the Congregational Church in Madison, Ohio, in 1816, contain the following entry: "This church considers the collecting of hay or grain on the Sabbath; attending to any part of the business of making sugar; the visiting of friends, except in cases of sickness; the prosecuting of journeys on that day, without special necessity, a violation of Christian duty." Among the articles of faith of the Congregational Church at Du Page, Cook County, Illinois, adopted in 1833, was the belief that the first day of the week is the Christian Sabbath and is to be sanctified by an holy resting all day, even from such worldly employments and recreations as are lawful on other days. At the annual meeting of the Illinois Congregational Association in 1836 it was resolved that it was the duty of all men, and especially all friends of the Redeemer, to refrain from traveling and all unnecessary business on the Sabbath, and in all respects to abstain from the heinous sin of Sabbath-breaking. It was further resolved that capitalists holding property in railroads, stages, and steamboats by which the Sabbath was desecrated were guilty of violating the spirit of the Fourth Commandment.

The advent of the railroad was most disconcerting to the Sabbatarians, because traveling on the Lord's day was an especially corrupting snare of Satan. In 1854 Thomas Beals, a devout member of the Congregational Church in Canandaigua, New York, told his grandchildren that "they used to be more strict about Sunday than they are now." He related how he had to go to Geneva one Saturday morning in the stage and expected to come back in the evening, but an accident delayed the stage until Sunday morning. He told the stage driver to leave him at the door of the church, which he entered. The next day he heard that he was to come before the minister and the deacons to explain why he had broken the Fourth Commandment. When he got to the meeting, the minister asked him what he had to say, whereupon he explained about the accident and asked them to read a verse from the eighth chapter of the Gospel of John, before they made up their minds what to do to him. The verse was "He that is without sin among you, let him first cast a stone at her." They all smiled, and the minister dismissed the meeting.

On April 4, 1843, the American and Foreign Sabbath Union was organized in Boston. Justin Edwards served as secretary of the new organization and traveled extensively, delivering sermons on Sundays and addressing national, state, and local Sabbath conventions, state legislatures, college and seminary students, and public meetings, besides preparing literature.

On November 27, 1844, a National Sabbath Convention was held at Baltimore, attended by about seventeen hundred delegates from eleven states, at which John Quincy Adams, former president of the United States, presided. Resolutions were adopted, expressing the sense of the sacredness, the divine authority, the obligations, and the benefits of the Sabbath. The convention adopted three public appeals for the true and proper observance of the Sabbath, addressed, respectively, To the People of the United States; To Canal Commissioners; and To Directors of Railroads.

The reports presented to the American and Foreign Sabbath Union by Justin Edwards during the seven years of his activity radiated optimism. The transportation of mails on Sunday had been discontinued on many routes and about forty railroad companies, including about four thousand miles of track, had stopped the running of trains on that day. "The communities through which they pass, and whose right to the stillness and quiet of the day had for years been grossly violated by the screaming and rumbling of cars in time of public worship, are now free from the nuisance, and are permitted to enjoy their rights and privileges without molestation." Laborers, in many cases, refused to work on the Sabbath, he said, because they viewed it as a degradation to be singled out from the rest of the community and obliged to labor when others were at rest. They found it hurtful to themselves and their families. Stockholders, directors, distinguished merchants, and civilians had expressed the conviction that it would promote the welfare of all if stage coaches, steamboats, trains, and canalboats ceased to run on Sunday.

There is a growing conviction, founded upon experience and observation, that property and life are more safe under the care of those who keep the Sabbath, than under the care of those who violate it; and that the one class are more likely to be blessed and to be a blessing, even in this world, than the other. As the principles and facts become known, all see new evidence that "the Sabbath was made for man" and that in the keeping of it, according to the will of God, there is great reward.

Reference has been made to the *Sabbath Manual* which was published coöperatively by the American Tract Society and the American and Foreign Sabbath Union and was widely distributed. Justin Edwards prepared "Permanent Sabbath Documents," five in number, which had extensive circulation in both England and the United States and were regarded as a standard work on the subject. These publications considered the ends for which the Sabbath was appointed and the reasons why it should be kept; the change from the seventh to the first day of the week; the Sabbath as a family institution; the proper mode of keeping the Sabbath as prescribed in the Scriptures; and more than a hundred facts illustrating the blessedness of keeping the day holy and the folly and sin of rebelling against God by profaning the Sabbath.

In considering the change from the seventh to the first day of the week, the author stated that after Christ's resurrection, when He became the headstone of the corner, He no longer went into the synagogue or any other place of worship, not even meeting His disciples on the seventh day; but on the first day He met them from time to time with abundant blessings.

Immigrants from Catholic and Lutheran countries of Europe had difficulty in understanding why Christmas and certain other church holidays were ignored in a country which kept the Sabbath holy. The first Christmas spent in America was for many emigrants from Germany, Sweden, Norway, and Denmark the dreariest day of their lives. In New England school was kept and stores were open on Christmas day. Parents told their children that nobody knew when Christ was born, and that there was nothing in the Bible to indicate the time for celebrating Christmas. In some homes, usually on Thanksgiving day or at New Year's, there was an interchange of presents, which had been prepared or purchased in secrecy and were opened in the presence of the family. As the years of the nineteenth century marched on— even before the Civil War—elderly folks told their grandchildren that when they were young, nobody observed Christmas, but that they always kept Thanksgiving. Schools and academies had Christmas trees laden with gifts. In *Poganuc People,* Dolly, the little daughter of the minister of the Presbyterian meeting-house, had never heard of Christmas, when the hired girl said to her: "Your papa ain't a 'piscopal, and he don't believe in keeping none of them 'ere Prayer-Book days— Christmas, nor Easter, nor nothin'."

Theodore Parker, the Boston radical, helped to organize an Anti-Sabbath convention which met in his Melodeon in 1848. In a sermon preached at the Melodeon on Sunday, January 30, 1848, he presented "Some Thoughts on the Most Christian Use of Sunday." He contrasted the use of the day in Catholic countries and in Protestant countries on the continent of Europe, where people flocked to church in the morning, but devoted the afternoon and evening to society and amusements of various kinds. Even the theaters were open. The Puritans, he said, went to the other extreme. "We think their mode of keeping Sunday is unholy; they, that ours is Jewish and Pharisaical." He made a plea for common sense in the observance of the day, and would remove the day from bigotry and superstition. "I would use the Sunday for Religion in the wide use of that word; use it to promote Piety and Goodness, for humanity, for science, for letters, for society. I would not abuse it by impudent license on the one hand, nor by slavish superstition on the other." He referred to the thirty thousand Catholics in Boston, twenty-five thousand of them probably too ignorant to read any book with pleasure or profit. In Ireland amusement was part of their Sunday service. Is it Christian in us by statute to interdict them from their recreation, he asked.

The Anti-Sabbatarians who met in the Boston convention objected to the penal laws that had been enacted to compel observance of Sunday which the American and Foreign Sabbath Union was proposing. Parker's speech before the convention was moderate and the resolutions adopted were in keeping with it. They pronounced the superstitious opinions pertaining to the origin of the observance of Sunday as a day devoted to religious purposes the chief obstacle to a still more profitable use of the day; but they considered it of great advantage to mankind to devote one day of the week to spiritual culture, rather than to see it devoted to labor or sport.

Sabbath observance became a political issue in states and communities where the immigrant vote was a factor. The Know Nothing party of the decade of the fifties was anti-Catholic and advocated political proscription of foreign-born citizens because of their alleged ignorance of American institutions. After the decline of the Know Nothing party, following the election of 1856, the two major parties tried to pin the stigma of nativism on the opposing party in order to win the votes of naturalized citizens. By virtue of the fact that in the northern states most of the former Know Nothings joined the ranks of the Republican party, Democratic newspapers and speakers "exposed" Republicans who had supported "Sunday laws" and complained that Republicans were temperance people and hated the Germans because they drank beer even on Sundays and sang and danced on the Lord's day. They shouted that if the Republicans had their way, a man could not cook meals on Sunday, or kiss his wife, or take a walk for pleasure.

The puritanical and pietistic strain among the Lutherans from the Scandinavian countries set them apart from the German Lutherans. The Swedish Lutheran immigrants were children of the second religious reformation in Sweden, which was just as radical as the one effected in the sixteenth century. The older reformation was German; the younger was Anglo-Saxon and, in the later stages, almost exclusively American. The protestants against the dry rot of Lutheran orthodoxy were sons of peasants and artisans, who drew their inspiration from the Scriptures as interpreted in sermons, songs, and tracts that breathed the practical religion of the American frontier. So far was the Church of Sweden from the ideal of the new reformers that even a pastor in its service could say in 1854: "The spiritual level in church and state is so low that conditions could hardly be worse if we were under the dominion of the papacy."

The continental reformers of the sixteenth century were not Sabbatarians. They were opposed to the application of the Fourth Commandment to the New Testament dispensation. The Augsburg Confession, which was adopted as the doctrinal basis of the Lutheran Church in 1530, contained the following paragraph in Article XXVII:

For those who judge that, by the authority of the Church, the observance of the Lord's day instead of the Sabbath day was ordained as a thing necessary do greatly err. Scripture has abrogated the Sabbath day; for it teaches that, since the Gospel has been revealed, all the ceremonies of Moses can be omitted. And yet, because it was necessary to appoint a certain day, that the people might know when they ought to come together, it appears that the Church designated the Lord's day for this purpose; and this day seems to have been chosen all the more for this additional reason, that men might have an example of Christian liberty, and might know that the keeping neither of the Sabbath, nor of any other day, is necessary.

The "ecclesiastical view" of the origin and obligation of the Lord's day is that it is not a Sabbath, or a successor to the Sabbath. It was not enjoined by the Fourth Commandment. The passages usually cited from the New Testament do not imply that it existed as an institution in the lifetime of most of the Apostles. This was the view held by many writers in the Church of England and was directly at variance with the Puritan conception of Sunday.

The Puritan version held that the observance of the Sabbath was enforced under the Jewish system and that the Old Testament was not contrary to the New Testament. Indeed, it was identical in all respects. It was admitted that the name "Sunday" was not found in Scripture, but there was a great deal about the Sabbath. Therefore, the Sabbath was to be enforced as a doctrine of Scripture. The theory that the essence of the Fourth Commandment was that one day in seven was to be kept holy disposed of the objection that the Sabbath was the seventh day. Nothing was made of the fact that the New Testament made a distinction between the Lord's day and the Sabbath. The Puritans preferred the appellation "Sabbath" because Sunday suggested heathenism.

"Sunday Sabbatarianism" was not officially sanctioned by the Church of England, nor did it pronounce in favor of the "ecclesiastical view." In the reign of Elizabeth in the last quarter of the sixteenth century Sunday was classed with other holidays, as it had been in Catholic countries. The fact that Sunday had been made coördinate with a crowd of saints' days and the like caused the people to rebel at the observance of so many days, and they became holidays that not even remotely suggested the religion of Christ and His disciples. The result was that in Catholic countries distinctions were not clearly drawn and the Lord's day was desecrated along with the rest. This explains in part why the Puritans in England and in America ignored Christmas day and saints' days, but kept the Lord's day holy and observed fast days and Thanksgiving day—a *sui generis* holy day.

The first Stuart king, who had already made himself unpopular with the Puritans, in 1618 issued the "Book of Sports" by which persons were allowed after church time on Sundays to indulge in athletic games and to engage in other pastimes. The document was to be read by clergymen in churches, but the order was not generally enforced. But the animus was there and it was augmented by Archbishop Laud who ordered a declaration in favor of Sunday sports to be read from every pulpit. Ministers who refused to conform with the archbishop's policy were either silenced or lost their livings.

The Puritans' reverence for the Sabbath was another manifestation of their veneration for the Holy Bible, of which the Old Testament, as an integral part and inspired by Jehovah, contributed to their heroic resolve to establish the kingdom of God in the New England wilderness.

The fruits of their resolution were commented on by an English Methodist who visited the United States in 1856. He found that the Sabbath was much better observed in New York than in London or Liverpool. The streets were quieter, pleasure-seekers were fewer, and purchases, if made, were more concealed from public observation. Among all classes more reverent attention seemed to be paid both to religion and to its ministers.

EIGHTEEN

THE TEMPERANCE MOVEMENT

THE American Temperance Society was organized in 1826, and its work was carried on the wings of the religious and humanitarian movements whose objectives were identical, whose methods were similar, and whose list of members revealed their common interests. With few exceptions, the Protestant churches, both as to individual members and corporate action, joined the temperance crusade. In Europe, on the contrary, the temperance agitation was associated with Methodism, sectarianism, and charlatanism, and was frowned upon by the upper and educated classes, including the clergy in the established churches. On the continent of Europe the temperance movement was looked upon as an Anglo-Saxon importation—a by-product of nonconformity. It is true that the methods of temperance workers were of an entirely different spiritual structure from that of state churches; and churchmen held aloof from a movement in which they could not participate wholeheartedly. They condemned extreme statements made by certain orators and objected to their alleged loose and unsound interpretation of certain Scripture passages. Moreover, worldly and sometimes dissolute parish pastors and priests felt the sting of invective directed against them by crusaders. Robert Baird's book, dealing with the history of temperance societies in the United States and with temperance movements in certain countries of Europe, was translated into several languages in the decade of the thirties, as were other books, sermons, and tracts before and after that time. Some of the reformers condemned the use of tobacco in any form, and even the use of coffee and tea.

The American concept of freedom was fundamentally different from the negative attitude of reformers, liberals, and radicals in Europe who conceived of freedom as the absence of restraint. Liberty sometimes took the form of license and the right of the individual to follow his natural impulse. As has been stated, the Puritans made fewer concessions to human nature than did the men who had taken holy orders in the sacramental and liturgical churches. In general, this was true of dissenters and nonconformists in every land. American freedom implied a moral self-determination working in harmony with law, order, and authority. American reformers, temperance and others, took the position that freedom rests upon moral groundwork and individual self-control.

By way of contrast, a communication from a missionary in the West written in 1857 may be cited. In the Thirty-first Annual Report of the American Home Missionary Society the communication bore the caption "Red Republican Liberty." The missionary wrote that the "infidel" Germans were assuming a lawless attitude. The village authorities required that all saloons be closed on the Sabbath. The Germans replied: "We sold ardent spirits under an arbitrary government, when we pleased, and this is a free country, and we are not to be controlled in the matter." They have hoisted their red-republican flag, he continued, and constructed a bower near the village, where, with their barrel of beer, they spend the Sabbaths.

The prevalence of excessive and moderate drinking in the first half of the nineteenth century is abundantly attested by a variety of sources, notwithstanding letters written by immigrants to relatives and friends who, by contrast with their native lands, found America almost a temperance paradise. After a residence of four years in southeastern Iowa, an immigrant testified in 1848 that he had "dined in hundreds of homes," and had "yet to see a whiskey bottle on the table." In 1850 an immigrant who wrote from Illinois found the advancement of temperance almost unbelievable. In a midwestern town of about two thousand inhabitants one had to be well acquainted in order to purchase whiskey or strong wine. "From this incident you may judge of the state of temperance in American cities," he confided. Making allowance for the enthusiasm of crusaders and of immigrants who had been freed from the class distinctions of an old-world society, and knowing that the map of mid-nineteenth-century America was dotted with thousands of oases, it is nevertheless a fact that America furnished a striking contrast to most countries of Europe.

Lyman Beecher, who delivered temperance sermons in America and England, in his early ministry in New England found the drinking habits of his brethren in the ministry shocking, as related in his Autobiography. At the ordination of a certain minister in Plymouth, Massachusetts, in 1812, the broad sideboard in his home was covered with decanters and bottles and sugar and pitchers of water. All the various kinds of liquor then in vogue were served. When the Consociation arrived, there was a round of drinks; also before and after services. There was a decanter of spirits on the dinner table to help digestion, and gentlemen partook of it through the afternoon and evening. The sideboard, with the spillings of water and sugar and liquor, looked and smelled like the bar of a "very active grog shop." None of the Consociation were drunk, but there was at times considerable hilarity. When they had done drinking, and had taken pipes and tobacco, in less than fifteen minutes there was "such a smoke you couldn't see," and there was a maximum of hilarity. "They were not old-fashioned Puritans," commented Beecher. He recollected that some animadversions were made at the time by people on the amount of liquor consumed, for "the tide was swelling in the drinking habits of society."

At the next ordination Beecher attended, a short time after, the scenes at the first were reënacted, followed by still louder murmurs from the society at the quantity and expense of the liquor consumed.

These two meetings excited in Beecher alarm and indignation; and he silently took an oath before God that he would not attend another ordination of that kind. As chairman of a committee subsequently appointed (1812) he brought in a report, which he regarded as the most important paper he ever wrote. The report in part read as follows:

The General Association of Connecticut, taking into consideration the undue consumption of ardent spirits, the enormous sacrifice of property resulting, the alarming increase of intemperance, the deadly effect on health, intellect, the family, society, civil and religious institutions, and especially in nullifying the means of grace and destroying souls, recommend . . .

The recommendations included appropriate discourses on the subject by all ministers of the association; the abstention from use of liquor at ecclesiastical meetings; the abstention of members of churches from the use and sale of ardent spirits; the substitution, by farmers, mechanics, and manufacturers, of palatable and nutritious drinks for alcoholic drinks; the circulation of tracts and sermons on the subject; and the formation of voluntary associations to aid the civil magistrate in the execution of law.

Individuals, congregations and larger ecclesiastical units took similar action. The General Assembly in 1812 recommended that all ministers in the Presbyterian Church deliver discourses on the sin and mischief of intemperate drinking. In 1816 the Synod of Pittsburgh, recognizing that the use of ardent spirits produced sickness, poverty, and wickedness, destroyed health and reputation, introduced discord into families and larger communities, enervated the strong and changed many of the wise into idiots, resolved that ardent spirits ought never to be used, except as medicine. It declared that the free and common use of alcohol at the raising of buildings, military musters, weddings, and other public and social occasions was unnecessary and pernicious. In 1838 at a meeting of the Illinois Congregational Association it was resolved to unite with the friends of temperance in petitioning that it be made a legal offense in candidates for office to "treat in order to secure their election."

Missionaries in the West reported that interest in the cause was increasing; but they lamented that there was opposition from some members of Christian and Baptist churches. One report from Kingston, Tennessee, in 1834, placed the blame for the opposition chiefly on Hardshell Baptist ministers, who were engaged in making and selling whiskey and excited prejudice against the temperance cause by charging its friends and advocates with being hostile to civil liberty and having designs to destroy both church and state with temperance societies. The same men were opposed to Bible and tract societies. As the numbers of temperance adherents increased, ministers tried, often successfully, to get congregations to make the use of ardent spirits by members a subject of discipline.

Even before the organization of the American Temperance Society, tract societies and local and regional societies, composed of church members, promoted the abstinence from intoxicating drinks as a measure to increase the spread of the Gospel. Temperate drinking was also condemned because it would lead to intemperance and by example would tempt others to moderate indulgence.

The inception of the American Temperance Society dates from a meeting of a few individuals in 1825 to consider the question: "What shall be done to banish intemperance from the United States?" Correspondence with men interested in the cause followed; and at a meeting in Boston in January, 1826, a committee was appointed to draw up a constitution, to be presented at the adjourned meeting. At the appointed time, February 13, 1826, the constitution was adopted and the society was organized. Immediately a publication program was launched. It was fortunate for the American Temperance Society that Justin Edwards was induced to turn aside from his pastoral duties in Boston to take over the duties as General Agent and Secretary in the late summer of 1829. Edwards brought to the society the enthusiasm and experience of a man who in the discharge of his pastoral duties had seen the evils of intemperance, and had preached and written against it.

In 1832 Edwards wrote a "National Circular," addressed to the head of each family in the United States, of which tens of thousands of copies were issued coöperatively by the American Temperance Society and the American Tract Society. It was religious in character and issued a special appeal to women to join temperance societies, because their influence as mothers and sisters would count heavily with youths and children. Moreover, thousands of women have been doomed to the curse of having drunken husbands and rearing their children under the "withering influence of drunken fathers." The document urged people to take the pledge which was printed and read as follows:

We whose names are hereunto annexed, believing that the use of intoxicating liquor as a beverage is not only needless, but hurtful to the social, civil, and religious interests of men; that it tends to form intemperate appetites and habits; and that, while it is continued, the evils of intemperance can never be done away; do therefore agree that we will not use it, or traffic in it; that we will not provide it as an article of entertainment or for persons in our employment; and that, in all suitable ways, we will discountenance the use of it in the community.

The use of the pledge was explained in a pamphlet by Henry Ware, Jr., Professor of Pulpit Eloquence in Harvard University, entitled "The Combination Against Temperance Explained and Justified." It was originally delivered as an address before the Cambridge Temperance Society, March 27, 1832. The speaker brushed aside objections to taking the pledge on the ground that it contained a snare to the conscience by inducing the individual to act from unworthy motives. He argued that taking a pledge set a good example and would bring others to a like decision. It is your duty to pay your debts, he said, yet you do not hesitate to give a promissory note. It is your duty to be faithful to your wife; yet you did not refuse when you took her for better or worse to engage to be so. He was aware of the delicacy of the subject of abolishing the traffic in liquor, and knew the risk of hurting the feelings of men engaged in a business which, when they entered it, was considered as reputable as any other. All their habits of education and of life, their business, their interest, and their connections concur to blind them. Even John Newton, for some time after his character became Christian, failed to see that his employment in the slave-trade was in contradiction to his religious principles. The professor asserted that no man can think or act on Christian principle and at the same time make or sell the instrument of intoxication. For let him consider what it amounts to; employing his time, capital, and industry to prepare for use and offer for use that thing which has been proved to be the principal source of misery and crime in modern society; providing for men the convenient and tempting means of ruining their health and business, beggaring their families, sinking prematurely to a dishonorable grave, and entering eternity—with what a preparation!

Several tracts prepared by Edwards were published by the American Tract Society. By 1836, 325,000 copies of temperance tracts had been put into circulation; and efforts had been made to supply copies to ministers, lawyers, physicians, magistrates, government officials, teachers, educated young men, foreign missionaries, and distinguished philanthropists in all parts of the world. Copies of tracts were translated and distributed to emigrants in Europe. The National Temperance Manual was translated into several languages, including Spanish. Tract No. 176 of the American Tract Society series was entitled "The

Well-Conducted Farm" and exhibited the excellent results of total abstinence upon a large farm in the County of Worcester, Massachusetts. Tract No. 249 was an address on temperance delivered by Dr. Sewell, a well-known physician and an active member of the Methodist Church.

In May, 1833, a National Temperance Convention, called by the American Temperance Society, was held in Independence Hall, Philadelphia, at which four hundred delegates from temperance societies in twenty-one states were present. Jurists, physicians, statesmen, and others participated in an extended discussion of a resolution declaring that traffic in ardent spirits to be used as drink was morally wrong and ought to be universally abandoned. The resolution was adopted. So deeply impressed by the deliberations in such a distinguished body, in which men of all Christian denominations and political parties were interested, was the Honorable Stephen Van Rensselaer that he bore the expense of publishing one hundred thousand copies of the proceedings of the convention.

The American Congressional Temperance Society was organized on February 26, 1833. Assured of support from members of the Senate and House of Representatives, Edwards made a special trip to Washington with that objective. Among the senators who were interested in the cause were Webster, Grundy, and Ewing. Upon invitation, Edwards preached in the Capitol on the subject of temperance. At about the same time he attended a meeting of the members of the legislature of Massachusetts, when the Massachusetts Legislative Temperance Society was organized.

These activities indicate the scope of the work of the American Temperance Society and its affiliated societies. A long list of state temperance conventions and state and legislative societies could be compiled; and of course the coöperation by churches was perhaps the greatest single factor in the success of the movement.

The temperance movement was but one of the humanitarian and philanthropic reforms that were products of the enlightened public opinion of the time. Temperance, for example, was regarded as a powerful means for the prevention of crime. In his charge to the grand jury in the County of Worcester, Massachusetts, in 1832, Judge Solomon Strong emphasized the intimate connection between intemperance and crime. Go to our jails and penitentiaries, he said, and inquire of the inmates, severally, by what means they have been brought to such misery, and nine times out of ten you will hear substantially the same story: social or club drinking, excessive drinking, intoxication, fraud, fighting, the brothel, the jail, the state prison. "The utility of temperance, as a preventive of crime, is not left to theory alone. It is practically proved," he said.

One of the famous temperance orators, who began his work in the decade of the forties, was John B. Gough. He made thousands of addresses and induced countless thousands to sign temperance pledges; and his fame spread to Europe, where religious and temperance papers published his biography. At the age of twenty-five he was a confirmed drunkard and a victim of delirium tremens. As an actor he appeared as a keeper of a temperance house in a play entitled "Departed Spirits, or the Temperance Hoax," in which Lyman Beecher and other prominent temperance men were held up to ridicule. On one occasion while Gough was staggering along the street, a shabby-looking drunkard touched his shoulder, called him by name, and urged him to sign a temperance pledge. The stranger promised to introduce him to good friends who would help him to keep his good resolutions. At a temperance meeting Gough stood up and related what rum had done to him. In his own words, he said:

I related how I was once respected and happy, and had a home; but that now I was a houseless, miserable, scathed, diseased, and outcast from society. . . . In my palsied hands I with difficulty grasped the pen, and, in characters almost as crooked as those of old Stephen Hopkins on the Declaration of Independence, I signed the total abstinence pledge, and resolved to free myself from the inexorable tyrant—rum. . . . I felt that I was relieved from a part of my heavy load. . . . I had exerted a moral power which had long remained lying by, perfectly useless. The very idea of what I had done, strengthened and encouraged me.

The Washingtonian revival, which got under way at the beginning of the decade of the forties, increased the number of pledge-signers. "Experience meetings" were held in schoolhouses, churches, and halls all over the country, at which three or four reformed drunkards would testify. John B. Gough was especially effective in gaining converts and pledge-signers. It was said that he could "make an audience laugh

as much by wagging his coattails as some men can by talking an hour."
When he spoke at Pittsfield, Massachusetts, in November, 1847, under
the spell of enthusiasm a huge blank book, elegantly bound, was circulated by the committee for the signatures of the whole town to the
pledge. Several hundred names had been procured, when the volume
suddenly and forever disappeared.

Father Theobald Mathew left his field of work in Ireland to under-
take an extensive speaking tour of the United States at the beginning
of the fifth decade. It was said that he induced about five hundred
thousand Catholics to take the pledge. Joseph Crétin (1799–1857),
the first Roman Catholic bishop of St. Paul, Minnesota, was a strong
advocate of the temperance movement and a bitter foe of the frontier
saloon. He ordered the cathedral bell to be rung in approval when the
Minnesota legislature enacted a liquor law.

A temperance reformer whose fame was world-wide was Neal Dow,
the "father of the Maine law" which was adopted in June, 1851. The
text of this prohibitory measure was published in temperance papers
in the United States and in Europe, and quotations from Dow's
speeches were used to justify similar legislation in other states and
countries. Church bodies adopted resolutions indorsing the "Maine
law." Horace Greeley's *New York Tribune*, whose columns were open
to the exposition of a variety of reforms, in 1854 regarded the "Maine
law" as the great legislative antidote to the "fearful tendency of our
time to a deluge of pauperism."

The fruits of the temperance movement which became more and
more in evidence as the years of the nineteenth century moved along
were listed among others which caused pietists and puritans in many
lands to cast longing glances toward the New World and its free and
humanitarian institutions.

NINETEEN

THE CHURCH AND THE COMMUNITY

THE first settlers of New England fled from religious persecution, and they were determined that their children should never become the slaves of any hierarchy. The clergy, therefore, were rendered dependent for their support and influence on their merit and their services; and they have ever remained, not as in other countries, a separate order of men, but as the most useful of citizens, blending their feelings and interests with those of the rest of the community, partaking of their prosperity and enjoying their unalloyed respect.

These are the words of an oration by Andrew Dunlap, delivered at the request of the Republicans of Boston at Faneuil Hall on the Fourth of July, 1822. Making some allowance for the spell of the moment, it is true that in the United States clergymen and laymen met on a common level and coöperated, unlike Europe where the clergy were a privileged estate and managed things for themselves. It is also true that in colonial New England the ministers were dictatorial and exercised political influence in selecting certain officers; but their prerogatives were limited in contrast with churchmen in Europe. The words of Ophelia, spoken in Hamlet, Act I, Scene iii, apply to the time and place: "But, good my brother, do not, as some ungracious pastors do, show me the steep and thorny way to heaven, whilst, like a puff'd and reckless libertine, himself the primrose path of dalliance treads and recks not his own rede."

Unlike the clerical estate in Europe, which was chiefly recruited from the so-called better classes, the profession in America sprang from the soil and understood the people whom it served. Moreover, the education provided in the universities of Europe, which was more classical than religious, was not adapted to the high calling of parish pastors, whereas the American clergymen's education, with all its deficiencies, made them better pastors and preachers. There was no social gulf fixed between clergy and laity. Religion in America was democratized.

The first half of the nineteenth century, with which we are chiefly concerned, was still the "age of homespun," although ready-made clothing was on the market and was worn by the well-to-do, especially in the cities. It was the simplicity of life that caused people who lived through the Civil War and the Reconstruction period to think longingly of "those quiet, simple times, when there was not a poor person in the parish, and the changing glories of the year were the only spectacle." So wrote Harriet Beecher Stowe in 1876–77 when she was about sixty-six years old.

Horace Bushnell, in his delightful "Age of Homespun," called it a life of honesty and simple content and sturdy victory. Immoralities were much less frequent because people had less thought of adventure, less to do with travel and trade and money, and were closer to nature and the simple life of the home. A later generation has called them "small," he wrote, because they were too simple and rustic to have any conception of the big operations by which other men got their money without earning it, and lavished it all the more freely because it was not earned. Probably the man who was heard threshing in his barn of a winter evening by the light of a lantern would be seen driving his team the next day to draw a load of wood for a present to his minister. The housewife who haggled with the merchant over some small transaction would board the schoolteacher without recompense.

Mrs. Stowe thought it worthy of special notice that in a community where life was marked by a minute economy, where every board, nail, drop of paint, and shingle in house or barn was counted and estimated, the spontaneous growths of the soil were free to the earliest comer— chestnuts, hickorynuts, butternuts, grapes, strawberries, huckleberries, and cranberries. From the beginning of New England poor people, widows, and fatherless children eked out their living by selling nuts and fruits which the custom of the country allowed them to gather on other people's land. What a contrast with the country from which the Puritans came! There game laws and other restrictions deprived the poor of the bounties of nature. In New England the Puritans applied the spirit of the Mosaic law which commanded that something should be left to be gathered by the poor.

In the "age of homespun" the matter of dress had not become a yoke and a burden, wrote Mrs. Stowe. While they had before their eyes the query of Sacred Writ, "Can a maid forget her ornaments?"— they felt that there was no call to assist the maid in her meditations on that subject. Little girls were taught that to be neat and clean was the main beauty; and good mothers who had pretty daughters were very reticent of any remarks that might lead to personal vanity.

A competent student of American history, James Truslow Adams, awards high praise to the political wisdom of the people during the Revolutionary and Confederation period. He states that the newspaper articles and pamphlets inspired by the struggle over the ratification of the Constitution called forth a concentration of thought that could hardly be counted on in this latter day in a decision of the people. In the days when newspapers were scarce and the means of communication were limited, a book was an event and became a topic of conversation. As a rule pietists and puritans frowned on novel-reading as a subtle poison for the mind prepared by Satan. However, even the strictest parents permitted teen-age daughters to read the Waverley novels, *David Copperfield,* and Shakespeare's plays.

The wise in every generation know that it is unwise to occupy the mind or devote the energies to those things that tend to weaken the will and to befog principles of morality. The character of the performances on the English stage and the low estate of the actors were indelibly impressed on the Puritan tradition. Churchmen and educators in the United States could cite devastating indictments of the English stage by men of note, notably by Jeremy Collier, a non-juring clergyman, who near the close of the seventeenth century wrote *A Short View of the Immorality and Profaneness of the English Stage,* and Colley Cibber, who in 1740 published his *Apology* and stated that the immoralities of the stage had been creeping up ever since the time of Charles II, until nothing could be too low for it. It was not until the Restoration period that women were actors on the stage; parts of women were played by boys or "effeminate men," he wrote. Cibber remembered the time when ladies were afraid of venturing bare-faced to a new comedy, until they had been assured they might do so; or if their curiosity was too strong for their patience, they took care, at least, to save appearances, and rarely came upon the first days of the performance except in masks.

The following quotation from Pollock's *Course of Time* states the puritan's position:

> The theatre was from the very first
> The favorite haunt of sin, though honest men,
> Some very honest, wise, and worthy men,
> Maintained it might be turned to good account;
> And so, perhaps, it might, but never was.
> From first to last it was an evil place,
> And now such things were acted there as made
> The devils blush.

In the winter of 1857–58 Mrs. Stowe made her first visit to a theater when she went to the National Theatre in Boston to see the stage performance of *Uncle Tom's Cabin*. In 1827 it was suggested to the mind of Justin Edwards in passing the Tremont Theatre in Boston, which was then under construction, "whether it is not the will of God that his people should agree together to pray that the building may be, as soon as the designs of infinite benevolence shall permit, consecrated as a temple for the worship of the living God" instead of a place in which multitudes would be ripened for perdition. He inquired of the secretary of the American Tract Society if it was too much for the Lord, in the course of no long period, to take possession of that theater, of Harvard College, of all Boston, and of the whole commonwealth.

The arguments against attending the theater mustered by pietists and Puritans both in England and the United States were strong. In the eighteenth century William Law, who was attracted to the Methodists and Quakers in England, wrote *The Absolute Unlawfulness of the Stage Entertainment Fully Demonstrated*. He asserted that there were just as strong arguments against the stage as any that could be urged against the worship of images, or any other corruption of the most corrupt religion. He alleged that the English playhouse was the sink of corruption and debauchery; that it was the general rendezvous of the most profligate of both sexes. The playgoer entertained his mind with extravagant thoughts, wild rants, blasphemous speeches, wanton amours, profane jests, and impure passions. He cited the authority of Scripture to affirm that "evil communications corrupt good manners." Let every man or woman who goes to a play, he said, ask themselves this question: Does it suit with their religion to act the parts that are there acted?

Hannah More, whose activity in behalf of the London Religious Tract Society and of the American Tract Society has been discussed, in her early life attended the theater and even appeared on the stage and wrote theatrical compositions. But she changed her mind. She said she wrote for the stage because she was led to entertain what she found was a delusive hope, that the stage, under certain regulations, might be converted into a school of virtue. She found that there almost inevitably runs through the whole web of the tragic drama a prominent thread of false principle. It is generally the leading object of the poet to erect a standard of honor in direct opposition to the standard of Christianity. Worldly honor is the very soul and spirit and life-giving principle of the drama. "There is a substantial difference between seeing and reading a dramatic composition. . . . It is the pageantry, the splendor of the spectacle, and even the show of the spectators, these are the circumstances which fill the theater, produce the effect, and create the danger."

Timothy Dwight, president of Yale College, voiced the sentiments of many fellow-Americans in *An Essay on the Stage: in which the Arguments in its Behalf, and those against it, are Considered; and its Morality, Character, and Effects Illustrated.* This essay of more than a hundred pages was published in 1824.

The teacher of morality whom God approves must himself be pure and holy. No clean thing can possibly come out of the unclean. The Yale president found in the Bible neither stage, nor stage minister, nor stage instruction. The scenes and phrases to be seen and heard in the theater on the subject of marriage, if exhibited at a private party, would fill every mind with disgust. Portrayal of crime and criminals, lust and passion, the liar, the thief, the drunkard does not cause offenders to amend base conduct. If a virtuous player be as rare a being as a white raven, we may hence infer that his profession has at least, in part, furnished coloring matter to dye its occupier. When a Christian attends or justifies stage exhibition, his departure from God is manifest; the prevalence of the unrenewed man in his heart seems so great, that little affection can be discovered in it.

Dwight admitted that recreation is necessary, perhaps, to all; but anything that engages the mind too much is unfit, in its nature, to amuse. It wearies and distresses, instead of invigorating the mind. The stage, on this very ground, is unfit for accomplishing the object of amusement. Its scenes of distress are such as to excite too strongly the passions and sympathies—they employ the mind too universally to give it relaxation. Stage audiences, though melted into tears at the sight of imaginary distress, discover no emotions of sympathy at the sight of the cottage of sorrow, the bed of anguish, or the house desolated by death. "Genuine sympathy denies relationship to those bastard spurious progeny of fiction," he said. "A life of perpetual amusement is a useless life—it yields no pleasure on review, but burdens its possessor, and is a public evil in the world."

The activity of college professors and presidents in Bible societies, tract societies, missionary movements, and temperance has already been noted, from which it appears that faculties were made up of religious men. Down to the end of the first half of the nineteenth century, at least, colleges, with few exceptions, were founded to promote the cause of Christian education. The baccalaureate sermon was a symbol of the religious and moral worth of a college education. The main function of a college was conceived to be to train the mind and to build character. Through its colleges and seminaries, the church provided facilities for the training of religious teachers. The day of specialization and vocational training had not dawned.

The character of education for men preparing for the ministry in American churches differed greatly from the formal education of ministers in the state churches of Europe. The fact that the pastoral office in Europe usually combined the duties of a clergyman and civil officer explains to some extent the characteristics of the men who were criticized by pietists and dissenters. Education was under the control of the church, and the teaching of religion was apt to be formal and lifeless, with heavy emphasis on dogma and doctrine. This was due in part to the lack of religious experience on the part of ministers and to the training they had received in the universities. They showed little interest in religious revivals, and many of them were actively hostile.

Before the establishment of theological seminaries was made possible by donations of philanthropists and by individual denominations, young men convinced of the "inner call," studied theology under an ordained pastor. In some cases the candidates resided in the home of the minister, and sometimes they boarded in homes near the parsonage. They had access to his library and their reading was directed and supervised by their tutor. For example, Lyman Beecher had at one time as many as fifty candidates at Litchfield, Connecticut, who were preparing themselves, under his direction, to enter academies and colleges. In frontier communities, almost without exception, the homes of ministers harbored young men in training for the ministry.

Education societies, supported by individual denominations or by bequests and donations from friends, gave stipends to enable men to prepare for the ministry. One of the first of these societies was the American Education Society, which was formed in Boston in 1816. For about fifteen years it published the *American Quarterly Register*.

The Charitable Collegiate Institution (Amherst College) was founded in 1821 by the people of the Connecticut Valley in the "conviction that the education of pious young men of the first talents is the most sure method of relieving our brethren, by civilizing and evangelizing the world." The president of Amherst College from 1823 to 1845, Heman Humphrey, in his inaugural address stated that "It is education that pours light into the understanding, lays up its golden treasures in the memory, softens the asperities of temper, checks the waywardness of passion and appetite, and trains to habits of industry, temperance, and benevolence." During the incumbency of Humphrey, seven hundred and sixty-five men graduated, of whom four hundred entered the ministry. He founded a society, the members of which pledged themselves to refrain from the use of alcoholic liquors, opium, and tobacco. More than three-fourths of the students took the pledge.

Upon the "defection" of Harvard from the faith, Andover Theological Seminary was founded in 1808. It was the forerunner of seminaries founded by denominations to supply the need for higher educational qualifications in the clergy. Undoubtedly through the years all too many men were ordained whose qualifications, spiritual and educational, left much to be desired, regardless of formal training or otherwise. On the other hand, it is easy to be unjustly critical of the clerical estate in American churches. Biographies and autobiographies of eminent clergymen, whose orthodoxy was unquestioned, reveal that their reading was broad, whether pursued in college, seminary, or in private study, and that there was no mental quarantine to prevent exposure to the products of men of different minds. For example, Justin Edwards, who was a student in Williams College from 1806 to 1810 and whose orthodoxy was above suspicion, read among other books, Bacon's *Essays,* Locke on the *Human Understanding,* Hume, Gibbon, Butler's *Analogy,* Jews' *Letters to Voltaire,* Montesquieu's *Spirit of Laws,* Blackstone's *Commentaries,* Addison's, Franklin's, and Priestley's *Works.*

On the frontier, where educational facilities were inadequate and the need for ministers was urgent, candidates were subjected to examination and were often found deficient and rejected. According to the minutes of the Transylvania Presbytery, dated April 9, 1806, a candidate produced a written discourse on John 3:36 which had been assigned to him, and it was found to be so defective that it was not accepted. The Presbytery, after having made "sufficient trial" of his qualifications, found that he did not possess the aptitude to teach and did not give promise of ever obtaining the degree of literary knowledge and distinctiveness of expression which would make him an edifying minister of the Gospel. So they decided not to continue his trials for the important office. In another case the Presbytery, after having heard an exegesis written by the candidate, were of the opinion that it did not embrace the main points contained in the subject. The candidate was also deficient in Latin and Greek.

At the first annual meeting of the Congregational Association of Illinois, on October 5, 1840, an interesting committee report was adopted. After laying down rules of procedure and qualifications for preachers of the Gospel, the report considered the case of an intelligent Christian man who should find himself cast among pagans with the Bible in his hands, and without any means of intercourse with the evangelical countries. If after a few months' residence he should find himself sufficiently acquainted with the language of those around him to enable him to give instruction in the Bible, and if he acquired the ability to speak in public, for him no ordination, no license, no examination would be a necessary preliminary to assuming the office of Christian preacher. He would be just as authorized to proclaim to those dying sinners the doctrines and invitations of the Gospel as if he had been consecrated by the hands of all the prelates and Presbyterians in Christendom.

Charles G. Finney would have agreed with the "doctrine" enunciated in this report. He avowed that it was a mistake for schools to require ministerial candidates to write sermons. Literary essays, he said, would not win souls. A man can never learn to preach except by preaching, he said. "Great sermons lead the people to praise the preacher. Good preaching leads the people to praise the Savior." Preachers must address people directly. All ministers ought to be so filled with the Holy Spirit that all who hear them will be impressed with the conviction that "God is in them of a truth."

The problem of discipline in the West was met in frontier fashion— tempered by fair play and common sense. Although rules of procedure varied according to individuals—clergy and laymen—and according to time and place, certain rules applied to all cases. Unless insuperable obstacles interfered, the accuser and the accused were brought face to face, and minutes of the proceedings were kept.

The Congregational Association of Illinois resolved on April 18, 1840, that it was the duty of any person aggrieved with a brother in the church to follow the rule laid down in the eighteenth chapter of Matthew until the case was fully presented to the church, after which the duty of prosecuting the case devolved on the church. In view of the fact that the Scriptures were silent in regard to rules to be followed in admitting or rejecting testimony "on account of interest or consanguinity," those rules must be determined by the common sense and the enlightened dictates of the human mind.

The flexible conscience of the pioneer with reference to government property—and the public domain, in particular—was a matter of concern and discipline for the churches. At the same meeting of the Congregational Association of Illinois, the prevalent practice of cutting timber without the owner's consent from the lands of non-residents was declared to be in open violation of the laws of God—impairing the moral sense of communities and hindering the progress of the Gospel. This practice was branded as sinful as any other act of trespass; and the churches were entreated to call offenders to account and to discipline them.

The morals and the conduct of ministers were under the scrutiny of members of the churches, and individuals who were found wanting were liable to reprimand and discipline. Clergymen who augmented their skimpy salaries by engaging in farming and business were sometimes accused of unethical practices. The Ohio Annual Conference of the Methodist Episcopal Church in 1835 resolved that it was inexpedient in ministers to connive at, and wrong for members, to attend shows, menageries, and theaters. A pious grandmother in 1857, who had seen the pictures on the handbills of Barnum's circus, would not allow her granddaughters to attend. She said it was all right to look at the creatures God had made, but she did not think He ever intended that women should go only half-dressed and stand up and ride on horses bareback, or jump through hoops in the air.

Of great concern to the churches was daily Bible-reading and instruction in Bible lessons. The Bible was generally used as a reading book in primary grades, though in some places the Roman Catholics had succeeded in excluding it. At a large meeting of teachers at Cincinnati, Ohio, in October, 1836, the following committee report was adopted:

Your committee, then, consider that the Bible—no selection from the Bible, but the Bible itself—ought to constitute the class-book in our common school. Only the Bible can spread over the whole ground. . . . We are convinced that the whole of the inspired volume should as soon as possible be placed in the hands of the learner.

A missionary in Ohio in the service of the Connecticut Missionary Society, in 1808, lamented that in some schools novels and romances were used in teaching children, instead of the Bible. Some objected to the use of the Scriptures by saying that they did not interest children and therefore retarded their progress in learning. The missionary stated, however, that reason, observation, and experience had demonstrated the danger of filling the youthful mind with vanities and neglecting the means of forming a taste for useful knowledge.

Novel-reading was placed in the same category of sinful indulgences as the theater, the opera, dancing, card-playing, billiards, and gambling. Raffling for the purpose of raising money for the church or for charitable purposes was deemed wrong in principle by many churches. "Pious gambling" was only one step among many toward overwhelming the Church of God with the spirit of the world.

Even before the dawn of the nineteenth century prominent men had favored a general system of common schools; but it was not until the forties that the idea bore the fruit that made American education unique. Horace Mann of Massachusetts stands out as the great leader in the twenty years before the Civil War. He was a Unitarian and believed that the Bible should be read in the public schools, but without comment. This proposal drew the fire of churchmen and educators who contended that it would create godless schools.

Liberals in European countries cited statistics showing the expenditure per child in Massachusetts for public education to prove that the American people were wiser than the people of Europe, because they had no fear that popular education would awaken dissatisfaction among people. They acted on the principle that an educated man was a better asset to the country than an ignorant man.

Notwithstanding pride in the developing system of public schools, the family was still regarded as the foundation of character. It was there that the mind should be disciplined at the age when impressions could be made; when parents could have a salutary influence over young minds. The child should be made to feel his dependence on, and the disciplinary power of, parents. It was in the Puritan tradition that children should be taught to regulate their conduct with reference to time and eternity. In the words of a jurist: "A deep sense of our final accountability to an infinitely holy and just Being, has an all-pervading influence on the prevention of crime."

The nineteenth century brought leniency in the punishment of criminals and a broader charity in the treatment of the unfortunate members of society. Public executions became incongruous, although as late as 1815, as a boy of about eight, Oliver Wendell Holmes witnessed such an execution in Cambridge, Massachusetts. Among the radicals were such reformers as Theodore Parker who wanted to abolish capital punishment. If the Bible sanctioned capital punishment, he said, the Bible was wrong. "It fills me with disgust that worthy men in these days should go back to such sources for their wisdom; should walk dry-shod through the Gospels, and seek in the records of a barbarous people to justify their atrocious acts."

George B. Cheever, a Congregational and Presbyterian pastor and an exponent of "New England Theology," thought otherwise. He was an uncompromising reformer and a pronounced evangelical. He was an abolitionist, a Sabbatarian who opposed the running of Sunday trains, attacked the Roman Catholics who opposed compulsory reading of the Bible in public schools, and opposed ritualistic tendencies in the Episcopal Church. In 1849 he published *Punishment by Death: its Authority and Expediency.*

Cheever's argument from Scripture was forthright and plain. The Mosaic Code was not of Moses, but of God. Jehovah himself was the lawgiver, and Moses acted simply as His agent or minister. The whole code was framed by divine inspiration. Not one of these precepts was ever abrogated by the Savior; on the contrary, they were sustained and sanctioned by His own declarations and example. They contain the great law of love, promulgated anew in the Gospel—in the Sermon on the Mount. These laws were, in that age and generation, a collection of superhuman wisdom, and stood out in such bright contrast with the statutes of the heathen world as to constitute a satisfactory and conclusive demonstration of their divine origin. The author argued that the Mosaic law recognizes in the crime of murder, not an injury to a man merely, or to society, but to God; the highest possible violation of His authority; the greatest possible insult, through His violated image; a degree of turpitude and enormity, of which the Divine Majesty requires the highest possible punishment of human law.

Cheever denied that Christ in the Sermon on the Mount reprobated the vengeful and retaliatory tenor of the laws before His time—that is, an eye for an eye, and a tooth for a tooth. He argued that Christ's teachings were not directed to the laws themselves, but to the abuse of them. Christ had in view the correction of the spirit of malice and private revenge. In other words, the duty of private forgiveness does not interfere with the course of public justice in punishment by death. "It is one of the greatest mistakes, both for this world and for eternity, to suppose . . . that punishment is always or exclusively designed for reformation. . . . Punishment is the end; the effort at reformation is subservient and secondary." The writer conceded that every possible effort ought to be made to reform the criminal, but he is not to be taught that he is punished solely for his own good, this being a perfect lie in the face of all legislation, human and divine. One of the strongest objections which a believer in Christianity must feel to the whole reasoning of some men on the subject of capital punishment is that they tend to weaken and destroy the sanctions not only of the human government, but of the divine.

Cheever's exegesis was challenged in his own generation by men of integrity and scholarship; but his exposition was consistent with his interpretation of other parts of Scripture and compatible with the puritan tradition. In a later address delivered in 1858 before the American Abolition Society, when the country was ablaze with the Dred Scott decision, he characterized the Word of God as a "park of artillery—a swift-rushing mountain of thunderings and lightnings against sin." "The power and glory of the Old Testament, the intense fire of God's love and justice, and his wrath against injustice and oppression, the forked and chain-lightnings of the prophets, and the thunderbolts of Hebrew history, are yet to be shot upon this nation's sins."

TWENTY

RELIGIOUS NATIVISM

MANY books and articles have been written to explain the remarkable transition caused by the sudden influx of immigrants alien to the language, religion, and social, political, and
economic institutions of the United States. The confluence of events
in the forties and fifties within the boundaries of the United States,
coupled with social and economic uneasiness, and the repercussions of
religious, political, and economic upheavals in Europe, raised the hue
and cry against individuals and creeds and cultures that were said to
be incompatible with, and antagonistic toward, the fundamental principles of the Constitution of the United States. In the din of the hub-
bub raised by the press and by agitators in hostile camps, it is easy to
lose sight of the fact that America was the freest country in the world;
that it was the "Land of Canaan" where Protestants, Catholics, and
Jews were free to work out their own religious, social, economic, and
political salvation; where the gates stood ajar to admit men and
women of all races and of all creeds who were clamoring for the wages
of the New England factory, the opportunities of the housemaid, and
the cheap lands of the West. They brought with them problems which
neither they nor the land of their adoption could solve within one or
two generations. In no country was a foreigner treated with more
respect and kindness, and in no country did he find less difference between the native and the foreign-born citizen.

Solon compared the people to the sea, and orators and counsellors
to the winds, and said that the sea would be calm and quiet if the
winds did not trouble it. When racial antipathy and religious intolerance become the football of politics, the less level-headed members of
society have their day; and the level-headed citizens either bide their
time or else trim the excesses of both sides. The arrogance of some

members of the foreign population tried the patience of the benevolent and the tolerant. They recognized that humanity and the liberal character of republican institutions required that everything be granted to the strangers that could be useful to them, provided that no injury resulted to the new country. They warned the foreign-born population against provoking a contest with native Americans, which could only result to their disadvantage. They told them that they had been imprudent and had committed serious mistakes. No nation was bound to admit foreigners to all the rights and immunities of natural-born citizens. The propaganda of their leaders had had the opposite effect from that which was intended, because naturalized citizens did not have rights in national and political affairs equal to those enjoyed by native-born citizens.

In the light of the situation that existed before thousands of Europeans landed on American shores, when poorhouses were almost nonexistent in many towns and counties—more especially in New England—the following resolution adopted by the Massachusetts legislature and presented to the Senate by Senator Davis of that state, on May 2, 1836, is significant:

Resolved that it is expedient to instruct our Senators and to request our Representatives in Congress to use their endeavors to obtain the passage of a law to prevent the introduction of foreign paupers into this country, and to favor any other measures which Congress may be disposed to adopt to effect this object.

Without pursuing this topic farther, it may be said that abundant evidence was extracted from the reports of American consuls stationed in England, Ireland, and Germany to prove that local governments paid the passage of paupers, criminals, and other undesirables to unload them on the American people.

The stream of emigration from every country carried with it radicals and agnostics and atheists, some of whom had fled with a price on their heads. In the United States they fomented discord by publishing newspapers and by agitating in favor of revolutions in Europe to the extent that they sought to involve the government of the United States in intervention in behalf of their causes. There were, among the Germans, Austrians, and Irish, radicals who capitalized on nationalistic solidarity to the degree that there was an "Irish vote" and a "German vote." Moreover, abolitionists, educational reformers, temperance advocates, Sabbatarians, and a motley army of crusaders found "foreigners" opposing their pet ideas.

In the years before the Civil War the bulk of immigrants came from England, Ireland, Scotland, Germany, Switzerland, The Netherlands, Norway, and Sweden. The Dutch and the Scandinavians and the Swiss were relatively few and their settlements were sparsely distributed and swallowed up by the vast distances of the Mississippi Valley. The English and the Scotch for obvious reasons were readily assimilated. The Germans were strangers to the English language and were repelled by certain mores and customs; but they were land-hungry and took advantage of the agricultural opportunities in the West, where there was a spirit of give and take and ample room for industrious and law-abiding citizens. Among the Germans with religious affiliations there were Roman Catholics and Lutherans, with a sprinkling of sects. (Catholics and Lutherans resent the term "sect" as applied to them.) From 1820 to 1865 one-half of the volume of immigration came from Great Britain and Ireland, with the numbers from the Emerald Isle taking on great proportions after the potato famine of 1846 and 1847, which has been pronounced as "probably the most potent factor which has ever influenced the flow of emigration."

The Irish were poor in the goods of this world and were compelled to seek employment as laborers in the cities of the East. They were without the means to continue their journey to the interior, and they were without the experience and the equipment to make a success of farming in a country where agricultural methods were so unlike those of their native land. It was the irony of fate that New England became the home of thousands of Irish immigrants; that Irish Roman Catholics, whose hatred of England knew no bounds, found a place of refuge among the descendants of English puritans who fled from the persecution of prelates who sought to introduce Catholic forms and practices into the Church of England. Boston's immigrants were overwhelmingly from Ireland. The Irish established an independent institutional life, for they brought with them problems with which they were unable to cope and which Old Boston was unable to solve. Native Bostonians and Irish immigrants were segregated in hostile camps. In the clash of cultures and creeds, the other immigrant groups allied themselves with the Bostonians against the Irish.

The heavy Irish immigration wrought a transformation in the Roman Catholic Church in the United States. In fact, in the minds of many Americans, Catholicism was synonymous with Irish patriotism. Moreover, the fact that Boston and New England became a Catholic stronghold in the stronghold of Congregationalism suggests the lying down together of the lion and the lamb.

It is not within the province of this study, which is concerned with religion, to recite the events—some of them sensational—which fanned the flames of political nativism and gave the opportunity to organize a new party which was nicknamed "Know Nothing." It is our purpose to bring Catholicism and Protestantism face to face in a predominantly Protestant country and to explain why a deluge of Catholic immigrants put an end to the religious tolerance that prevailed in the early nineteenth century.

The Roman Catholic Church and the Lutheran Church were the major "foreign-language churches." The membership of the Lutheran Church was recruited from the German and Scandinavian immigrants. By virtue of the fact that the Lutheran Church was divided into a number of synods, whose independence or autonomy was based on language, doctrine, or geographical location, its influence and effectiveness in American Protestantism was impaired. Conservative along social and doctrinal lines, it emphasized creeds and confessions, liturgy, and sacraments. Before the advent of Lutherans from Germany and Scandinavia, who had been confirmed in the established churches of those countries, the American Lutheran Church had imbibed freely of the spirit of the so-called Reformed churches—so much so that its members were called "American Lutherans" or "New Lutherans," in contrast with "Old Lutherans" or "European Lutherans." The fact that the various synods differed in doctrine and forms of service made it impossible to form a general body to which anything more than advisory power could be delegated. This explains the characteristics of the General Synod, which was organized at Hagerstown, Maryland, in 1820, and embraced fully two-thirds of the Lutherans in America.

The powers of the General Synod were mainly advisory; the district synods retained in the essentials the jurisdiction which was theirs be-

fore the union. It has been said that the agreement to disagree was
the highest unity the General Synod ever proposed. Not only was the
organization founded on a broad doctrinal basis, but it was avowedly
unionistic. For example, at the Baltimore convention in 1845 it was
voted to approve of the practice "which has hitherto prevailed in our
churches, and those of the Presbyterian Church," of mutually inviting
the ministry to act as advisory members in each body, of inviting
communicants in regular standing in either church to partake of the
Lord's Supper in the other; and of dismission of church members at
their own request from the churches of the one to those of the other
denomination.

By 1850 the cleavage in the General Synod between the "American
Lutherans"—the liberals—and the "Old Lutherans"—the conservatives—was marked. The most prominent of the "Americans," or "new
measures" men, was S. S. Schmucker, Professor of Theology in
Gettysburg Theological Seminary. This able man had received his
theological training in Princeton Theological Seminary and had thus
acquired a liberal point of view with respect to Lutheran doctrine;
but he was interested in committing the Lutheran synods to a confessional position, despite the fact that he employed his prolific pen to
counteract the influence of those who planted themselves on the his-
toric Lutheran symbols. He preferred the constitution of the General
Synod, which went no farther than to state that "the fundamental
doctrines of the Word of God are taught in a manner substantially
correct in the doctrinal articles of the Augsburg Confession." He
argued that since Lutheranism in the various countries of Europe had
acquired a distinctive flavor, the Lutheran Church in America should
adapt itself to the genius of American institutions and society.

The influence of the "Old Lutherans," or symbolists, augmented
each year by the immigration of Germans and Scandinavians, called
forth editorials and speeches which lamented the bigotry of the ministers and members of these churches. They cited their exclusiveness,
sacramental superstition, and strong leaning toward semi-Roman rites.
They conceded their learning in scholastic theology, but mourned over
their ignorance of the genius of American institutions. In the opinion
of one editor, to expect Christians under a free government and an
untrammeled church to think and believe on all points, major and

minor, exactly as they do under a despotism in state and church, and to look for the same development of the Gospel in a republic that it exhibits where the adulterous and hampering union of church and state exists, was so verdant, so puerile, so absurd as to awaken pity and ridicule. The militant editor saw little hope for improvement in a people who fancied that they had the truth and nothing but the truth and that all the rest of the world was in error and blindness.

In a vain attempt to stem the tide of confessional Lutheranism, Schmucker, in 1855, published the "Definite Synodical Platform," whose authorship he later acknowledged. This "American Recension of the Augsburg Confession," as Schmucker called it, was intended to furnish a doctrinal basis for Lutheran synods in the United States. It was prepared in consultation and coöperation with Lutheran ministers of eastern and western synods, at the special request of "western brethren," whose churches particularly needed it, being intermingled with German churches, which avowed the whole mass of the former symbols. The revision added nothing to the Augsburg Confession, but omitted those points of doctrine which were unscriptural and remnants of Romish error. The "errors" omitted were approval of the ceremonies of the mass, private confession and absolution, denial of the divine obligation of the Christian Sabbath, baptismal regeneration, and the real presence of the body and blood of the Savior in the eucharist. In listing the "errors" of the symbolical books, it was asserted that the extraordinary length of these books was sufficient reason for rejecting them as a prescribed creed, "because neither the Scriptures nor the practice of the early centuries affords any warrant for an uninspired and therefore fallible creed nearly as large as the entire Old and New Testament together. The exaction of such an extended creed is subversive to all individual liberty of thought and freedom of Scriptural investigation."

The introduction to the platform also stated that Luther and his coadjutors had changed their views on some subjects contained in the Augsburg Confession; and that a quarter-century after Luther's death certain writings of Luther and Melanchthon and the Formula of Concord, which neither of them ever saw, were made binding on ministers and churches, not by the Church acting on its own free choice but by the civil authorities of certain kingdom and principalities.

The reception of the platform was disappointing to Schmucker and his followers and was indicative of the profound change which the Lutheran Church had experienced in the years immediately preceding the publication of the document. The emigrant ships depositing hordes of Germans and Scandinavians on American shores proved to be more powerful than the facile pens of Schmucker and his "American" followers. Down to 1850 the Lutheran Church in America was in a fair way to develop a liberal theology; but this tendency was checked by the influx of symbolists from Germany and Scandinavia, who would not admit that the Augsburg Confession was an antiquated document; that it had been superseded by the superior knowledge of succeeding generations. They would not recede one step from the position that the framers of the Augsburg Confession had formulated for all time the tenets of the Christian religion. What was the truth in Luther's generation was the truth in theirs and would be the truth in the church of their children.

The position of the "Americans" was stated in an article by Francis Springer in the *Evangelical Review* for July, 1859, which was a red flag in its critical attitude toward the "European Lutherans, with their tenacity of language, European ecclesiasticism, and worship of symbols."

The declaration of Augsburg is the exponent of the degree of intellectual and social development of which the most active and vigorous race of mankind was then capable; and that instrument is scarcely more the property of the Lutheran Church than it is of the entire human race. But, though it is a fixed point in human progression, we are not hence to infer that progression itself has been arrested and can advance no further. It is the right, nay, the duty of any generation having attained a clearer light and superior advancement over preceding generations, to mark, by a suitable monument, the point of progress they have reached. . . . The people of a subsequent generation may, of right, make a new declaration, standard or confession; or, if not quite prepared for this, they may proclaim a qualified adherence to the one made previously.

Notwithstanding the triumph of symbolism and the repudiation of a latitudinarian basis in the American Lutheran Church brought about by the infiltration of European Lutherans, there remained a leaven of

Calvinism and Methodism. The orthodoxy of the Germans was unquestioned; but among the Scandinavians, who were divided, there were liberals who were glad to be emancipated from the deadly and sterile orthodoxy of established churches. The Norwegians were distributed mainly in three synods which were miles apart on certain items of doctrine and polity, whereas the Swedes were concentrated in one group. The German Missouri Synod sowed discord among them by attacking the alleged "unholy alliance" between the Scandinavians who were affiliated with the General Synod. The Norwegian clergy who had been indoctrinated in the strait-laced symbolism at the University of Oslo remained coldly outside the General Synod and fulminated against their countrymen who were affiliated with a heretical synod.

It is significant that the founders of the Swedish Lutheran Church who left Sweden at the close of the forties and in the fifties were strongly influenced by the pietistic reformation in Sweden which was Anglo-Saxon and, in its later stages, almost exclusively American. They took care that the church they founded in the New World should bear little resemblance to the Church of Sweden. It was a virtue in the new church to be apart from and unlike the old church. The preëminent leader in the pioneer Swedish Lutheran Church was Tuve Nilsson Hasselquist, who had been closely associated in Sweden with men known for their piety and free-church tendencies. He could never reconcile himself to a state-church system. After eighteen years' experience with free churches in America he wrote: "For my part I cannot love the state church; it is most certainly inconsistent with both the Word of God and all experience. . . . Church and state are so interwoven that it is often difficult to distinguish between them."

Hasselquist saw no danger to Lutheran doctrine if the liturgy and certain forms were laid aside and if his church coöperated with other denominations. In his earlier years he would appear at the Sunday morning service dressed in a white linen coat; and as he walked to the front of the church he would sing a gospel hymn, in which the congregation joined. In the pulpit he was equally informal, often interrupting his sermon by singing a familiar song. Throughout the many years he served as theological professor, editor, and pastor he wielded an influence that placed the stamp of pietism and low-church form so securely on the Swedish Lutheran Church that it occupied a unique place among Lutheran synods.

It is significant that the architecture of many Lutheran churches constructed in the nineteenth century, especially in the earlier years, was more "Reformed" than Lutheran. The altar did not have a prominent place, and altar and pulpit were one. It is also significant that the American Scandinavian Lutheran churches did not adopt the episcopate. Bishops were painful reminders of haughty prelates in Europe. Moreover, many Lutheran ministers were prejudiced against vestments and gowns, partly because they reminded their parishioners of worldly and overbearing parish pastors. In polity the Scandinavian churches were Congregational and Presbyterian.

Necessity dictated the licensing of laymen to preach the Gospel, in spite of Article XIV of the Augsburg Confession which taught that no one should publicly teach in the Church or administer the sacraments unless he was regularly called. The strictly orthodox Norwegian Lutheran Synod was in disagreement with the Swedes and their Norwegian allies in the General Synod in the interpretation of this article. The former group held that exhortation and praying by laymen publicly in church could be allowed only in cases of necessity, whereas their "low-church" brethren believed that this should be allowed at all times under careful supervision of the pastor. On the far-flung frontier, lay preachers rendered services to the widely scattered Scandinavian Lutheran congregations similar to those rendered by the Methodist circuit-riders and by the agents and colporteurs sent out by the American Home Missionary Society, the American Tract Society, and the American Bible Society. In a sense, some of the immigrant churches were in their inception laymen's missionary movements, a fact which explains to a degree the representation of laymen in the government of the churches.

Although the immigrants from the various political divisions of Europe had some things in common, and exhibited a certain solidarity, there were many evidences of disharmony. Although they had no use for the Know Nothing party, they had their own brands of nativism. The churchly elements looked with hostility on the radicals, especially the "forty-eighters" who carried on their agitation for reforms and changes that were said to be inconsistent with the American idea of liberty. They feared the influence of skeptics and atheists. Moreover, some of the immigrants, editors and speakers, who ransacked their vocabularies for epithets to apply to the nativists, exceeded them in the violence of their denunciations of Roman Catholics. A Minnesota editor of a German language newspaper, who was a refugee from the Metternich system, wrote: "Americans, tear asunder the bonds between Romanism and Republicanism, while it is yet time, by a law making it impossible for a Roman Catholic to become a citizen of your republic."

TWENTY ONE

THE OLD WORLD AGAINST THE NEW WORLD

IN RELIGIOUS controversies the contending parties are equally adept in hurling such epithets as "bigotry," "intolerance," "clannishness," and "nativism"; and fumbling historians have appropriated the vocabulary of propaganda without a clear understanding of the milieu and without measuring the width and the depth of the chasms that divide nationalities, religions, and classes. In all generations followers of the lowly Nazarene have been willing to lose their lives as members of a minority—a remnant—and to bide their time. They humbled themselves in the hope that in God's own time they would be exalted. Creeds, dogmas, and ecclesiastical systems were of minor importance to them, because these factitious standards represented what Christ meant when He condemned those who made the commandment of God of none effect by their tradition and taught for doctrines the commandments of men. In all generations those who made broad their phylacteries, and enlarged the borders of their garments, and loved to be called of men, Rabbi, have been uncomfortable in minorities.

It is significant that in the nineteenth century, emigrants from Europe—from Protestant countries—quickly sensed the difference between pastors in America and in Europe. They found ministers in America democratic and warm-hearted; they sought the sheep, unlike ministers in Europe where the sheep sought the shepherd and were careful to address him by the proper gradation of titles—"Very Reverend," "Most Reverend," "Curate," "Rector," "Bishop"—which the church had awarded him. An emigrant from Sweden wrote in 1850 that "there is as great difference between the pastors here and in Sweden as there is between night and day."

Clergymen, whether visiting or otherwise, trained in the state churches of Europe did not relish being "mistered" in America. Men who had taken holy orders could not adjust themselves gracefully to public criticisms of themselves and of the church which had ordained them. In Europe the clergy stood out as a separate estate, with property and interests peculiarly their own, and enjoyed the special privileges and exemptions written into law at the dictation of a hierarchy. In America the safety of republican institutions depended on the free and enlightened play of public opinion; and in the churches the priesthood of the common man and the representation of laymen in congregations and synods and conferences justified the fears of James I of England, who in 1604, angrily told certain Puritan clergymen that a Scottish Presbytery "agreeth as well with a monarchy, as God and the devil." In New England the clergy were not spared the invectives of men like Whitefield and Davenport and Theodore Parker; and in the fullness of time the Puritan oligarchy was broken and church establishments were abolished.

Churchmen trained in Europe were unable to understand the nonconformist temper of their countrymen in the New World. Some of them never learned that a frontier environment was not fruitful soil for planting stiff, formal, liturgical churches; others pleaded that their church in the New World was different from the institution professing the same faith in the Old World.

Politics perverts whatever it touches; and when a church, through its recognized leaders, takes sides on political questions, it exposes itself to political criticism. Fear of foreign influence was present before the extraordinary outburst of nativism in the two decades preceding the Civil War; and with the invasion of hordes of Germans and Irish, newspaper editors of the forties and fifties were not afraid to record their misgivings on the editorial page. Editorials and articles in the religious press raised apprehensions as to the safety of America's heritage of religion, morals, and culture. Was not the American conception of freedom vastly different from that of Europe? Would not the naturalization of Catholics, radicals, and revolutionists be an empty formality? The law naturalized the old Adam and did not suffice. Naturalized citizens, as well as native-born, needed to be born again and to be admitted into American citizenship on confession of faith in the Declaration of Independence and in the First Amendment to the Constitution. Separation of church and state was a *fait accompli* and was no longer debatable by 1840.

The English historian James Anthony Froude, who wrote with strong convictions on the Protestant Reformation and on the Catholic Counter Reformation, is the author of the following paragraph in an article on "Romanism and the Irish Race in the United States," which appeared in the *North American Review* for December, 1879:

> A prophet, who had foretold at the time of the Declaration of Independence that within a century the Roman Catholics would be the largest single religious community in the United States, would have deserved a place in a lunatic asylum, so absurd such an anticipation would have seemed. . . . That in New York and New England, the chosen home of Calvinism and Puritanism, the woman of the seven hills should have set up her standard, and that American citizens would be gathered round it in millions, would have seemed an hypothesis so wild, that every man or woman with ordinary sense would have agreed that it could not be.

Froude pointed out that in 1785 there was only one Roman Catholic bishop in the United States, with fifty priests and five churches. The Catholic population was French or Spanish and had neither school, college, nor monastery. The population was declining in numbers or was being absorbed into the preponderating Anglo-Saxon element. At the time Froude's article was written the Roman Catholic population numbered six and a half million.

The English historian quoted a statement in a communication written by a Catholic to a New York newspaper to the effect that Protestants must tolerate Catholics, but Catholics must not tolerate Protestants. "The Church is in possession of absolute truth; she alone has the right to be, she alone must be intolerant." Froude commented that language of that kind was permitted in the New World because of its absurdity. Americans were complacent and in their ignorance underestimated the power of the Catholic Church, he wrote. He predicted that as their numbers grew, Catholics would assert their principles more and more; and that a Catholic majority, under spiritual direction, would forbid liberty of worship and would try to forbid liberty of conscience. This majority would control education; it would put the press under surveillance; it would punish opposition with excommunication, and excommunication would be attended with civil disabilities. To the republic as it stood, concluded Froude, the Catholic system was a direct menace.

Another English historian, even more distinguished than Froude, whose wide experience, careful research, and powerful pen joined forces in producing a monumental history of England during a time when the issue of constitutional government and religious toleration hung in the balance, was a keen judge of character and an excellent judge of value. The following quotation from the writings of Lord Macaulay was pointed to the schemes of James II (1685–1688) to produce a conflict between the Church of England and the Protestant dissenters, and thus facilitate the victory of the Catholics over both.

Every sect clamors for toleration when it is down. . . . The doctrine which, from the very first origin of religious dissensions, has been held by all bigots of all sects, when condensed into a few words, and stripped of rhetorical disguise is simply this: I am in the right, and you are in the wrong. When you are the stronger you ought to tolerate me; for it is your duty to tolerate truth. But when I am the stronger, I shall persecute you; for it is my duty to persecute error.

It is difficult for Americans of the twentieth century to comprehend the character of the religious, ethical, cultural, social, and political barriers that divided Catholics and Protestants from 1840 to 1860. There were no barriers so long as the Atlantic was the boundary between Catholics and Protestants as individuals. The Monroe Doctrine was a protest against an old-world system that threatened to nullify yearnings for freedom in the Western Hemisphere. Austria and the Austrian statesman Metternich symbolized and personified the "system" which President Monroe pronounced "dangerous to our peace and safety." During these early years of the century sermons preached in American meeting-houses and churches furnished evidence that the Protestant Reformation and the Puritan Revolution had not been forgotten. These remote events were vivified by the almost daily arrival of emigrant ships with refugees from persecution and by newspaper reports of the downfall of Metternich and the flight of the pope from Rome, with Republican rebels at his heels.

When Harriet Beecher Stowe erected a white marble cross on her son Henry's grave in the Andover, Massachusetts, cemetery, that evangelical community was shocked. In a communication to the editor of the *New York Courier and Enquirer* for May 2, 1855, Senator Erastus Brooks made sarcastic reference to the practice of Archbishop Hughes signing his name prefixed with a cross. Nicholas Murray, who was born a Roman Catholic in Ireland and became a convert to Protestantism in New York and was employed by the American Tract Society as a student in college and in the theological seminary, made an appeal to "All Roman Catholics," after having addressed a series of letters to Archbishop Hughes. "I have appeared before you with no crosses before my name—with no ecclesiastical titles after it—making no flourish of trumpets from the places of brief authority, and with one single desire to unfold before your eyes the religious system which has oppressed your fathers. . . ." Frederick J. Jobson, a visiting English Methodist in 1856, was disturbed over the number of Irish Catholics in Boston. This fact, he said, to a mind under the influence of spiritual and saving Christianity, threw a gloomy cloud over the city and darkened its character. In Albany, New York, after having "looked in" at a Roman Catholic service, and after having seen the "show and glare of popery," and the priests and their attendants bowing and chanting before the crucifixes, he was minded to shout "Idolatry! Idolatry!" as loudly as Latimer himself.

Protestants pointed to the contrast between Catholic and Protestant countries—intellectually, morally, and socially. They attributed the Protestant superiority to an unshackled conscience and an open Bible. They asserted that the Catholic Church suppressed the preaching of the Gospel and substituted for it the mass. The apostles turned the world upside down by preaching, they said; but in papal countries there was generally no preaching. Some of the anti-Catholic propagandists pointed to the "vicious morals" in Spain, Austria, France, and especially in Italy. They alleged that to an inquiring mind, which knows nothing of the Bible, infidelity is the "fruit of popery." In papal countries, where the masses are superstitious, the intelligent and the educated are infidel, they said. They pointed to France which legislated God out of existence—decreed religion to be a fable, and death an eternal sleep. Voltaire was said to be the mind of France, and Eugene Sue the high priest of the people. From his Journal written in Paris, January 15, 1846, Horace Bushnell recorded that France "wants a religion; and nothing is more manifest to me than that she can never humble herself to contentment under the shams and mummeries of an unintellectual religion."

The two most striking objects which Bushnell found in Belgium were the magnificent churches and cathedrals and the profligate-looking priests. In the cathedral at Antwerp he saw the "gorgeous rites transacted before the images" and the "multitude famishing for lack of knowledge in the service of an unknown tongue." Near the close of the service, he saw the "ghostly procession winding through the crowd . . . the central figure of which was as bloated, sin-worn, sorry-looking miscreant as I ever beheld, walking in a cloud of incense, and trying to draw an air of sanctimony upon features that refused to be sanctified."

Lyman Beecher alleged that three-fourths of the foreign emigrants were through the medium of their religion and priesthood as accessible to the control of the potentates of Europe as if they were an army of soldiers, enlisted and officered, and spreading over the land. This would mean union of church and state. He called the pope a creature of Austria. He sensed the danger of a priesthood, educated under the despotic governments of Catholic Europe, and dependent for their office, support, and honors upon a foreign prince—a priesthood not elected by the people or dependent on them during good behavior.

The temporal power of the pope was the text for anti-Catholic propagandists. They insisted that the distinction between the authority of the pope as the spiritual head of the church and as the ruler of the Papal States was in reality slight—nominal. They charged that the bishops' oaths bound them to sustain the pope in all his characters, powers, rights, and claims. They avowed that no bishop dared publicly to disown the temporal power. After the Papal States were restored to the pope following the downfall of Napoleon, the government was in the hands of priests. It was a corrupt and bigoted government, and its finances were in deplorable shape. An important source of revenue was a lottery, which was administered by religious ceremonies and even kept running on Sundays. The inquisition was restored; education was controlled by the clergy; and the curriculum of universities was controlled. At the peace congress in Paris after the Crimean War, when the Italian question was discussed, Clarendon representing England denounced the government of the Papal States as a disgrace to Europe.

The controversy between Catholics and Protestants cannot be understood without taking into account events in Europe, where revolutionary disturbances tumbled kings from thrones and disturbed the ancient privileges of established churches—Protestant and Catholic. The papacy defended its position against its adversaries, and became militant and active on mission fields, even in Protestant countries. In England the Oxford movement made rapid strides toward Rome, and a considerable body of the Anglican clergy seriously contemplated secession.

The citizens of a country whose national life was rooted in revolution and documented in the Declaration of Independence could not approve of the action of the pope against Italian revolutionists. A pamphleteer attacked the statement attributed to Archbishop Hughes, namely, that the Catholic Church did not recognize the principle that people may change their government when they will. He ridiculed the archbishop's statement that the Americans of 1776 had the right to do this because of oppression and because leading men of the Revolution were religious men.

Agnostics, radicals, and revolutionists from Europe joined forces with nativists in charging the Catholic Church with opportunism: stating that in Austria it was in league with despotism; in England with the high-church Tory party; in Rome against the liberties of the Italian people; and in America sympathetic with Republican principles.

Lyman Beecher, with his eyes fixed on the Mississippi Valley and fearful that the pope was planning to exchange the plains of the Arno and the Tiber for that garden of the world, in the middle of the thirties launched this thunderbolt:

Who is it then that makes the proclamation, that the Catholic Church has discovered her mistakes in past ages and is reformed? Has the pope announced it? Has the general council decreed it? Has the Catholic convention at Baltimore placed it upon their records? . . . When and where has it been decreed that liberty of conscience, and civil liberty are the birth-right of man—that reading the Bible is the right of man and not a privilege to be conferred—that private interpretation is the duty of man instead of implicit confidence in the exposition of others—that persecution for conscience sake is tyranny, and the deeds of the inquisition an abomination in the sight of God? . . . What are the powerful principles of collision which now agitate Europe and South America but those of civil liberty and despotic power? And on which side, when uncoerced, is his holiness and his cardinals?

The Index was a target for the shafts of those who alleged that the papal system was hostile to the cause of popular education and the progress of the arts and sciences. The Address of the Board of Managers of the American Protestant Association (1843) asked how a system could be otherwise than hostile to American interests and to the improvement of man which prohibited the publication or the reading of the works of Algernon Sidney, Addison, Lord Bacon, Chief Justice Hale, John Locke, Milton, Robertson, Cowper, Young, and other great names of English literature? "Are the American people prepared to say that we are doing a needless or an unchristian service, in resisting a system which, if it had the power, would preclude them from reading 'Locke On the Human Understanding' or 'Paradise Lost' without permission of a priest?"

In the Catholic-Protestant controversy the rule of faith was inevitably brought into the public forum. Archbishop Hughes asserted that religion had been robbed of the very privilege and principle of self-preservation by private interpretation of the Bible, and thus denied the fundamental principle of American Protestantism. The irreconcilability of Catholicism and Protestantism has never been more clearly and forcefully stated than it was in Luther's "Address to the Christian Nobility of the German Nation" in 1520.

The Romanists, with great adroitness, have built three walls about them, behind which they have hitherto defended themselves in such wise that no one has been able to reform them. . . . First, when pressed by the temporal power, they have made decrees and said that the temporal power has no jurisdiction over them, but, on the other hand, that the spiritual power is above the temporal power. Second, when the attempt is made to reprove them out of the Scriptures, they raise the objection that the interpretation of the Scriptures belongs to no one except the pope. Third, if threatened with a council, they answer with the fable that no one can call a council but the pope.

Catholics speak of the pope as the "Holy Father," not necessarily in the holiness of the man himself, but in his office. They believe him to be the lawful and historical successor to Peter, whom they believe to be the first pope. They believe him to be the vicar of Christ on earth. Every one of these beliefs was rejected by the Pilgrims and the Puritans and by Protestants in every land.

In a letter dated January 21, 1833, to John Breckenridge of the Presbyterian Church, Bishop Hughes contended that the Redeemer of the world never intended that the Bible alone should be the rule of faith, because it was not universally known until the end of the fifth century what books were to be regarded as inspired scripture. Moreover, no part of the New Testament was written for several years, and some of it not until more than half a century after Christ's ascension into heaven. The bishop also cited the fact that there were millions who believed in Christ and could not read, or could not possess a Bible before printing was invented. Are Protestants now who cannot read destitute of a rule of faith, he asked. The churchman stated that the Bible alone, or the Bible operated upon by private interpretation, had given rise to all the heresies that existed, and that Socinians, Universalists, and Swedenborgians had as good a right to understand its meanings as Presbyterians.

Nicholas Murray took up the cudgel by harking back to his early life in Ireland, where he was born in 1802. He informed Bishop Hughes that for years he sat daily with a Catholic priest, who was a member of the family and the curate of the parish, and never saw a Bible used in the family. He never heard at the table, or in the morning, or in the evening, a religious service; and he never heard a sermon preached in a Catholic chapel in Ireland, nor a word of explanation on a single Christian topic, doctrine, or duty.

Turning to the bishop's assertion that private interpretation of the Bible was the root of heresy and that the Bible had no authority save what his church gave it and must be understood and received as his church interpreted it, Murray inquired how he might obtain the church's sense of it. He asked at what period in the life of the church he would most likely get a true interpretation. When the Church was Arian with Pope Liberius? Or pagan with Marcellinus? Or Pelagian with Pope Clement XI? Or infidel with Leo X? Or when strumpets were her waiting maids with John XXII and Alexander? Or when she was drunk with the blood of martyrs? Or when rival popes were tearing out each other's bowels? Or was it when in the height of her charity she was thundering her curses from Trent against all who refused to say "Amen" to her decisions?

A prolific propagandist, William C. Brownlee, reminded the bishop that Pope Pius VII in 1816 issued a bull against Bible societies and pronounced them "a shocking and most crafty device, to sap the very foundations of religion." He turned the tables, or thought he did, on the bishop who attributed the spread of heresy to private interpretation of the Bible, by asserting that popery was the parent and nurse of Deism. He stated that it was a matter of recorded history, that just in proportion as popery prevails in any land is the Sabbath of the Lord desecrated and despised. He alleged that Catholic priests in the United States attended the theater on the Sabbath day and that every traveler knew that this was practiced in Catholic Europe and in South America.

The issue between Bible Christianity and Roman Catholic Christianity resolved itself into a political conflict with farreaching consequences. The issue concerned civil and religious liberty and the separation of church and state, with implications and ramifications. If Calvinists did not cry "persecution" when their creed and conduct were analyzed, why should the Catholic religion be exempted from scrutiny? Has it disclosed more vigorous republican tendencies? These questions were asked by Lyman Beecher.

He stated that if Catholics regarded themselves only as one of many denominations of Christians, entitled only to equal rights and privileges, there would be no cause for apprehension. Unfortunately, he said, Catholics are taught to believe that their church is the only church of Christ and that none may read the Bible but by permission of the priesthood, and no one is permitted to understand it and worship God according to the dictates of his own conscience. Through the confessional it searches the heart, learns the thoughts, and thus acquires the means of an unlimited ascendancy over minds by the united influence of both worlds. When Catholics get power, said Beecher, they can intimidate the press, boycott merchants, lawyers, and physicians, if they do not favor their church. Denying animosity against individual Catholics, Beecher directed his fire against the political claims and character of the Catholic religion, and its church and state alliance.

Perhaps public schools against parochial schools was the major issue. This controversy has been even more acrimonious and has wrought more havoc in Catholic countries than in Protestant countries. In the United States it was complicated by the opposition of certain Catholic leaders to the reading of the Bible in the public schools. The King James Version, the Bible of the Protestants, was the translation used. Certain Protestant leaders complained that the concessions that were made to Catholics in regard to the reading of the Bible and the choice of textbooks did not solve the problem, because priests raised a new issue and began to complain that the public schools were "godless" and "atheistical"—just as they had required them to be.

The school controversy took on serious proportions in New York, more especially in New York City, at the beginning of the decade of the forties, when Archbishop Hughes attacked the public school system. Inevitably the issue became polluted when it was dragged into politics. It is not to our purpose to review the events and pass judgment on the conduct of the men, large and small, who waged this battle. It has been debated from that day until this. The Roman Catholic Church, with some minor exceptions, is the only Christian denomination which has not accepted the American public school system. For over a century the respective positions of Catholics and Protestants have remained essentially the same.

The Protestant point of view has never been more clearly stated than it was by Horace Bushnell in a sermon preached in March, 1853, on common schools and the modifications demanded by Roman Catholics. His text was Leviticus 24:22: "Ye shall have one manner of law, as well for the stranger, as for one of your own country: for I am the Lord your God." Bushnell complained that while Catholics accept the common rights of the law, the common powers of voting, the common terms of property, the common privilege in the new lands and the mines of gold, they will not be common in the matter of common schools. They require of us instead, he said, either to give up our common schools, or else, which in fact amounts to the same thing, to hand over their proportion of the public money, and then let them use it for the kind of schools as they happen to like best.

Bushnell argued that common schools are wanted for the common training of so many classes and conditions of people. "There needs to be some place where, in early childhood, they may be brought together and made acquainted with each other." He maintained that ecclesiastical distinctions are themselves class distinctions in another form and are even more dangerous than distinctions of wealth. "Let the Catholic children, for example, be driven out of our schools by unjust trespasses on their religion, or be withdrawn for mere pretexts that have no foundation, and just then commences a training in religious antipathies bitter as the grave. They grow up in the conviction that there is nothing but evil in each other. . . . The arrangement is not only unchristian, but it is thoroughly un-American, hostile at every point to our institutions themselves."

No bitterness is so bitter, no seed of faction so rank, no division so irreconcilable, as that which grows out of religious distinctions, sharpened by religious animosities, and softened by no terms of intercourse; the more bitter when it begins in childhood; and yet more bitter when it is exasperated also by distinctions of property and social life that correspond; and yet more bitter still when it is aggravated also by distinction of stock or nation.

In a letter dated May 17, 1844, prompted by the activity of the Native American party and the agitation by press and pulpit, Bishop Hughes denied that he was an enemy of the Bible, an intriguer with political parties, and a blackener of public school textbooks. The bishop deplored any distinction between natives and foreign-born in his church and was vigilant to suppress tendencies among the various nationalities in the church to divide according to respective nationalities. He was severe against efforts by American Catholics to carry their own nationality into the church. He opposed the policy of Orestes A. Brownson, who became converted to Catholicism after having been a Universalist and having associated with Transcendentalists. His periodical—*Brownson's Quarterly Review*—assumed the militant intensity of a neophyte; but it ran afoul of Archbishop Hughes and the hierarchy by advocating the liberalizing and Americanizing of the church. Brownson was interested in affecting a reconciliation of Catholicism and so-called modern civilization. He stated that he found the Jesuits in the way of his policy.

With the springing up of Catholic schools, colleges, and seminaries in many parts of the country, the Protestants became fearful that they were proselyting institutions. They pointed to the activity of the Leopold Foundation, which was organized in Austria, a country whose church was friendly to Metternich, the exponent of legitimacy and autocracy.

The speeches of Erastus Hopkins of Northampton, Massachusetts, on the bill to incorporate the College of the Holy Cross in Worcester, in April, 1849, reveal the fear of proselyting and of Jesuit influence. Before granting the prayer of the petitioners, said Hopkins, the legislature ought to consider whether it was expedient to sanction a system of education which committed the entire training of youth from the age of eight years, and even less, to celibates—men who, by their religious views and vows, had separated themselves from all the refining and beneficial influences of social life. He also objected to the censoring of the press which the Jesuits exercised over their community. By enacting the bill, the legislature would allow the use of the Douay Version of the Bible and permit the placing under the ban of proscription the Protestant Version, which the state applied only to obscene publications.

By granting the charter, Hopkins maintained that it would give power to Jesuits, the distinctive feature of whose order was that of entire, inflexible subordination and obedience to their superiors in office, through various grades up to a vicar general, a high functionary who resides at Rome. Therefore by granting the charter, the legislature would incorporate an institution really under the control and absolute direction of a foreign power, which in its alliances with monarchical governments constituted the essence of tyranny.

Political nativism in the form of the Know Nothing party was overwhelmed by the slavery agitation; and the new-born Republican party became the major party in opposition to the Democratic party. The war for the preservation of the Union allayed religious strife for a season; but it was only a respite. The fundamental causes of the controversy remained.

TWENTY-TWO

THE ABOLITION CRUSADE

S LAVERY was a blot on the charter of American liberty; and from the beginning there were men and women in the slave states as well as in the free states who hoped and prayed for the early extinction of the institution. Their hopes would probably have been realized sooner had it not been for the "peculiar" character of American slavery. The fact that the slaves were of a race different from that of their masters raised the problem of the relation of the races after emancipation. The further fact that in the nineteenth century the institution was localized in a section brought additional complications with which statesmen were unable to cope. It is the judgment of history that slavery was an anachronism and had been extended to its "natural limits" on the eve of the Civil War, after which its decline and extinction were inevitable. It has been said that if the South had been left to itself, slavery would have been abolished by the action of the states themselves. A certain school of historians has pronounced harsh judgment on the abolitionists whose vituperation and intransigence retarded rather than hastened emancipation. The abolitionists stigmatized slavery as a moral iniquity, inconsistent with Christian civilization, and felt that in dealing with it no compromise was possible.

The American churches divided among themselves and against themselves on the subject of slavery. The multiplicity of sects and their democratic form of government gave free play to the expression of sentiment, with the result that the same denomination harbored within its membership wide differences of opinion with respect to the right of slavery to exist. Within churches there were seceding factions who were impatient and rebellious and demanded positive action by the authorities. On the other hand, there were clergymen and laymen who advised caution and restraint for what they conceived to be the best interests of church and country. It was impatience with men of this persuasion that caused firebrands like William Lloyd Garrison, Wendell Phillips, and Theodore Parker to move far away from orthodoxy into the camp of extreme liberals. Some, like James G. Birney, called churches the "bulwarks of American slavery," and like Stephen Symonds Foster, called churches and clergy the "brotherhood of thieves." Some historians have minimized the influence and activity of the churches in the years from 1815 to 1860, and have magnified the conservative slant of professors of religion in times of crisis. They have also concluded that the abolitionists were at a disadvantage in their long fight against slavery because they were outside the pale of orthodox churches.

It is, however, easy to underestimate the role of the churches in promoting abolition and in setting bounds to the territorial expansion of slavery. The list of clergymen, eminent and little known, who preached against slavery and joined anti-slavery and abolition societies is a long one. The First Annual Report of the American Anti-Slavery Society (1834) shows a large number of clergymen active and holding important offices, and the speeches and resolutions were strongly religious in content. The courageous and well-balanced William Ellery Channing, who disclaimed being an abolitionist and denied any responsibility for the movements of the abolitionists, honored them as advocates of the principles of freedom, justice, and humanity, and for having clung to these principles amidst threats, perils, and violence.

Slavery was perhaps the greatest stain on the record of American churches, and many just and also unjust criticisms were leveled against them by foreigners and Americans. In general, church bodies in the North went on record to urge kind treatment of slaves and to prevent separation of husband and wife and parents and children. Resolutions also expressed the hope that in the fullness of time the institution would be abolished.

About 1830 slavery rose to new significance with the movement of population westward and the mounting emigration from Europe; and the rising tide of abolitionism was registered by the establishment of Garrison's *Liberator* in 1831, and by the increasing number and activity of anti-slavery societies. Increasing sectionalism raised the fear in serious minds of internal discord and even violence. A New England clergyman, John Todd, who learned that a national anti-slavery society was about to be formed at Philadelphia wrote on December 6, 1833, that it marked the beginning of a warfare such as the country had never seen. He breathed the prayer that nothing worse would result than the outpouring of passions in words.

A Thanksgiving discourse entitled "The Census and Slavery" delivered by Horace Bushnell on November 28, 1860, a few weeks after the election of Abraham Lincoln, charted the course of religious statesmanship, professed and practiced by a substantial body of church members, clergymen and laymen. In broad outline Bushnell's sermon also expounded the philosophy and religious beliefs of the great president who became known as the Great Emancipator and who stated publicly that "if slavery is not wrong, nothing is wrong."

Bushnell began his discourse by positing the statement that the returns of the census of 1860 presaged the inevitable extinction of slavery at no very distant day. Changes in the distribution of population will be as silent as the movements of the stars, he said. Whether the slave states secede or not, slavery in those states will be extinguished by the operation of irresistible forces. If their population does not increase, he said, they will be overwhelmed by the population of free laborers; and if their population does increase by increase of their own population, the result will be the same.

No wisdom of man, or tempest of man's obstinacy can save it; and what is about equally plain, no agitations of philanthropy, or objurgations of reform, can very much hasten it. About the only thing we can do with much effect of benefit, is to limit the spread of the fire, and leave it to burn itself out. . . . Why should I be contriving the abolition of slavery and raising little storms and thunders of human campaigning against it when the Almighty Himself has a silent campaign of inevitable doom against it, marching on the awful census tramp of south and north to push it forever away. This campaigning, too, of God, if we look upon it rightly, has a moral significance more deep and vast than the fussing and the noisy chatter of a whole million of reformers.

Notwithstanding this reliance on the purposes of the Almighty, the speaker recalled things in human slavery against which he could not withhold his testimony, even if it were not to exist a year longer: the tearing asunder of parents and children, husbands and wives; compulsory concubinage substituted for marriage among human beings; a form of society that denies the right of chastity, the right of a Sunday, the right of serving God with a free conscience, the right of any sort of culture. With these unspeakable wrongs of slavery, the minister could not be at peace for an hour.

He repudiated the efforts of both sides to justify or to condemn slavery by quoting Scripture. One side made Scripture an authority to support the eternity of wrong in the world; the other side tortured the meaning out of it to save it from being shamed by the progress of society. Were the question between them polygamy and not slavery, they would have the same precise treatment or course of practice to go over, he said. Opposite to all such low conceptions of Scripture and its authority, what does it real honor is that it expects a growth in the moralities, and that God is all the way through putting in new germs of possibility, to raise the conceptions of men and make them capable of better things. "Polygamy, slavery and the slave trade, war, persecution—all these, by the appointed progress of moral opinion, are to be finally outlawed out of the world."

Making no concessions on moral grounds to certain aspects of slavery, including the Fugitive Slave Act, Bushnell expressed sympathy with the condition of the slaveholding states, because slavery was upon them without their consent, in the sense that men naturally approve that into which they have been trained by their laws and by their condition. "The sentiment of the world is against them . . . while they have no power to change it. . . . Let us have patience with it, speak of it with allowance, bathe it with all heavenly charity."

In an Anti-Slavery Tract entitled "The Infidelity of Abolitionism," published in 1860, William Lloyd Garrison wrote that the American Anti-Slavery Society, which was organized in December, 1833, had never criticized any religious body on account of its peculiar creed and had never discussed or attempted to settle the question whether or not the Bible was plenarily inspired. Of the Bible, as an anti-slavery instrumentality, it had made constant and powerful use against the pro-slavery interpretations of a "time-serving clergy." Of Jesus it had affirmed that He was ever with the downtrodden and the oppressed. "If, therefore, it be an infidel Society," he said, "it is so only in the sense in which Jesus was a blasphemer, and the apostles were 'pestilent and seditious fellows, seeking to turn the world upside down.' . . . It is infidel to a church which receives to its communion the 'traffickers in slaves and the souls of men'; it is loyal to the church which is not stained with blood, nor polluted by oppression. It is infidel to the Bible as a pro-slavery interpreted volume."

The Second Annual Report of the American Anti-Slavery Society (1835) dealt with the argument that Christianity, at its first promulgation, found slavery in the world, and by its general transforming influence upon the hearts of individuals, destroyed it. Hence it was inferred that no special effort should be made by abolitionists; the matter should be left to the reforming influence of Christianity. The conclusion was branded as false because the cases were not parallel. Granting that the apostles made no special attack upon slavery, yet they were not slaveholders. They made no compromise with sin. In America, however, slavery nestled in the church. In all leading denominations a large portion, both of members and ministers, held slaves and trafficked in them. Say what you will of the silence of the apostles on the subject of slavery, said the report, if their lips did not preach directly against slavery, their practice did.

Books, pamphlets, tracts, and sermons were published to present the scriptural, ecclesiastical, and historical view of slavery from the time of Abraham to the nineteenth century. Harriet Beecher Stowe paid her respects to complacent clergymen when she reported the conversation at the Sunday dinner table in the home of Arthur St. Clare, Uncle Tom's second master. Mrs. St. Clare had attended the morning service, while her husband sat at home smoking a cigar and reading the *New Orleans Picayune.* She waxed enthusiastic about the sermon which portrayed slavery as a part of God's plan of society. The sermon was fortified by selected quotations from the Old and the New Testaments. This was too much for the cynical St. Clare. He said he did not need to go to church to hear such drivel; he could learn what did him as much good as that from the *Picayune,* and smoke a cigar besides. He shocked his wife by admitting that the whole framework of society in Europe and in America would not stand the scrutiny of any very high standard of morality and by expressing his opinion of a minister who would quote Scripture to justify it. He concluded his part of the conversation by asserting that if it could be proved to church members that slavery was economically unprofitable, a flood of light would at once pour into the church, and it would immediately be discovered that everything in the Bible and in reason went the other way.

In the realm of Bible Christianity, where there was no ecclesiastical authority clothed with power to suppress the right of private judgment or to impose its own interpretation of the Bible, it was the sense of the ordinary man that finally counted, just as it was in the interpretation of the Constitution of the United States. In the words of Professor Moses Stuart of Andover Theological Seminary, who quoted Scripture to justify slavery, a thorough Protestant professes to believe that "the Scriptures are the sufficient and only rule of faith and practice." He said the Bible must be the ultimate test to which all sincere Christians were bound to appeal.

The majority of abolitionists within the fold of the Christian church were in agreement with the Andover professor as to the authority of the Bible, but they took violent exception to his exegesis. "Show me a Bill of Sale from the Almighty!" is what Lydia Maria Child would say to "Southern tyrants" who would enforce the Fugitive Slave Law. No other proof should be considered valid in a Christian country, she said. The abolitionists contended that they had a right to address the American people in the words of Paul to the Galatians: "Am I therefore become your enemy because I tell you the truth?" They maintained that they quoted Scripture as much as their opponents, but always on the side of right and justice. Finding Onesimus to have been sent back to Philemon not as a servant, but above a servant, a brother beloved, they could not see in that message any justification of the Fugitive Slave Law. At the head of the title page of Garrison's *Liberator* appeared the picture of Jesus with appropriate quotations from His words: "I come to break the bonds of the oppressor." "Thou shalt love thy neighbor as thyself."

In advocating resistânce to the enforcement of the Fugitive Slave Act, Lydia Maria Child asked if resort should be had to the Old Testament argument, "that anodyne for the consciences of 'South-Side' divines." Suppose the descendants of Ham were ordered to be slaves to the end of time, for an offense committed thousands of years ago, by a progenitor they never heard of, she said, still, the greatest amount of theological research leaves it uncertain who the descendants of Ham were, and where they were. "Then again, if we admit that Africans are descendants of Ham, what is to be said of thousands of slaves, advertised in the Southern newspapers as passing themselves for white men or white women? . . . Are these sons and daughters of our Presidents, our Governors, our Senators, our Generals, and our Commodores, descendants of Ham? Are *they* Africans?"

A former resident of a slave state, Mrs. L. J. Barker, presented an aspect of Christian hope that ran counter to the exegesis of men who preached to slaveholders. Sunday after Sunday she had seen pious church members meet to listen to the "garbled presentation of God's Word," members of one church claiming one God as their Father, one Christ for their Savior, striving for the blessed promises of one heaven, to which there is but one strait and narrow way of entrance; yet the "visible church" divided black from white by a wooden fence. On "sacrament days," after the white members had partaken of the bread and wine, the black members crawled through a little gate, left open only on that day, and came forward, four or five at a time, to take the bread and wine.

The action of the General Assembly of the Presbyterian Church in 1845 with reference to numerous memorials and petitions pertaining to slavery sheds light on the interpretation of the Bible by a representative and influential church body. The question which the Assembly was called upon to decide was: "Do the Scriptures teach that the holding of slaves, without regard to circumstances, is a sin, the renunciation of which should be made the condition of membership in the Church of Christ?" The Assembly resolved that it was impossible to answer this question in the affirmative without contradicting some of the plainest declarations of the Word of God. Facts which meet the eye of every reader of the New Testament made it impossible for the Assembly to denounce the holding of slaves as necessarily a heinous and scandalous sin. These facts were listed as follows: Slavery existed in the days of Christ and his apostles. They did not denounce the relation itself as sinful, as inconsistent with Christianity. Slaveholders were admitted to membership in the churches organized by the apostles. Although slaveholders were required to treat their slaves with kindness and as rational, accountable, immortal beings, and, if Christians, as brethren in the Lord, they were not commanded to emancipate them. The Assembly resolved that since Christ and His inspired apostles did not make the holding of slaves a bar to communion, as a court of Christ the Assembly had no authority to do so. The Assembly felt constrained to say that however desirable it might be to ameliorate the condition of the slaves in the Southern and Western states, or to remove slavery from the country, these objectives could never be secured by ecclesiastical action. The apostles sought to ameliorate the condition of slaves, not by denouncing and excommunicating their masters, but by teaching both masters and slaves the glorious doctrines of the Gospel, and enjoining upon each the discharge of their relative duties.

It will be noted that the General Assembly made no reference to the Old Testament, but justified its action as consistent with, and enjoined by, the example of Christ and His apostles as recorded in the New Testament. Moses Stuart, the professor in Andover Theological Seminary who was attacked by abolitionists as a betrayer of Christianity by his "pro-slavery" attitude, cited the Old Testament to prove the great antiquity of slavery—before the flood. Under many modifications, he said, slavery existed among patriarchs of the Jewish nation. He did not defend certain practices among Jews, who were immoral judged by Christian standards. He cited the Mosaic law which made heathen bondmen perpetual slaves; and this law was not to be erased by the hands of abolitionists. In his judgment, the position of the abolitionists plainly taxed high heaven with misdemeanors and alleged that the God of the Hebrews had sanctioned the commission of a crime as great as that which is forbidden by the Sixth or Seventh Commandment.

Moving into the New Testament, Stuart found that while almost every prevailing sin of the day was expressly denounced by the Savior, he did not once touch on the abuses of slavery. Stuart's explanation was that Christ purposely and carefully abstained from meddling with those matters which belonged to the civil power. Slavery was one of these. "An undertaking to dictate on this subject, would have subjected him to the accusation of being pragmatical in the affairs of civil government." It would seem, he said, that Christ believed that the sudden breaking up of the then existing framework of society would have occasioned greater evils than slavery. He quoted Paul to prove that servants were bound to be obedient and condemned the abolitionists for telling the slave that he owed no duty to his master and that he ought to escape from his service if possible. He found it stated nowhere in the New Testament that to be the master of a slave proves the want of Christianity. "On the other hand, one may with very much more reason say, that a refusal to obey Paul, an ignoring of what he has taught respecting slavery . . . is unspeakably stronger evidence of the want of Christian principle."

Every one of these conclusions and interpretations was challenged or rejected by abolitionists, who also pointed out that the status of the slave under the Mosaic law and the Roman law was essentially different from his legal status in the American colonies and states, where he was a chattel. In her Appeal to the Christian Women of the South (1836), Angelina E. Grimké stated that the fact of slavery having been the subject of prophecy furnished no excuse to slave-dealers, because no such system flourished under the patriarchal system. Slavery in America, she wrote, reduced a man to a thing, a chattel personal, and robbed him of all his rights as a human being and threw him out of the protection of the law.

The institution of slavery as it developed on the large plantations in the Cotton Kingdom symbolized the iniquity that drew the fire of the anti-slavery forces; and it was that militant slave power which produced the statesmanship symbolized by the "fire-eaters." During the period of the Revolution and the early years of the republic, the sentiment of the country as a whole was unfriendly to slavery. It was regarded as inconsistent with Christian civilization and out of accord with the principles for which the colonies had contended. Recognizing the problem of the African race, the American Colonization Society was organized in 1816 with the purpose of colonizing free Negroes outside the United States. James Madison and Henry Clay saw in this organization the most promising solution of the problem. Ralph Randolph Gurley, Connecticut-born, a Yale graduate and prominent Presbyterian layman, was for twenty-five years the leading advocate and director of the colonization cause.

The managers of the American Colonization Society argued that if free Negroes remained in the United States, they would have to contend, not only with law and prejudice, but also with superior knowledge, wealth, and influence, with a competition to which they were not equal, and with a deep sense of the thralldom of the past, which no benevolence nor even religion, could for ages, if ever, remove. Moreover, by establishing colonies of freedmen at proper intervals along the whole coast of western Africa, the slave trade would eventually be destroyed, and a knowledge of the Christian faith would be communicated to African tribes. A friend of the American Colonization Society suggested to a committee of the American Tract Society (1824) the importance of establishing a depository in Liberia, to aid in promoting religion among Negroes who were to become members of the republic which was then springing into existence.

The African Education Society was instituted on December 28, 1829, at Washington, D. C. Citizens of the District of Columbia and members of Congress conferred on the subject of establishing a society for the education of Negroes for influence and usefulness in Africa. The names of members and officers included many who were active in tract societies, home missionary societies, and Bible societies. There was no direct connection with the American Colonization Society, but at the meeting it was mentioned that it was logical to do something for the education of freedmen who were sent to Liberia.

The managers of the American Colonization Society appealed to the clergy of every denomination to make an annual appeal, "in or near the day consecrated to the memory of our independence," to bring the claims of the society before their people and to receive free-will offerings. Congregations and larger ecclesiastical units responded favorably, especially in the early years of the Society. For example, successive General Assemblies of the Synod of New York and Philadelphia of the Presbyterian Church ordered collections to be taken up. In 1818, in recommending its members to patronize and encourage the American Colonization Society, the Assembly adopted the following resolution:

As our country has inflicted a most grievous injury upon the unhappy Africans, by bringing them into slavery, we cannot indeed urge that we should add a second injury to the first by emancipating them in such a manner as they will be likely to destroy themselves or others. But we do think that our country ought to be governed in this matter by no other consideration than an honest and impartial regard to the happiness of the injured party, uninfluenced by expense or inconvenience which a regard may involve. We therefore warn all who belong to our denomination of Christians against unduly extending this plea of necessity; against making it a cover for the love and practice of slavery, or a pretence for not using efforts that are lawful and practicable to extinguish the evil. And we at the same time exhort others to forbear harsh censures and uncharitable reflections on their brethren who, unhappily, live among slaves whom they cannot immediately set free; but who at the same time are really using all their influence and all their endeavors to bring them into a state of freedom as soon as a door can be safely opened.

This school of Christian statesmanship was too cautious to win the approval of William Ellery Channing, who thought colonization might do good in Africa but only harm at home. He thought it had confirmed the prejudice, to which slavery owed much of its strength, that the colored man could not live and prosper as a freeman in America. Colonization darkened the prospect of humanity at home, however it might brighten it abroad. It had done much to harden the slave-holder in his purpose of holding fast his victim, he said. Lyman Beecher, on the other hand, wrote to Arthur Tappan on April 23, 1833, that he was not apprized of the ground of controversy between the colonizationists and the abolitionists. "I am myself both," he wrote, "without perceiving in myself any inconsistency."

There is abundant documentary evidence that in the slave states there were many yearnings for the day when slavery should be no more. Devout church members spoke of slavery as a "national sin." A clergyman of Murfreesboro, Tennessee, wrote on October 22, 1805: "I wish I never owned, or was master of Negroes! They are a hell to us in this world. I fear they will be so in the next. . . . We can't live with them or without them; and what to do is a question. If they make a little, they steal it as soon as they can; and unless the whip is for-ever on the creatures' backs they do nothing. . . . Is this a life for a Christian to lead?" In 1827 a Circular from ministers and delegates composing the annual meeting of Baptized Children of Christ, Friends of Humanity in Kentucky and Illinois, expected an awful storm to fall on a guilty land. "And may we not look for the heaviest punish-ment to fall on the professors of the most benign religion that ever existed who keep in continual countenance this shocking system by their unprecedented example." In the Transylvania Presbytery, 1787, the question, "Is slavery a moral evil?" was determined in the affirmative. The question, "Are all persons who hold slaves guilty of a moral evil?" was voted in the negative. In the same Presbytery in 1794 it was ordered that all persons under the care of the Presbytery holding slaves should teach all slaves not above the age of fifteen years to read the Word of God and to give them such education as might prepare them for the enjoyment of freedom. Masters should urge the attendance of slaves at public and family worship. The Forks of Elkhorn Baptist Church, Kentucky, from 1800 to 1820 received slaves into membership on the same grounds as free persons: experience, repentance, letter.

In 1842 the General Association of Massachusetts addressed a letter to thirty ecclesiastical bodies in the slave states, belonging to both divisions in the Presbyterian Church. Returns were received from only seven Presbyteries. Replies from two Presbyteries in Tennessee were pessimistic. The Presbytery of West Tennessee reported that the whole South was groaning under the evils connected with slavery. It extended an invitation to ministers from the North to come down to preach to the slaves and their masters; but it warned that any direct action taken in the North would be viewed by the majority in the South as an unwarrantable interference with their prerogatives as sovereign states. The reply from the Kingston Presbytery reflected the prevailing sentiment of the non-slaveholding majority in the population of East Tennessee. It lamented that influence and fashion gave slaveholders a preponderancy in legislative councils. These slaveholders were never asleep but sought to exercise censorship of the press, pulpit, and post office. Throughout the eastern division of the state few slaveholders dared to justify the system of slavery; they barely ventured to palliate it in their "particular cases."

The Presbytery of South Alabama replied that God had sanctioned and given laws for the government of the institution of slavery, and neither Christ nor His apostles condemned it. The untempered spirit of abolitionism had added "not a little in putting off the day of slave emancipation"; and had led to state enactments which precluded hope of ever bettering the condition of the slave spiritually or morally, except to a very limited extent. The efforts of the abolitionists had diffused a general distrust of ministers of the Gospel, and few were permitted to preach to Negroes free of suspicion. A letter from North Carolina, dated September 15, 1839, informed the American Home Missionary Society that the Southern people were not opposed to the preaching of the Gospel to their slaves; but they were opposed to ignorant preachers who endeavored to work more upon the passions and sympathies of the Negro "by loud unmeaning bawling instead of truth."

The Grimké sisters, who were members of the Society of Friends and changed their places of residence from their native South to the North, addressed the people of the South through the printing press. Angelina wrote an "Appeal to the Christian Women of the South"; Sarah wrote "An Epistle to the Clergy of the Southern States." Both were published in 1836. In reply to the accusation that the abolitionists abused their Southern brethren, Angelina asked if the prophet Isaiah abused the Jews when he addressed to them the cutting reproofs contained in the first chapter of his prophecies. Did Peter abuse the Jews when he told them they were the murderers of the Lord of Glory? "No man will now accuse the prophets and apostles of abuse, but what have the abolitionists done more than they?" Sarah compared the horrors of the Inquisition and "all the cruelty exercised by the Church of Rome" with the iniquity of slavery, and asserted that the abominations of Catholicism would not surpass those of slavery.

Almost without exception the churches were torn with the slavery controversy; and some of the major denominations divided into Northern and Southern bodies. Churchmen usually lament schism in their own denominations; but in the nature of the case Protestantism is sectarian and schismatic. Sectarians and schismatics could cite a number of New Testament passages to justify their positions and actions. The Reverend George Gordon in 1850 preached a sermon on "Secession from a Pro-Slavery Church a Christian Duty" and chose as his text Revelation 18:4: "Come out of her my people, that ye be not partakers of her sins, and that ye receive not of her plagues." The sermon presented the pastor's reasons for seceding from the Old Style

Presbyterian Church and his subsequent separation from the people of his charge.

The minister began his sermon by asking that if it be duty to leave one church on account of her errors in doctrine, or corruptions in practice, why should not another church be left in like circumstances. The act of secession is essentially the same as that of suspending or excommunicating a disorderly or reprobate member. When a church has grown corrupt, there is the same demand for secession on the part of her pious and orderly members that there is for a profession of religion at first. All Protestants agree, he said, that there is a point in a church's declension at which secession becomes a duty. Without such a concession, we must condemn the course of Luther and be consistent and go back to Rome. The preacher called to mind that the General Assembly of the Presbyterian Church had declared that American slavery was no bar to Christian communion. He stated that the members of the Old Style Presbyterian Church owned eighty thousand slaves. He quoted Scripture passages to prove that the spirit of Christianity was against slavery and that the Church ought to condemn members who lived in open sin; and he quoted many other passages to support his contention that Christians should have "no fellowship with the unfruitful works of darkness."

About fifteen years before Gordon preached his sermon, Beriah Green, president of Oneida Institute, expounded a radical doctrine in a sermon delivered Sunday evening, July 17, 1836, in the Presbyterian Church at Whitesboro, New York. The discourse was entitled "Things for Northern Men to Do." Before assuming the presidency of Oneida Institute, Green occupied the chair of sacred literature in the theological department of Western Reserve College. In December, 1833, he presided over the convention in Philadelphia at which the American Anti-Slavery Society was formed. Under his leadership students of every nationality and color were admitted on terms of equality into Oneida Institute. His uncompromising and fearless abolitionism and his liberal theology made him so unpopular that orthodox pulpits were closed against him.

He advocated the immediate dissolution of ecclesiastical connections with churches which tolerated in their members the sin of slaveholding. Until that was done, he said, the vitals of the evil against which he contended could never be reached. "Let all professed Christians, who enslave their brethren, know that no honest man can 'give them the hand of fellowship,' as the disciples of the Savior," he said. "Our compromise with slavery is full of ruin. Our covenant with death shall be disannulled, and our agreement with hell shall not stand." He asked if the North had nothing to do with a system of oppression, which was corrupting the morals, and wasting the strength, and blasting the character of the nation. Had the North nothing to do with a system which was poisoning the heart of the church and eating up the vitals of the republic? American slavery, he said, had deeply involved the North in guilt.

The abolitionists were aware of the argument used by men of the South that men in the North had been engaged in the slave trade and that therefore the North was partly responsible for fastening the institution of slavery on the country. They pleaded guilty to the indictment and turned the admission to their own advantage by assuming the obligation to remove it. William Ellery Channing admitted that the abolitionists deserved rebuke, but he thought it ought to be proportioned to the offense. They were wrong in making angry denunciations of slaveholders, but he asked if calling the slaveholder bad names was a crime of unparalleled aggravation? Is it not, at least, as great a crime to despoil a man of his rights and liberty, to make him a chattel, to trample him in the dust, he asked. Channing did not regard slaveholding as a proof of the necessary absence of a moral and religious principle. He held firmly to the conviction that the people of the North had reason and were bound to condemn the enormous wrongs practiced in the South; but he denied that they had the right to boast of themselves as better than their neighbors. He admitted that the selfish spirit of gain, which was blinding multitudes in the South to the injustice of slavery, was rife in the North. If the institution was rooted in the North, he asked, would not its people cling to it as obstinately as others. If the slaveholder could look upon slavery from the point of view of the North, he would not blame the remonstrances against it. Unfortunately, he said, long habit had hardened him to slavery.

The principle of action followed by the American Anti-Slavery Society was to overthrow slavery by revolutionizing public sentiment; and in effecting this objective it was necessary to begin with those who were not slaveholders. The Second Annual Report of the American Anti-Slavery Society (1835) denied that division in the church was the worst of all possible evils. The day was coming when Christ Himself would make a division.

TWENTY - THREE

CAESAR OR CHRIST

As THE sectional controversy over slavery grew in intensity, the anti-slavery forces were recruited by citizens in all walks of life who were outraged by what they conceived to be the threatening and aggressive slaveocracy. With each successive crisis precipitated by the annexation of Texas, the War with Mexico, the events which produced the Compromise of 1850, the Kansas-Nebraska Act, the Dred Scott decision, the enforcement of the Fugitive Slave Act, the assault on Senator Sumner, and the Harper's Ferry raid, the abolitionists gained allies among persons who were more moderate in speech and action. The abolitionists were relatively few in number. Their demand for immediate and unconditional emancipation was too radical for the much larger number of people who favored congressional action to prohibit the further expansion of slavery into territories but who were convinced that Congress had no power to interfere with slavery in the states where it was already established.

Slavery in the colonies and in the states rested on a legal system that was indigenous to them. There grew up a body of customary law, modified and amplified by statutory law, which governed the institutional development of slavery. Moreover, the existence of slavery was recognized in the Constitution of the United States by provisions pertaining to the slave trade, fugitive slaves, and the enumeration of slaves for purposes of representation and direct taxes. The abolitionists were taunted by their adversaries who insisted that slavery was an established institution—established by state laws—and recognized in the Constitution. They argued that slavery was local and not a proper subject for federal legislation or interference of the sort demanded by abolitionists.

The Reverend Nehemiah Adams, a New England clergyman active

in the American Tract Society, wrote a *South-Side View of Slavery* after a visit to the South in the decade of the fifties. He stated it mildly when he wrote: "There is a law of the land, a Constitution, to which we must submit, or employ suitable means to change it. While it remains, all our appeals to a 'higher law' are fanaticism." Abolitionists and anti-slavery clergymen pointed to Adams as an example of complacent churchmen who did the church much injury. They rejoiced when in 1856 Adams was defeated for reëlection to the board of the American Tract Society; every other member was unanimously reëlected. The only cause for lamentation was the fact that the defeat was not by a unanimous vote.

Even more unpopular was Moses Stuart, the Andover professor who in 1850 published *Conscience and the Constitution,* which was a defense of Webster's Seventh-of-March Speech. Stuart himself stated that within a week after his name was signed to a paper approving of Webster's speech, he began to receive anonymous letters. One letter stated that the professor, who had attained to the age of seventy, was in his second childhood; and another correspondent wondered how a man could study the Bible for forty years without having learned that slavery was a sin.

Stuart argued that the compacting states had the right to write into the Constitution of the United States Article IV, Section 3, with reference to the rendition of fugitive slaves. This provision was not inconsistent with the Declaration of Independence—that all men are created equal—because each state was, and is, a sovereignty within itself. Each state could, and can now, make laws regulating for itself all rights of property or of citizenship. Massachusetts cannot decide for Virginia on such a question. Virginia may do wrong, but Massachusetts is in no degree accountable or responsible for her actions or sins.

Turning to the contention that there is a law higher than the Constitution, the law of heaven written on our hearts and consciences, and that we are to follow that law and to disobey the Constitution, he asked what the *Christian* conscience did say. Stuart found the answer in the action of Paul when he sent the slave of Philemon back, because Paul's Christian conscience would not permit him to injure the vested rights of Philemon. Paul's conscience, he said, sent back the fugitive slave; the abolitionist's conscience encourages him to run away.

The theological professor cited cases where conscience went wrong: Loyola founded the Inquisition; Mary, Queen of England, had a conscience; James II and Judge Jeffreys made noisy claims to a conscience; hangers of witches had a conscience. Did the framers of the Constitution have conscience, he asked. What would these exalted and noble patriots think of certain anti-slavery meetings, was another question.

In conclusion the book listed a formidable number of evils of slavery. The author, in the interest of Christian justice, advocated patience and understanding and final and gradual, compensated emancipation.

A minister who had burned all bridges between himself and institutional Christianity did not chop logic when it was a question of slavery and the Constitution, nor did he spare the feelings of these two New England clergymen. This fearless preacher was Theodore Parker. In expounding the "Function of Conscience in Relation to the Laws of Men" he said: "The law of God has eminent domain everywhere . . . over all official business, all precedents, all human statutes, over all conventional affairs of mankind." Directing his words against Adams, Stuart, and others, Parker expressed amazement that Christianity of the Puritan stock should prove false to the only principle which at once justifies the conduct of Jesus, of Luther, and of the Puritans themselves. If obedience to the established law be the highest virtue, "then the Patriots and Pilgrims of New England, the Reformers of the Church, the glorious company of the Apostles, the goodly fellowship of the prophets, and the noble array of martyrs, nay, Jesus himself, were only criminals and traitors." This language was restrained in contrast with Parker's blistering attack on Webster's speech:

Metropolitan churches toppled, and pitched, and canted, and cracked, their bowing walls all out of plumb. Colleges broken from the chain which held them in the stream of time rushed toward the abysmal rent. Harvard led the way, *Christo et Ecclesiae* in her hand. Down plunged Andover, *Conscience and the Constitution* clutched in its ancient failing arm. New Haven began to cave in. Doctors of Divinity, orthodox, heterodox, with only a doxy of doubt, "no settled opinion," had great alacrity in sinking, and went down as ever into the bottomless pit of lower law.

Three tracts published by the American Anti-Slavery Society, numbered 7, 11, and 19, respectively, and entitled "Revolution the Only Remedy for Slavery," "Disunion our Wisdom and our Duty" (by Rev. Charles E. Hodges), and "Relations of Anti-Slavery to Religion" (by Charles K. Whipple) proposed extreme measures. The first tract attributed the grand secret of the strength of the slave power to the federal Union. It could command the militia to put down insurrection. It had awed prominent men into submission; it had awed the pulpit into submission; it had corrupted the heart óf the church. Only a remnant had not bowed the knee to this political Baal. Southern slave-breeders and slave-mongers as Christians and ministers of Christ visit Northern cities and large towns and are taken to the bosom of churches and afterward made welcome to pulpits. The only practical way of cutting any of these cords is to sever them all at a single stroke. "May God hasten the day when it shall be our happiness to hail for our beloved country a new State and a new Church, 'wherein dwelleth righteousness.' "

The tract written by Hodges maintained that it was the duty of every honest man to free himself of the prejudice that the Constitution was as sacred as a divine revelation and that the Union was of divine origin. "Have we a right for the sake of national greatness and power, or territorial integrity, or any conceivable material property . . . to sustain a union, which demands, and for its preservation must secure, from its citizens, a sacrifice of the fundamental and eternal laws of religion and morality?" Whipple's tract enumerated instances where church and clergy were derelict in speech and action.

In a speech before the second annual meeting of the Anti-Slavery Society (1835) James G. Birney compared the Constitution to a treaty. He said the Constitution bound the people of the free states to aid the South in suppressing insurrections and domestic violence. Suppose, he said, that the United States were bound by a treaty with Russia to suppress insurrection against that government, would the American people be guiltless of all participation in the oppression of her Polish subjects? And suppose that after a Polish insurrection had been suppressed, and thousands driven into exile, and others had escaped to the United States, the United States should stipulate by treaty to aid the autocrat in recovering his prey, would anyone pretend to say that the American people had no participation in the subsequent oppression that might ensue? And yet where is the difference between this case and our constitutional stipulations with the Southern slaveholders, he asked.

The Fugitive Slave Laws, whether enacted in 1793 or in 1850 were the targets of the most bitter invectives, even by such men as Horace Bushnell and William Ellery Channing, who usually trimmed the excesses of extremists.

After the election of Lincoln in 1860, Bushnell admitted that the Constitution plainly gave a right to the recovery of fugitives which good citizens could not deny; and he thought that "our part" of the bond ought to be religiously fulfilled. However, the plain truth in regard to the act of 1850 was that it was passed "in high blood and carries the plantation airs in its nod." He alleged that the law was meant to insult the people of the North and to crack the lash in their faces. He denied that the right to such a law was given by the Constitution; it was not fit to be passed. Let it be repealed in its obnoxious features, he said, and put in some guise of decency and good manners, allowing the masters to arrest their own fugitives and take them away on some adequate proof and trial of their ownership.

In his "Remarks on the Slavery Question," published in 1839, Channing stated that he knew of no provision of the Constitution at which his moral feelings revolted but that pertaining to the rendition of fugitive slaves. It did not satisfy him to be told that this provision was a part of "that sacred instrument, the Constitution, which all are solemnly bound to uphold." No charter of man's writing can sanctify injustice, or repeal God's Eternal Law, he said. He could not escape the conviction, that every man who aided in the restoration of a fleeing slave was a wrongdoer. He was well aware how these views would be received at the North and the South; but he looked "above scoffers and denouncers to that pure, serene, almighty Justice, which is enthroned in Heaven, and inquire of God, the Father of us all, whether he approves the surrender of the flying slave."

The argument in justification of slavery based on vested interests and property rights did not silence Channing. He replied that an evil did not lose its deformity by becoming an institution, that is, an established thing, held up by laws and public force. Slavery entrenched behind institutions, was on that very account to be assailed with all the weapons of reason, of moral suasion, of moral reprobation, which good men could wield. He lamented that multitudes knew no higher authority than human government and were possessed of the idea that a number of men, perhaps little honored as individuals for intelligence and virtue, were yet competent, when collected into a legislature, to create right and wrong. The most immoral institutions thus gained a sanctity from law. He admitted that he was bound to submit to the laws, in the sense of abstaining from physical resistance; but he denied the obligation to bow his own moral judgment, his free thoughts, his free speech. "Is conscience to stoop from its supremacy, and to become the echo of the human magistrate?" he asked. "Is the law, written by God's finger on the heart, placed at the mercy of interested statesmen?"

Channing asked what ought to be done if the Constitution bound citizens to an unlawful act. He answered his own question by stating that the individual must abstain from what he deemed wrong. He also asked whether a citizen, who viewed the government which he sustained as pledged to wrong deserved reproach for laboring to bring it into harmony with truth and rectitude. He answered that question by putting another: "Does not the Constitution, in making provision for its own amendment, imply the possibility of defect, and warrant free discussion of its various clauses? What avails our liberty of speech, if, on a grave question of duty, we must hold our peace?"

Channing took issue with lawyers who held that property was the creation of law; as if it had no natural foundation, as if it were not a natural right. Of all radicals, he said, the most dangerous, perhaps, was he who made property the creature of law; because what law created, it could destroy. There were principles of property which no law could move, he said.

The argument that slavery in the South was no concern of people in the free states—that those states stand on the same ground with foreign countries—was disposed of by positing a series of questions: "Is humanity a local feeling? Does sympathy stop at a frontier? . . . Has duty no work to do beyond our native land? Does a man cease to be a brother by living in another state?" Christianity taught different lessons. Under its impulses, Christians sent the preachers of the cross to distant countries, to war with deep-rooted institutions.

Channing did not live to face the dilemma created by the Dred Scott decision; but Chief Justice Taney might have read a terrific excoriation of himself if he had read a speech delivered by George B. Cheever at the anniversary of the American Abolition Society in May, 1858. It was entitled "The Fire and Hammer of God's Word against the Sin of Slavery." The speaker asserted that our iniquitous and cruel career against the African race came to its climax in the Dred Scott decision; for when iniquity took the place of national law, and was enthroned in the tribunal of justice, it could not well go higher. "The Sabbath after that prodigious judicial crime, it seemed as if the very Bibles would have burst open of their own accord, and that in living fire the lightnings of God's word would almost have burned its sentence on the walls and hissed along the congregations." If ever the Church and the ministry were going to speak out, it should have been then, he said. He asked if the country could go any lower, any deeper, than the Dred Scott decision and its consequences. "Our public officials of justice and of policy, from the highest to the lowest, every time they are about to enact a new violence against the oppressed, only have to refer to the Dred Scott decision, and the basest, meanest, most detestable acts of fraud and cruelty are converted into righteousness."

Abolitionists compiled digests of slave codes in order to bring home to people in the North the wide gulf that existed between the white and the black races and to illustrate the injustice of the laws governing the relation between master and slave. Apologists for the institution, like Thomas R. Dew, Professor of Political Law in the College of William and Mary, were convinced that slavery was intended by the Creator for some useful purpose and that it had been the principal means for impelling forward the civilization of mankind. One of the stock arguments in defense of slavery was that it brought the black man out of barbarism, made him a useful member of society, and conferred upon him the blessings of Christianity.

The abolitionists denied that slavery Christianized the Negro. The Reverend T. W. Higginson wrote an Anti-Slavery Tract (No. 4) in which he quoted from reports of Southern religious bodies to prove that the moral and spiritual condition of Negroes was heathenish. "Their depravity, their spiritual ignorance and destitution, are amazingly and awfully great," he wrote.

The defenders of slavery contended that through the leniency of the master, the slave suffered less than the laborer in most other countries. He had more comforts and was happier. William Ellery Channing thought it honorable to his time that such a defense as that was urged and required. The fact that the master held himself bound to maintain that his victim was happier for his bondage showed the progress of civilization and Christianity. The ancient Roman never thought of seeking a justification of slavery in its blessings, he said. He never took the ground of his being a benefactor to those whom he oppressed. "The lenity which quiets you in wrong-doing becomes a crime. Do not boast of your humanity to those whom you own, when it is a cruel wrong to be the owner." He brought in the example of some highwaymen who have taken pride in the gentlemanly, courteous style in which they have eased the traveler of his purse. They have even given him back a part of the spoils, that he might travel comfortably home. But they were robbers still.

Channing stated that the master's kindness to the slave was not of the right stamp. It was lacking in moral character. The master was kind to his slaves because they were his own, not because they were fellow-creatures. Little good could be expected from religious instruction to the slave, because it was hard to graft good on what was essentially evil and corrupt; hard for the man who oppressed to exalt his victim. "It is hard to comprehend how the slaveholder can preach the grand precepts of Christianity; how he can set forth God as the Universal Father, who looks on all men with an equally tender love, and watches, with an equal severity of justice, over the rights of all."

The *Antislavery Record* for February 9, 1836, printed results of a query presented to the Savannah River Baptist Association of Ministers with reference to remarriage in the case of separation of husband and wife by sale, so as to preclude reunion in the future. The ministers answered that such separation among persons situated as the slaves were, was civilly a separation by death. They believed that in the sight of God it would be so viewed. The slaves were not free agents; and a dissolution by death was not more entirely without their consent and beyond their control than separation by sale. Channing's comment was: "What a comment on Southern institutions! It shows how religion is made their tool, how Christianity is used to do violence to the most sacred feelings and ties, that the breed of slaves must be kept up. It shows us, that this iniquitous system pollutes by its touch, the divinest, the holiest provision of God for human happiness and virtue."

The slavery controversy involved collateral issues that were just as vital as the abolition of slavery and the setting of bounds to its territorial extent. In both sections of the country efforts were made to deny the right of petition, to exclude anti-slavery literature from the mails, and to deny the right of free speech and of publication. At a meeting held in Faneuil Hall in November, 1837, the attorney-general of Massachusetts referred to Channing as a clergyman "marvellously out of place" mingling in the debates of a popular assembly, whereupon Wendell Phillips asked the gentleman if he remembered that freedom to preach was first gained, dragging in its train freedom to print.

The cause of academic freedom was one of principles at stake in the Lane Seminary debate which resulted in the dismissal of a member of the faculty and the withdrawal of most of the students who were loyal to him. The debate and the train of consequences that followed hard upon it gave a tremendous impulse to abolitionism throughout the nation. Lane Seminary was located in Cincinnati, Ohio, about a mile from the boundary of the slave state of Kentucky. Many of the students were sons of slaveholders. The debate within the student body was held in the winter of 1833–34 and lasted eighteen evenings. The subject was divided into two questions: (1) Ought the people of the slaveholding states to abolish slavery immediately? (2) Are the doctrines, tendencies, and measures of the American Colonization Society, and the influence of its principal supporters, such as to render it worthy of the patronage of the Christian public?

The Lane Seminary crisis was precipitated by the Board of Trustees who, in the absence of President Lyman Beecher in the East, abolished the Lane Seminary Anti-Slavery Society and prohibited the discussion of slavery in any public room of the seminary. The trustees discharged the head of the Preparatory Department, who was an abolitionist, and forced out Theodore Dwight Weld, one of the ablest members of the faculty. Had it not been for the action of the trustees, who acted without due consideration for the authority of the faculty, the imbroglio might not have occurred. Beecher and the faculty were not entirely blameless, and neither were the students. The whole affair was poorly handled. Beecher won concessions from the trustees, but Weld would not reconsider his decision to change his field of activity. He had before him the prospect of the opening of Oberlin College, to which most of the seceding Lane students went with the exception of a few who enrolled at Western Reserve College, the "Western Yale."

The Lane Seminary crisis gave a serious setback to the prospects of that institution; but the founding of Oberlin College, which grew directly out of the controversy, gained more for the anti-slavery cause than was lost by the action of the seminary authorities. One of the trustees who dissented from the action of his colleagues was Asa Mahan, minister of the Sixth Presbyterian Church in Cincinnati. In 1835 he was elected first president of Oberlin College; and he accepted the position on condition that students be admitted without discrimination as to race or sex. Charles G. Finney was made head of the Department of Theology. Arthur Tappan, a wealthy businessman, became the Maecenas of the institution. He gave a donation and made a private pledge of his entire income in order to assure the establishment of the college. Finney and Weld were instrumental in training some of the greatest speakers in the anti-slavery cause; and many pulpits were filled with Oberlin graduates.

William Lloyd Garrison took sweet revenge when in January, 1835, his *Liberator* published the statements of both the seceding students and faculty of Lane Seminary. Garrison commented that Lane Seminary was now to be regarded as strictly a Bastille of oppression—a spiritual Inquisition. Statements and comment were reprinted in a pamphlet, eighteen thousand copies of which were circulated by Arthur Tappan and other New York abolitionists. It was most effective in influencing the class of people who sent sons to divinity schools. Garrison had not forgotten the slight he had received in 1830 when he solicited Beecher's support for the projected *Liberator*. At that time Beecher was the most prominent orthodox clergyman in Boston; and Garrison was charmed by the spell of his eloquence. Beecher listened patiently to Garrison's project and then informed him that he had too many irons in the fire to put in another. Garrison retorted:

"Doctor, you had better take them all out and put this one in, if you mean well, either to the religion or to the civil liberty of our country."

The comment of Wendell Phillips on this episode was made public in a speech at the Melodeon in Boston on January 27, 1853, and was published as an Anti-Slavery Tract in 1860. The title was "The Philosophy of the Abolition Movement." Phillips stated that the "great orthodox leader" did not rest with merely refusing to put another iron into his fire; he attempted to limit the irons of other men. As president of Lane Seminary he endeavored to prevent the students from investigating the subject of slavery. The result was the strenuous resistance of a large number of the students, led by that remarkable man, Theodore Dwight Weld. "The right triumphed, and Lane Seminary lost her character and noblest pupils at the same time."

There were among the clergy and the laity those who believed that slavery was a subject that ought to be excluded from the pulpit; that it was a proper subject for the political forum. The abolitionists pinned their hope on a fearless and unmuzzled ministry. Flavel Bascom, pastor of a Presbyterian Church in Chicago, appointed prayer meetings in behalf of the anti-slavery cause. In his Autobiography he wrote that it was esteemed a great privilege that they might present their petitions to the Supreme Ruler of Heaven and Earth, seeing that they were unheeded by the rulers and lawmakers of the nation and that nearly all the religious denominations were implicated in the responsibility of lending their sanction to slavery. The same year (1840) at a meeting of the Congregational Association of Illinois at Payson it was resolved that the subject of slavery, like any other question of morality, was a proper subject to be introduced into the pulpit.

At a meeting of the Congregational Association of Illinois at Warsaw on April 18, 1839, a communication signed by fifty-six citizens of Warsaw protesting the preaching of an anti-slavery sermon was presented. The communication stated that the preaching of the sermon would be against the almost unanimous wishes of the citizens of that community. In reply to the communication it was resolved to maintain the privilege of expressing opinions wherever and whenever the cause of truth could be promoted. It was further resolved that the Association adopted the resolution from a sense of duty to God and man.

Moreover, it was stated, that if they once adopted the principle of consenting to renounce their own principles and inalienable rights out of regard to the feelings of others, they would frequently have occasion to turn aside from the path of duty or to relinquish those rights.

The most influential abolitionist, whose power of expression touched the hearts and fired the determination, was neither a speaker nor a pulpit orator. An Englishman, Alfred Bunn, in his book, published in London in 1853, entitled *Old England and New England, in a Series of Views Taken on the Spot*, stated that anyone writing at the present moment on America and not mentioning Mrs. Harriet Beecher Stowe, would lay himself open to a charge of high crimes and misdemeanors. Mrs. Stowe wrote that the object of publishing *Uncle Tom's Cabin* was to awaken feeling and sympathy for the African race; but Bunn did not believe one syllable of that assertion. The first aim of the authoress, said Bunn, was to enlist the sympathies of the churches and array them in open hostility to the established institutions of the country. The second aim was that of self-aggrandizement and reward. "The book of this priestess is one far more of fiction than of fact, conceived in a coarse spirit, and executed in vulgar style." The falsity of its premises renders the communication little less than criminal. Mrs. Stowe, he stated, held up ministers to contempt by charging them with harboring sentiments unworthy of men and Christians. The English author then referred to the controversy with Joel Parker to prove Mrs. Stowe's contempt for ministers.

The controversy with Parker stems from an article in the *Independent* of May 15, 1851, which was a reprint of an article that appeared originally in the *Mercury*, published in Bristol, England. The article was read by Mrs. Stowe in her kitchen in Brunswick, Maine. It was concerned with the propriety of admitting to English pulpits certain American clergymen who were planning to attend a convention in London. To justify English concern for the purity of its pulpits, the *Mercury* published a list of utterances on slavery attributed to a number of American clergymen. Among the ministers quoted was Joel Parker, a Presbyterian minister in Philadelphia, a former president of Union Theological Seminary, and a personal friend of Mrs. Stowe's husband, father, and brothers. The statement attributed to Parker was: "There are no evils in slavery but such as are inseparable from any other relation in civil and social life." Mrs. Stowe's brilliant biographer, Forrest Wilson, states that these statements made her seethe; and the complacent attitude of the Northern clergy became her obsession. In this mood, says Wilson, she brought seven preachers into *Uncle Tom's Cabin* as characters, but only one in a favorable light.

The sequel to this episode is found in Chapter XII of Mrs. Stowe's masterpiece, entitled "Select Incidents of Lawful Trade." This chapter tells the story of Lucy who with her infant was tricked aboard an Ohio River steamboat, after having been secretly sold to the trader who was taking Tom down the river. When the boat stopped at the wharf at Louisville, the infant was carried away by stealth in the arms of a man who had purchased him. The heartbroken mother ended her wretched existence by suicide. In relating this incident, Mrs. Stowe remembered Dr. Joel Parker's "comfortable sophistry," as Forrest Wilson called it, and used it in a "piece of blazing sarcasm," and then cited the name of the clergyman in a footnote. Mrs. Stowe contrasted these "little incidents of lawful trade" with the precepts of the Christian religion.

Forrest Wilson's explanation of the circumstances of the writing of *Uncle Tom's Cabin,* and of the aims of the author, is decidedly at variance with that of the English author. This is Wilson's version: During the communion service in the First Parish Church in Brunswick, Maine, Mrs. Stowe fell into a spiritual state. When the communion service began after the conclusion of the sermon, she went forward mechanically, returned to her pew in a daze, fighting back her tears. After the benediction had been pronounced, she walked home in a trance; and she remained in a reverie at the dinner table. Then she went to her bedroom and wrote out the picture in the vision, even to the names of characters in the story: Uncle Tom, Sambo and Quimbo, Simon Legree.

The story ran serially in the *National Era.* "The Lord himself wrote it. I was but an instrument in his hands," she said afterwards. *"Uncle Tom's Cabin* is an event rather than a book," wrote Wendell Phillips in 1853. He said that if the anti-slavery movement had not roused the sympathies of Mrs. Stowe, the book would never have been written; and if the movement had not raised up thousands of hearts to sympathize with the slave, the book would never have been read. He admitted that the genius of the author had increased tenfold the number of readers; but "there must be a spot even for Archimedes to rest his lever upon, before he can move the world; and this effort of genius, consecrated to the noblest purposes, might have fallen dead and unnoticed in 1835. It is the antislavery movement which has changed 1835 to 1852."

Does the huge success of the book in Europe, where the landscape was bare of abolitionist crusaders and tracts, contradict the judgment of Phillips? For example, *Uncle Tom's Cabin* began to run serially in *Aftonbladet,* a Stockholm daily, on October 25, 1852. It aroused so much interest that, in response to letters from individuals and from newspapers throughout Sweden, arrangements were made with Albert Bonnier to publish it in book form from the translation in *Aftonbladet.* On November 20, 1852, the daily published a biographical sketch of Mrs. Stowe, in response to the interest shown in her book.

The chief indictment of the institution in the pages of *Uncle Tom's Cabin* is in the very concept of slavery itself; and the prodigious success of the book may be attributed to the skill of a Christian mother in bringing to homes in the North the horrible implications of the concept of slavery.

In 1851 while sitting in the Melodeon, Wendell Phillips was startled by the assertion of his friend Parker Pillsbury that the theaters would receive the gospel of anti-slavery truth earlier than the churches. A hiss went up from the galleries, and many in the audience were shocked. Speaking in the same hall in 1853, Phillips admitted that he could not believe it to be true; but the lapse of two years proved it. "The theater bowing to its audience, has preached immediate emancipation, and given us the whole of 'Uncle Tom'; in the theological papers, the work is subjected to criticism, to reproach, and its author to severe rebuke." Exactly two years after Phillips made that speech, newspapers reported that "Uncle Tom's Cabin" continued to draw good houses at the New York theaters. By the end of March, 1854, it had played at the National Theater for the 226th time.

At the Eighteenth Annual Meeting of the Massachusetts Anti-Slavery Society in Faneuil Hall in January, 1850, Wendell Phillips reported scathing resolutions against the church. He charged that the church disowned the principles which had sprung from her bosom and branded them as infidel; that she kept the sword of the Spirit sheathed, while other men contended for the faith once delivered to the saints. In view of these facts and others, the resolutions pronounced her claim to be the church of Christ an idle blasphemy.

The ten years before the Civil War were pregnant with stirring events; and within about four years after these resolutions were read in Faneuil Hall, the *Liberator* reported that more than three thousand clergymen of all denominations resident in Massachusetts and the other New England States had formulated and signed petitions against the repeal of the Missouri Compromise. They protested against the Kansas-Nebraska bill as a great moral wrong and a breach of faith eminently injurious to the moral principles of the community. Subsequent issues of the *Liberator* printed similar protests from clergymen in many parts of the country.

Perhaps the consensus of opinion among clergymen in the North was stated by Albert Barnes in his *Inquiry into the Scriptural Views of Slavery,* published in 1846: "Christianity was not designed to extend and perpetuate slavery, but . . . the spirit of the Christian religion would remove it from the world, because it is an evil, and is displeasing to God."

After his conviction and sentence to death by hanging, John Brown expressed satisfaction with the treatment he had received at the trial, but felt no consciousness of guilt. "I went against the laws of men, it is true, but 'whether it be right to obey God or men, judge ye,' " he wrote. It was his Puritan conscience that took comfort in the thought that God could make his death more valuable to His own cause than his life.

TWENTY-FOUR

EPILOGUE

During the three centuries which have passed since the Puritans established their commonwealth in the New World, successive generations have passed judgment upon them, and historians have arrived at radically different appraisals of their character and achievements and influence upon posterity. It is the judgment of the historian Macaulay that the Puritans were perhaps the most remarkable body of men which the world has ever produced. Their achievements prove that they were no mere vulgar fanatics, he said; and most of their absurdities were mere external badges. No other Christians, whether as individuals or groups or sects, have exceeded the Puritans in their veneration of the Bible. In that respect, as well as others, Puritanism was elemental Protestantism. One of Cromwell's biographers calls Puritanism the "Protestantism of the Protestant religion." For Cromwell, whose fame transcends that of all Puritans, the Bible comprehended all literature.

A distinguished church historian attempted to give an answer to "What Is Christianity?" in sixteen lectures delivered in the University of Berlin in the Winter Term, 1899–1900. In a sense, Professor Harnack's lectures were a "confession of faith." He told his students that when a man grows older and sees more deeply into life, he does not find that he is advanced by the external march of things, by "the progress of civilization." He is forced to seek the source of strength where his forefathers also sought. It is the man who knows religion only as usage and obedience that creates the priest, he said, for the semi-religious prefer an ordinance to a Gospel. This scholar whose prolonged research was crowned by a monumental history of dogma quoted with approval Goethe: "Let intellectual and spiritual culture progress, and the human mind expand, as much as it will; beyond the grandeur and the moral elevation of Christianity, as it sparkles and shines in the Gospels, the human mind will not advance."

Twentieth-century America appears to have lost the Puritan heritage. A generation whose "literature" is more akin to the licentiousness of the press which ridiculed the Puritans in England, whose "movies" revel in the filth of the muckrake, whose radio and television programs serve a fare of vulgarity, and whose mechanism has degraded the superior man and has enhanced the power of the inferior man, is incapable of understanding a religious movement whose appeal is to the "remnant," to those who are conscious of the brevity of human life and recognize the spiritual life as the one great reality.

Puritanism laid emphasis on Christian intelligence, not primarily on theology. The letters that were written, and the sermons that were preached, bespeak an interest in dogma far more intense than letters and sermons of today; but they also reveal a more vital faith and a more strenuous morality. The vocabulary is more dignified and seasoned with biblical wisdom, indicating deep sources of faith and hours of meditation and devotion. It has been said that Calvin sought to answer the question: "How could the church be made not simply an institution for the worship of God, but an agency for the making of men fit to worship Him?"

The age-old problem as to whether or not creed forms character or character forms creed has not been answered. "Calvin shaped the mold in which the bronze of Puritanism was cast," wrote John Morley in his *Oliver Cromwell*. The same English author agrees with Hobbes that it is not points necessary to salvation that have raised all the quarrels, but questions of authority and power over the church, or of profit and honor to churchmen. "In other words," he writes, "it has always been far less a question of what to believe, than of whom to believe."

The Puritans sought to know God and to serve Him, without doing homage to ecclesiastical dignitaries and their rites and ceremonies. They were deeply read in the Word of God; and in the inspired Book terrestrial distinctions vanished. In order to counteract the doctrine of predestination, which leveled all classes before God, Archbishop Laud seized upon the doctrine of free will expounded by the Dutch theologian Arminius to displace it. As the conflict between Laud and the Puritans unfolded, predestination implied parliamentary government against an arbitrary government. The fact that Arminianism was espoused by churchmen with high-church tendencies and leanings toward Romanism, who were in the good graces of the king, was so alarming that Parliament adopted a resolution declaring that whoever sought to introduce "Popery or Arminianism, or other opinions disagreeing with the true and orthodox church," should be reputed a capital enemy to the kingdom and the commonwealth. This resolution was adopted in March, 1629. In 1628 and 1629, respectively, two expeditions established the settlement at Salem, Massachusetts. The religious development of New England was shaped by the colonists themselves, without interference from the Mother Country. They were beyond the reach of Archbishop Laud's strong arm.

The first settlers of the Massachusetts Bay Colony were the vanguard of twenty thousand Englishmen who fled from Laud's persecution between 1628 and 1640. In that sense Laud was the founder of Anglo-Saxon supremacy in the New World. As these words are written in 1951, the passage in Trevelyan's *England under the Stuarts* is even more prophetic than when it was written almost a half-century earlier:

In the new folk-wanderings of all peoples, nations and languages, which in North America today are preparing the future of the world, English speech and in some sort English ideas and customs have become the mould into which the outpourings of all Europe are cast year by year to dissolve, mingle and be transformed; because far back in a more quiet spot of space and time, William Laud determined that the village churches of England should have a seemly service. How can we praise or blame him? Love or hate of Laud and of what he purposed, pales before the gigantic hopes and fears of all who contemplate what he has accomplished.

The descendents of the Puritans played a leading part in the grand experiment of the Mississippi Valley in the nineteenth century, where the fabric of a new society was woven. The quickening spirit of Puritanism was augmented by the levelling process of the frontier. Asa Turner, a member of the "Iowa band," gave the following advice to prospective missionaries in the West:

Don't come here expecting a paradise. Our climate will permit men to live long enough, if they do their duty. If they do not, no matter how soon they die. Office and station are but little regarded here. People will not speak of you or to you, as the Rev. Mr. So-and-So, but will call you simply by your name, and your wife Peggy or Polly, or whatever her name may be.

Come prepared to expect savage things, rough things. Lay aside all your dandy whims boys learn in college, and take a few lessons of your grandma there before you come. Get clothes, firm, durable, something that will go through the hazel brush without tearing. Don't be afraid of a good, hard hand, or of a tanned face. If you keep free from a hard heart, you will do well. Get wives of the old Puritan stamp, such as honored the distaff and the loom, those who can pail a cow, and churn the butter, and be proud of a jean dress or a checked apron.

In the crusading zeal of the emissaries and colporteurs of the nineteenth century there was little of the persecutions instituted by the founders of New England, whose superstition and bigotry have been the themes of polemics in the twentieth century. Without condoning the sins and shortcomings of the men who banished Roger Williams and Anne Hutchinson, we may justly exclaim in the words of Lyman Beecher: "Would to God that the ancestors of all the nations had been not almost, but altogether such bigots as our fathers were."

It was not given to the founders and supporters of the American Home Missionary Society, the American Tract Society, the American Bible Society, and the American Sunday School Union to peer over the boundaries of the nineteenth century into the twentieth. Those who brought the Gospel to immigrants who in America found a haven of refuge from the trammels and injustices of an old-world society did not live to see and hear about the victims of totalitarian governments, who lived like cavemen in air raid shelters. Refugees from concentration camps and displaced persons made the "hard way" in America seem easy.

The depression that struck like a thunderbolt at the end of the third decade of the twentieth century and the war that added to the chaos in the following decades brought a catastrophe that shattered the dream of making a heaven on earth. What past generations prayed to God for was to be brought to pass by the help of science and technocracy. By eating the fruit of the tree of knowledge, we would become gods ourselves. The catastrophe has not only silenced such thoughts but it has pronounced a doom over the generation and civilization that gave birth to them. Science has given man great power and strength; but he has not learned that knowledge, power, and strength are not of themselves good.

The twentieth century needs such sermons and writings as Puritans of colonial New England heard and read. Their preachers and writers delivered a message for their time, just as all great preachers must, instead of appeasing or flattering their hearers and readers. William Ellery Channing had a message for all generations:

Erase all thought and fear from a community, and selfishness and sensuality would absorb the whole man. Appetite, knowing no restraint, and suffering, having no solace or hope, would trample in scorn on the restraints of human laws. Virtue, duty, principle, would be mocked and spurned as unmeaning sounds. A sordid self-interest would supplant every feeling; and man would become, in fact, what the theory of atheism declares him to be,—*a companion for brutes.*

BIBLIOGRAPHICAL NOTE

THE author of this volume is indebted to the authors of general works in the fields of European and American history and more especially monographic and biographic material pertaining to religious history. His main reliance has been on periodicals, pamphlets, tracts, sermons, diaries, autobiographies, and reports of organizations and societies. The character of this material is suggested by references in the text. This bibliographical note is intended to include only a few titles.

Brief biographical sketches of most of the personalities mentioned in the book are easily accessible in the *Dictionary of American Biography* for the American background and the *Dictionary of National Biography* for the English background. Appended to each article is a brief bibliography.

THE EUROPEAN BACKGROUND. Adolf Harnack, *What is Christianity?* (New York, 1904); Adolf Harnack, *The Constitution and Laws of the Church in the First Two Centuries* (London, 1910); George M. Trevelyan, *England under the Stuarts* (London, 1910); Frederic Seebohm, *The Oxford Reformers* (New York, 1914); Rufus M. Jones, *Spiritual Reformers of the 16th and 17th Centuries* (London, 1914); Charles Firth, *Oliver Cromwell and the Rule of the Puritans in England* (New York, 1900); Charles C. Butterworth, *The Literary Lineage of the King James Bible, 1340–1611* (Philadelphia, 1914).

THE PURITANS IN NEW ENGLAND. Samuel E. Morison, *The Founding of Harvard College* (Cambridge, 1935); Perry Miller, *The New England Mind. The Seventeenth Century* (New York, 1939); Williston Walker, *A History of the Congregational Churches in the United States* (New York, 1907).

THE QUAKERS. The following books by Rufus M. Jones are indispensable: *George Fox. Seeker and Friend* (New York, 1930), *New Studies in Mystical Religion* (New York, 1927), and *The later Periods of Quakerism* (2 vols., London, 1921). William C. Braithwaite, *The Beginnings of Quakerism* (London, 1923), and *The Second Period of Quakerism* (London, 1921); Stephen Hobhouse, *William Law and Eighteenth Century Quakerism* (London, 1927); Thomas E. Drake, *Quakers and Slavery* (New Haven, 1950).

THE GREAT AWAKENING. Joseph Tracy, *The Great Awakening* (Boston,

1842); Jonathan Edwards, *Some Thoughts Concerning the Present Revival of Religion in New England*. 1736; Thomas Prince, *The Christian History, Containing Accounts of the Revival and Propagation of Religion in Great Britain and America. For the Years 1743 and 1744* (2 vols., Boston, 1744, 1745).

THE METHODISTS. J. Brazier Green, *John Wesley and William Law* (London, 1945); William Law, *A Practical Treatise upon Christian Perfection* (London, 1807); Frederick J. Jobson, *America and American Methodism* (New York, 1857); John Emery, *A Defense of "Our Fathers" and of the Original Organization of the Methodist Episcopal Church, Against the Rev. Alexander McCaine and Others*, etc. (New York, 1838).

REVIVALS. William W. Sweet, *Religion on the American Frontier. A Collection of Source Materials:* Vol. I, *The Baptists* (New York, 1931); Vol. II, *The Presbyterians* (Chicago, 1936); Vol. III, *The Congregationalists* (Chicago, 1939); Vol. IV, *The Methodists* (Chicago, 1946); Whitney R. Cross, *The Burned-over District. The Social and Intellectual History of Enthusiastic Religion in Western New York, 1800–1850* (Ithaca, 1950); Frank G. Beardsley, *Religious Progress through Religious Revivals* (New York, 1943).

THE UNITARIAN MOVEMENT. *American Unitarian Association Tracts;* . William E. Channing, *Unitarian Christianity. A Discourse on Some of the Distinguishing Opinions of Unitarians Delivered at Baltimore, May 5, 1819;* Henry Ware, *Memoirs of the Rev. Noah Worcester* (Boston, 1844); Henry S. Commager, *Theodore Parker* (Boston, 1936).

ANTI-MASONRY. Charles McCarthy, *The Anti-Masonic Party*, in the *Annual Report of the American Historical Association*, 1902, Vol. 1; Charles G. Finney, *The Character, Claims, and Practical Workings of Freemasonry* (Cincinnati, 1869); *Anti-Masonic Review and Magazine; Published Monthly in the City of New York*, Vols. 1 and 2. 1829, 1830.

THE AMERICAN HOME MISSIONARY SOCIETY. Robert Baird, *Religion in America* (New York, 1844); Lyman Beecher, *A Plea for the West* (Cincinnati, 1836); Colin B. Goodykoontz, *Home Missions on the American Frontier* (Caldwell, 1939); William A. Hallock, *Justin Edwards* (New York, 1855).

THE AMERICAN TRACT SOCIETY. *American Tract Society Publications; American Tract Society: Proceedings of the First Ten Years* (Andover, 1824); Helen C. Knight, *Hannah More or Life in Hall and Cottage* (American Tract Society, 1855).

THE AMERICAN BIBLE SOCIETY. *Annual Reports of the American Bible Society: With an Account of its Organization*, etc. (New York, 1838);

W. P. Strickland, *History of the American Bible Society,* etc. (New York, 1849).

THE AMERICAN SUNDAY SCHOOL UNION. *Annual Reports of the American Sunday School Union;* Stephen H. Tyng, *The American Sunday-School Union and the "Union Principle"* (New York, 1855).

THE OBSERVANCE OF THE SABBATH. James A. Hessey, *Sunday: Its Origin, History, and Present Obligation Considered in the Bampton Lectures Preached before the University of Oxford in the Year 1860; American Tract Society Publications; American Home Missionary Society Annual Reports.*

THE TEMPERANCE MOVEMENT. Lyman Beecher, *Autobiography, Correspondence,* etc. (2 vols., New York, 1865, 1866); Lyman Beecher, *Six Sermons on the Nature, Occasions, Signs, and Remedy of Intemperance* (Boston, 1827); John B. Gough, *Autobiography and Personal Recollections* (Springfield, 1869).

THE CHURCH AND THE COMMUNITY. Robert Baird, *State and Prospects of Religion in America* (New York, 1856); Horace Bushnell, *Life and Letters* (New York, 1903); John E. Todd, Editor, *John Todd* (New York, 1876); Elizabeth Payson Prentiss, *Life and Letters* (New York, 1882).

RELIGIOUS NATIVISM. Ray A. Billington, *The Protestant Crusade, 1800– 1860: A Study of the Origins of American Nativism* (New York, 1938); Oscar Handlin, *Boston's Immigrants, 1790–1865* (Cambridge, 1941); Vergilius Ferm, *The Crisis in American Lutheran Theology* (New York, 1927).

THE OLD WORLD AGAINST THE NEW. John Hughes, *The Decline of Protestantism, and Its Cause* (New York, 1850); Joseph F. Berg, *A Lecture . . . in Answer to Archbishop Hughes* (Philadelphia, 1850); Horace Bushnell, *Life and Letters* (New York, 1903); Nicholas Murray, *Letters to the Rt. Rev. John Hughes, Roman Catholic Bishop of New York*. By "Kirwan" (Philadelphia, 1904).

THE ABOLITION CRUSADE. *American Anti-Slavery Society Annual Reports;* Reports of various Anti-Slavery Societies and Conventions; the *Liberator.*

CAESAR OR CHRIST. Anti-Slavery Tracts; William E. Channing, *Remarks on the Slavery Question, in a Letter to Jonathan Phillips, Esq.* (Boston, 1839; Forrest Wilson, *Crusader in Crinoline: The Life of Harriet Beecher Stowe* (Philadelphia, 1941).

INDEX